Hands-On Chatbots Conversational UI Development

MW01077115

Build chatbots and voice user interfaces with Chatfuel, Dialogflow, Microsoft Bot Framework, Twilio, and Alexa Skills

Srini Janarthanam

BIRMINGHAM - MUMBAI

Hands-On Chatbots and Conversational UI Development

First published: December 2017

Production reference: 1261217

Published by Packt Publishing Ltd.
Livery Place
35 Livery Street
Birmingham
B3 2PB, UK.
ISBN 978-1-78829-466-9

www.packtpub.com

Credits

Author
Srini Janarthanam

Reviewer
Vamsi Venigalla

Commissioning Editor
Kunal Chaudhari

Acquisition Editor
Siddharth Mandal

Content Development Editor
Arun Nadar

Technical Editor
Prajakta Mhatre

Copy Editor
Safis Editing

Project Coordinator
Sheejal Shah

Proofreader
Safis Editing

Indexer
Pratik Shirodkar

Production Coordinator
Melwyn D'sa

About the Author

Srini Janarthanam is an expert in conversational systems and has been working in the field for over 15 years. He has led and worked on several projects, building conversational systems for a variety of domains including tourism, healthcare, and education. He obtained doctorate in Philosophy (PhD) from the University of Edinburgh for his work in Artificial Intelligence and Natural Language Processing.

He is currently the co-founder and director of Chatomate, a UK brand building tailored chatbots, AI, and automation solutions for businesses. Previously, he worked as a research associate at Heriot-Watt University and the University of Edinburgh. He has published over 50 articles and papers in online chatbot magazines, journals, and international research conferences.

I am eternally grateful to everyone who supported me on this incredible journey. I thank my wife, Jayanthi, my son, Advaith, my parents, and everyone in the family for their encouragement, support, and help in this project. I want to thank my friends, Priyanka, Anup, Thiru, Suresh, Jaya, Nara, Diwakar, and many others, for encouraging me to take up this project and for keeping an eye on its progress throughout.

I want to thank the reviewers of the book for lending a hand to shape the book to make it what it is now. I also want to thank the entire team at Packt Publishing who have an enormous share in getting this book to you.

Finally, I want to thank God for giving me an opportunity to discover my strengths and for his grace and support to accomplish writing this book.

About the Reviewer

Vamsi Venigalla is a technology leader with over 12 years of experience in building technology organizations, strategic planning, rolling out multiple transformational platforms/products, IT program and project management, strategy and transformation (business, people, process, and technology), and delivering results for various business functions across mobile, sourcing, financial systems, HR, retail and supply chain in the food production and manufacturing domains.

Vamsi graduated with a master's degree in computer science from North Carolina State University, NC.

www.PacktPub.com

For support files and downloads related to your book, please visit `www.PacktPub.com`. Did you know that Packt offers eBook versions of every book published, with PDF and ePub files available? You can upgrade to the eBook version at `www.PacktPub.com` and as a print book customer, you are entitled to a discount on the eBook copy. Get in touch with us at `service@packtpub.com` for more details.

At `www.PacktPub.com`, you can also read a collection of free technical articles, sign up for a range of free newsletters and receive exclusive discounts and offers on Packt books and eBooks.

`https://www.packtpub.com/mapt`

Get the most in-demand software skills with Mapt. Mapt gives you full access to all Packt books and video courses, as well as industry-leading tools to help you plan your personal development and advance your career.

Why subscribe?

- Fully searchable across every book published by Packt
- Copy and paste, print, and bookmark content
- On demand and accessible via a web browser

Customer Feedback

Thanks for purchasing this Packt book. At Packt, quality is at the heart of our editorial process. To help us improve, please leave us an honest review on this book's Amazon page at https://www.amazon.com/dp/1788294661.

If you'd like to join our team of regular reviewers, you can e-mail us at customerreviews@packtpub.com. We award our regular reviewers with free eBooks and videos in exchange for their valuable feedback. Help us be relentless in improving our products!

Table of Contents

Preface

Building chatbots is fun. Although chatbots are just another kind of software, they are very different in terms of the expectations that they create in users. Chatbots are conversational. This ability to process language makes them project a kind of human personality and intelligence, whether we as developers intend it to be so or not. To develop software with a personality and intelligence is quite challenging and therefore interesting.

This is a book for programmers who are interested in exploring the world of conversational user interfaces. This book is organized as eight chatbot projects that will introduce the ecosystem of tools, techniques, concepts, and even gadgets relating to conversational interfaces. We will start exploring basic chatbots using button interfaces and move toward using text utterances and finally voice. We will begin with a no-code platform to build our first chatbot and move on to exploring libraries and services to program the modules ourselves. Every chapter is a unique project with the objective of building a conversational interface to a data source. We will seek to understand the data, identify conversational tasks, carry out conversation design, and finally follow step-by-step instructions to implement the interface.

What this book covers

Chapter 1, *Introduction*, begins by teaching you what conversational user interfaces are, and their history and recent developments. We will then explore their basic architecture, applications, and benefits, and some factors that suggest why conversational interfaces are here to stay.

Chapter 2, *Tour Guide for Your City*, explores how to build chatbots without having to code. We will explore a development and hosting platform called Chatfuel, using which we will develop a tour guide for your city. We will design and build a simple button-based chatbot and learn how to deploy the chatbot to Facebook Messenger, one of the most popular channels for chatbots.

Chapter 3, *Let's Talk Weather*, follows on to build a chatbot for the same channel, but by building it from scratch this time, using Java and Node.js. We will build a chatbot that can tell us about the weather using an open data source called OpenWeatherAPI, host it as a Cloud application, and link it to a Facebook App that connects to a Facebook Page. We will explore Facebook Pages and the Messenger SDK from the perspective of building and deploying chatbots.

Chapter 4, *Building a Persona Bot*, moves away from button-based chatbots to ones that can understand natural language. We will explore a popular tool called API.AI (now known as Dialogflow) which can be used to build chatbots that can understand natural language. We will build a persona bot that emulates a popular personality, Albert Einstein. We will then take a look at how to integrate the chatbot into a website and Facebook Messenger.

Chapter 5, *Let's Catch a Train*, delves into a more traditional channel of communication—Short Messaging Service (SMS). We will analyze how to build a chatbot for the SMS channel. Using a data service called Transport API, we will build a chatbot that can talk about train schedules over SMS. We will also integrate an API.AI module for the chatbot in order to allow it to understand what the user says.

Chapter 6, *Restaurant Search*, seeks to build a chatbot using Microsoft Bot Builder. This is fast becoming a popular tool for building bots and can be used to design an efficient conversation manager, rather than building it from scratch, as we did previously. We will build a chatbot to search for restaurants using a data service called Zomato. This will then be exposed on the Skype channel.

Chapter 7, *The News Bot*, explains a totally different channel of engagement—Twitter. We will develop a Twitter bot that can listen to the tweets of users, understand their interests, and send them personalized news on an hourly basis by connecting to a data source called the News API.

Chapter 8, *My TV Guide*, seeks to understand the rise of voice-activated bots like Alexa. We will then build an Alexa skill to talk about your TV schedule. We will build a skill that can access the TV schedule data from the TVMaze data service and respond to user requests made over Amazon Echo.

Chapter 9, *My Man Friday*, continues working on voice bots and builds a Google Assistant action. This action will allow users to manage their to-do list using their Google Home device. We will build a Cloud app that will integrate with the Todoist online service to create tasks and retrieve pending tasks.

Appendix, *More Resources*, explains various articles, list of magazines, list of conferences and so on to gain more knowledge about the chatbots.

What you need for this book

Here are some tools that we use extensively throughout the book. I recommend that you get them installed on your computer and get acquainted with them, as that will help you as we move through the projects:

- **Heroku**: Heroku is a cloud platform that allows you to host your web apps in the cloud. To get started, sign up to a free account at www.heroku.com and install the Heroku command-line tool from https://devcenter.heroku.com/articles/heroku-cli. You may also want to learn how to deploy apps on Heroku. I recommend that you go through some of the tutorials at https://devcenter.heroku.com/start.

- **Git**: Git is a version control tool that you might be familiar with. We will use Git extensively as it is part of the Heroku process. You will have to install the Git command line on your system. You should be able to find it at https://git-scm.com/downloads.

- **Node.js**: Node.js is a JavaScript runtime that we need to build web apps in most of our projects. You can find it at https://nodejs.org/en/download/.

- **Java SDK and Eclipse**: Java 1.8 is used to build the chatbot in Chapter 3, *Let's Talk Weather*. You need to install the Java SDK and the development environment called Eclipse to follow the instructions in the chapter. Alternatively, you can try to code the chatbot using Node.js or another programming language supported by Heroku. You can find Java 1.8 at http://www.oracle.com/technetwork/java/javase/downloads/index.html and Eclipse at https://www.eclipse.org/downloads/.

Who this book is for

This book is for developers who are interested in creating interactive conversational UIs/chatbots. You need to be able to program in Node.js and Java. Experience in using Node.js libraries such as request and express, and a basic understanding of tools such as Git and Heroku CLI will be helpful.

Conventions

In this book, you will find a number of text styles that distinguish between different kinds of information. Here are some examples of these styles and an explanation of their meaning.

Code words in text, database table names, folder names, filenames, file extensions, pathnames, dummy URLs, user input, and Twitter handles are shown as follows: "Create the index.js file."

A block of code is set as follows:

```
// EddieBot webhooks

const express = require('express')
const bodyParser = require('body-parser')
const app = express()
app.set('port', (process.env.PORT || 5000))
```

Any command-line input or output is written as follows:

```
npm init
```

New terms and **important words** are shown in bold. Words that you see on the screen, for example, in menus or dialog boxes, appear in the text like this: "Click on the **Get Started** button at the bottom of the chat window."

Tips and important notes appear in a box like this.

Tips and tricks appear like this.

Reader feedback

Feedback from our readers is always welcome. Let us know what you t
book--what you liked or disliked. Reader feedback is important to us a
titles that you will really get the most out of. To send us general feedb₂
feedback@packtpub.com, and mention the book's title in the subject of your ....
there is a topic that you have expertise in and you are interested in either writing or
contributing to a book, see our author guide at www.packtpub.com/authors.

Customer support

Now that you are the proud owner of a Packt book, we have a number of things to help you
to get the most from your purchase.

Downloading the example code

You can download the example code files for this book from your account at
http://www.packtpub.com. If you purchased this book elsewhere, you can visit
http://www.packtpub.com/support and register to have the files e-mailed directly to you.
You can download the code files by following these steps:

1. Log in or register to our website using your e-mail address and password.
2. Hover the mouse pointer on the **SUPPORT** tab at the top.
3. Click on **Code Downloads & Errata**.
4. Enter the name of the book in the **Search** box.
5. Select the book for which you're looking to download the code files
6. Choose from the drop-down menu where you purchased this book from.
7. Click on **Code Download**.

Once the file is downloaded, please make sure that you unzip or extract the folder using the
latest version of:

- WinRAR / 7-Zip for Windows
- Zipeg / iZip / UnRarX for Mac
- 7-Zip / PeaZip for Linux

code bundle for the book is also hosted on GitHub at `https://github.com/` `acktPublishing/Hands-On-Chatbots-and-Conversational-UI-Development`. We also have other code bundles from our rich catalog of books and videos available at `https://github.com/PacktPublishing/`. Check them out!

Errata

Although we have taken every care to ensure the accuracy of our content, mistakes do happen. If you find a mistake in one of our books-maybe a mistake in the text or the code-- we would be grateful if you could report this to us. By doing so, you can save other readers from frustration and help us improve subsequent versions of this book. If you find any errata, please report them by visiting `http://www.packtpub.com/submit-errata`, selecting your book, clicking on the **Errata Submission Form** link, and entering the details of your errata. Once your errata are verified, your submission will be accepted and the errata will be uploaded to our website or added to any list of existing errata under the Errata section of that title.

To view the previously submitted errata, go to `https://www.packtpub.com/books/content/support` and enter the name of the book in the search field. The required information will appear under the **Errata** section.

Piracy

Piracy of copyrighted material on the Internet is an ongoing problem across all media. At Packt, we take the protection of our copyright and licenses very seriously. If you come across any illegal copies of our works in any form on the internet, please provide us with the location address or website name immediately so that we can pursue a remedy.

Please contact us at `copyright@packtpub.com` with a link to the suspected pirated material.

We appreciate your help in protecting our authors and our ability to bring you valuable content.

Questions

If you have a problem with any aspect of this book, you can contact us at `questions@packtpub.com`, and we will do our best to address the problem.

1
Introduction

The age of intelligent machines has arrived, and conversational interfaces are leading the charge. Over the past couple of years, we have been swarmed by a number of new kinds of machines and software collectively known as bots. **Bots** are automated hardware or software machines that are powered by the advances in **Artificial Intelligence (AI)** technologies. Recent developments in machine learning algorithms, such as deep learning and deep reinforcement learning, have improved the performance of AI tasks such as **Automatic Speech Recognition (ASR)**, **Natural Language Understanding (NLU)**, **Text to Speech Synthesis (TTS)**, and Image Recognition. This has accelerated humankind's journey toward the technological singularity, the point in time when AI surpasses natural human intelligence by leaps and bounds.

One of the long-term goals in the field of AI is to build computer systems that can have human-like conversations with users. With recent advances in AI technologies, we are now one step closer to achieving this goal. Now, it is no longer fictional that we are able to interact with devices and gadgets in our homes and offices using nothing but voice. We still have a long way to go toward creating standards and building digital beings that are capable of seamless natural language conversation. However, a recent surge in interests and massive investments in pursuing these ideas suggest that we are on track toward evolving such a global standard. If you are excited about the recent developments in AI and automation technologies, this book is for you. We will embark on a journey toward a point in time in the future that the design guru Mark Curtis calls *conversational singularity*, when conversational devices disappear and conversation between man and machine is seamless and natural.

This is a book for programmers beginning to build conversational interfaces. Today, basic button-based chatbots can be built without even having to write a single line of code. In this book, that is where we will start. We will gradually move toward more complex and flexible architectures, and we will explore channels to use, such as Facebook Messenger, SMS, and Twitter. We will also be exploring tools for understanding natural language and conversation management as we proceed. Finally, we will end our journey by building voice-enabled bots on platforms such as Amazon Alexa and Google Assistant.

Conversational user interfaces

Conversational user interfaces are as old as modern computers themselves. ENIAC, the first programmable general-purpose computer, was built in the year 1946. In 1950, Alan Turing, a British computer scientist, proposed to measure the level of intelligence in machines using a conversational test called the Turing test. The test involved having the machine compete with a human as a dialogue partner to a set of human judges (yet another human). The judges would interact with each of the two participants (the human and the machine) using a text type interface that is not unlike most of the modern messaging chat applications. Over chat, the judges were supposed to identify which of the two participants was the machine. If at least 30% of the judges couldn't differentiate between the two participants, the machine was considered to have passed the test. This was one of the earliest human thoughts on conversational interfaces and their bearing on the intelligence levels of machines that have such capabilities. However, attempts to build such interfaces have not been very successful for several following decades.

For about 35 years, since the 1980s, **Graphical User Interfaces** (GUI) have been dominating the way in which we have been interacting with machines. With recent developments in AI and growing constraints such as the shrinking size of gadgets (from laptops to mobile phones), reducing on-screen real estates (smart watches), and the need for interfaces to become invisible (smart home and robots), conversational user interfaces are once again becoming a reality. For instance, the best way to interact with mobile robots that are distributed gadgets in smart homes would be using voice. The system should, therefore, be able to understand the users' requests and responses in natural human language. Such capabilities of systems can reduce human effort in learning and understanding current complex interfaces.

Conversational user interfaces have been known under several names: natural language interfaces, spoken dialogue systems, chatbots, intelligent virtual agents, virtual assistants, and so on. The actual difference between these systems is in terms of the backend integrations (for example, databases, and task/control modules), modalities (for example, text, voice, and visual avatars), and channels they get deployed on. However, one of the common themes among these systems is their ability to interact with users in a conversational manner using natural language.

A brief history of chatbots

The origins of modern chatbots can be traced back to 1964 when Joseph Weizenbaum at Massachusetts Institute of Technology (MIT) developed a chatbot called Eliza. It used simple rules of conversation and rephrased most of what the users said to simulate a Rogerian therapist. While it showed that naive users may be fooled into thinking that they are talking to an actual therapist, the system itself did not understand the user's problem. Following this, in 1991, the Loebner prize was instituted to encourage AI researchers to build chatbots that can beat the Turing test and advance the state of AI. Although no chatbots beat the test until 2014, many notable chatbots won prizes for winning other constrained challenges. These include ALICE, JabberWacky, Rose, and Mitsuku. However, in 2014, in a Turing test competition to mark the 60th anniversary of Alan Turing's death, a chatbot called Eugene Goostman, portraying a 13 year old kid, managed to fool 33% of the judges—thereby beating the test. **Artificial Intelligence Markup Language (AIML)** and ChatScript were developed as a way to script the knowledge and conversational content for most of these chatbots. Scripts developed using these scripting languages can then be fed into interpreters to create conversational behavior. Chatbots developed to beat the Turing test were largely chatty with just one objective—to beat the Turing test. This was not considered by many as advancement in AI or toward building useful conversational assistants.

On the other hand, research in artificial intelligence, specifically in machine learning and natural language processing, gave rise to various conversational interfaces such as question answering systems, natural language interfaces to databases, and spoken dialogue systems. Unlike chatbots built to beat the Turing test, these systems had very clear objectives. Question answering systems processed natural language questions and found answers in unstructured text datasets. **Natural Language Interfaces to Database Systems (NLIDBS)** were interfaces to large SQL databases that interpreted database queries posed in a natural language such as English, converted them into SQL, and returned the hits as response. **Spoken Dialogue Systems (SDS)** were systems that could maintain contextful conversations with users to handle conversational tasks such as booking tickets, controlling other systems, and tutoring learners. These were the precursors of modern chatbots and conversational interfaces.

Recent developments

In 2011, Apple released an intelligent assistant called Siri as part of their iPhones. Siri was modeled to be the user's personal assistant, doing tasks such as making calls, reading messages, and setting alarms and reminders. This is one of the most significant events in the recent past that rebooted the story of conversational interfaces. During the initial days of Siri, users used it only a few times a month to perform tasks such as searching the internet, sending SMS, and making phone calls. Although novel, Siri was treated as a work in progress with a lot more features to be added in the following years. In the early days, Siri had many clones and competition on Android and other smartphone platforms. Most of these were modeled as assistants and were available as mobile apps.

In the same year (2011), IBM introduced Watson, a question answering system that participated in a game show called Jeopardy and won it against previous human winners, Brad Rutter and Ken Jennings. This marked a milestone in the history of AI as Watson was able to process open domain natural language questions and answer them in real time. Since then, Watson has been refashioned into a toolkit with an array of cognitive service tools for natural language understanding, sentiment analysis, dialogue management, and so on.

Following Siri and Watson, the next major announcement came from Microsoft in 2013, when they introduced Cortana as a standard feature on Windows phones and later in 2015 on Windows 10 OS. Like Siri, Cortana was a personal assistant that managed tasks such as setting reminders, answering questions, and so on.

In November 2014, Amazon invited its Prime members to try out its very own pe
assistant called Alexa. Alexa was made available on Amazon's own product calle
Echo was a first-of-its-kind smart speaker that housed within it an assistant like a "ghost in
the machine. Although called a speaker, it was actually a tiny computer with the voice as its
only interface, unlike smartphones, tablets, and personal computers. Users can speak to
Alexa using voice, ask her to do tasks such as setting reminders, playing music, and so on.

Recently, in April 2016, Facebook announced that it is opening up its popular Messenger
platform for chatbots. This was a radically different approach to conversational interfaces
compared to Siri, Alexa, and Cortana. Unlike these personal assistants, Facebook's
announcement led to the creation of custom built and branded chatbots. These bots are very
much like Siri, Cortana, and Alexa, but can be custom tuned to the requirements of the
business building them. Chatbots are now poised to disrupt several markets, including
customer service, sales, marketing, technical support, and so on. Many messaging
platforms, such as Skype, Telegram, and others, also opened up to chatbots around the
same time.

In May 2016, Google announced Assistant, its version of a personal chatbot that was
accessible on multiple platforms such as Allo app and Google Home (a smart speaker like
Echo). All assistants like Siri, Cortana, Alexa, and Google Assistant have also opened up as
channels for third-party conversational capabilities. So, it is now possible to make your
Alexa and Google Assistant personalized by adding conversational capabilities (called
skills or **actions**) from a library of third-party solutions. Just as brands can develop their
own chatbots for various messaging services (for example, Skype and Facebook Messenger),
they can also develop skills for Alexa or actions for Google Assistant. Apple's very own
smart speaker, Homepod, powered by Siri, is slated to be released in 2018.

Parallel to these developments, there has also been major growth in terms of tools that are
available to build and host chatbots. Over the last two years, there has been an exponential
growth of tools to design, mock, build, deploy, manage, and monetize chatbots. This has
resulted in the creation of an ecosystem that designs and builds custom conversational
interfaces for businesses, charities, governmental, and other organizations across the globe.

Architecture of a conversational user interface

In this section, let's take a look at the basic architecture of a conversational interface:

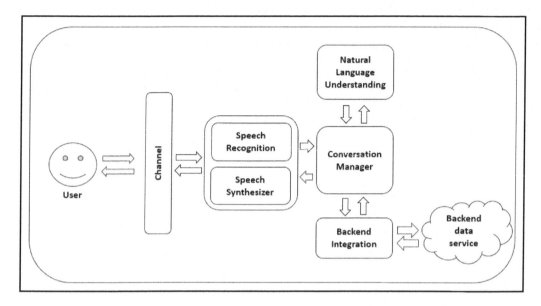

The core module of a conversational interface is the conversation manager. This module controls the flow of the conversation. It takes the semantic representation of what the user says as input, and decides what the response of the system should be. It will maintain a representation of the conversational context in some form, say a set of key value pairs, in order to meaningfully carry out the conversation over several turns between the user and the system.

The semantic representation of the user input can be directly fed from button pushes. In systems that can understand language, user utterances will be translated into semantic representation, consisting of user intents and parameters (slots and entities), by a natural language understanding module. This module may need to be previously trained to understand a set of user intents identified by the developer pertaining to the conversational tasks at hand.

Voice-enabled interfaces that accept user's speech inputs also need a speech recognition module that can transcribe speech into text before feeding it into the natural language understanding module. Symmetrically, on the other side, there is a need for a speech synthesizer (or text-to-speech engine) module that converts the system's text response into speech.

The conversational manager will interact with backend modules. It can be a database or an online data source that gets queried in order to answer a user's question (for example, TV schedule) or an online service to carry out a user's instruction (for example, booking a ticket).

The channel is where the chatbot actually meets the user. Depending on the channel, there may be one or more modules that make up this layer. For instance, if the chatbot is on Facebook Messenger, this layer consists of a Facebook Page and a Facebook App that connects to the rest of the chatbot modules wrapped as a web app.

Classification

Conversational user interfaces have found themselves applied in various scenarios. Their applications can be classified broadly into two categories: **enterprise assistants** and **personal assistants**.

Enterprise Assistants are chatbots and other conversational user interfaces that are modeled after customer service representatives and store assistants. Just like human customer service representatives, the bots engage customers in conversation carrying out marketing, sales, and support tasks. Most chatbots deployed on channels such as Facebook Messenger, Skype, Slack, and many more are enterprise assistants. They are designed and built to do tasks that store assistants and customer service representatives would do. Enterprise assistants are being developed in many business sectors, automating a variety of conversational tasks.

On the other hand, personal assistants are bots like Alexa, Siri, and Cortana, which act as a user's personal assistant, doing tasks such as managing a calendar, sending texts, taking calls, and playing music. These personal assistants can be extended in terms of their capabilities. For instance, Alexa allows for such augmentation by letting developers build skills that users can choose to add to their own Alexa. Brands can, therefore, develop skills for Alexa or actions for Google Assistant that will enable Alexa and Assistant to interact with the brand's IT services and perform tasks such as placing orders, checking delivery status, and many more. For instance, popular brands like PizzaHut, Starbucks, and Domino's have developed skills that can be enabled on Alexa.

:ations

Although chatbots have been under development for at least a few decades, they did not become mainstream channels for customer engagement until recently. Over the past two years, due to serious efforts by industry giants like Apple, Google, Microsoft, Facebook, IBM, and Amazon, and their subsequent investments in developing toolkits, chatbots and conversational interfaces have become a serious contender to other customer contact channels. In this time, chatbots have been applied in various sectors and various conversational scenarios within these sectors: retail, banking and finance, governmental, health, legal and third sector, and many more.

In retail, chatbots have been applied for product marketing, brand engagement, product assistance, sales, and support conversations. Brand-engagement chatbots offer tips and advice to loyal customers of a brand related to the use of products sold by the brand. For instance, Sephora chatbot advises users on how to select their ideal lipstick. Similarly, TK-Maxx chatbot assisted users in choosing gifts for their friends and family during Christmas 2016. One of the first retailers to explore chatbots for sales was H&M. The H&M chatbot helped users browse through the product catalogue and add products to their shopping carts. Car manufacturers like Tesla, Kia, and Mercerdes have developed chatbots that can help car users with information regarding their cars.

Chatbots have been very successful in the banking and finance industry. Banking was one of the first sectors that experimented with conversational interfaces. Banking chatbots can answer generic questions about financial products, secure banking, and so on, along with providing specific and personalized information about user's accounts. Many global banks and financial service providers including Bank of America, ICICI bank, HSBC, Royal Bank of Scotland, Capital One, Mastercard, and so on have deployed chatbots to assist their customers. Many fintech companies are building chatbots that can act as financial assistant to users. Ernest.ai and Cleo are chatbots that can link to your bank accounts and talk to you about your spending, balances, and also provide tips to save money. Chatbots are also being widely deployed in the insurance sector, where they act as assistants that can get you tailored quotes (for example, SPIXII).

Chatbots are also being used in legal, health, governmental, and third sectors. A chatbot called DoNotPay has assisted people to challenge parking tickets in London and New York in over 160,000 cases. Following this, more chatbots have been developed to help people access justice and legal services: assessment of crime (LawBot), business incorporation (LawDroid), help tenants (RentersUnion), help with legal questions and documentation (Lisa, LegaliBot, Lexi, DocuBot), and find lawyers (BillyBot).

In the third sector, chatbots have been used to spread awareness of issues that charities care about. Stoptober is a Facebook chatbot that was developed by the **National Health Services (NHS)** in the UK to help sn   o quit. Another chatbot, Yeshi, was developed to draw awareness to Ethiopia's water   tbots are beginning to make their entry into healthcare as well. Chatbots like You   lthTap were designed to   gnose health issues based on symptoms. Emily is a chatbot designed by LifeFolder to help make the end of life decisions (for example, legal documentation, life support, organ donation, and many more).

Chatbots are not only being used to be customer facing but also internally, to face employees. Chatbots, in a sense, are becoming coworkers by helping fellow employees with tasks that are repetitive, mundane, and boring. Messaging services such as Slack and Microsoft Teams have been encouraging chatbots on their platforms to automate office communication. These bots aim to engage coworkers in chat on fun and essential tasks. For instance, there are bots to help coworkers share knowledge (Obie.ai), access other services such as GDrive (WorkBot), set up meetings (Meekan), discuss lunch (LunchTrain), and even help with decision making (ConcludeBot, SimplePoll).

If you are interested in finding out more use cases, I would recommend you to take a look at some of the bot directory services like `botlist.co` and `www.chatbots.org`, where you can find more information and inspiration.

Developer's toolkit

Over the last few years, an ecosystem of tools and services has grown around the idea of conversational interfaces. There are a number of tools that we can plug and play to design, develop, and manage chatbots.

Mockup tools

Mockups can be used to show clients as to how a chatbot would look and behave. These are tools that you may want to consider using during conversation design, after coming up with sample conversations between the user and the bot on the back of a napkin. Mockup tools allow you to visualize the conversation between the user and the bot and showcase the dynamics of conversational turn-taking. BotSociety.io (`https://botsociety.io/`) and BotMock.com (`https://botmock.com/`) are some of the popular mockup tools. Some of these tools allow you to export the mockup design and make videos.

nnels

Channels refer to places where users can interact with the chatbot. There are several deployment channels over which your bots can be exposed to users. These include messaging services such as Facebook Messenger, Skype, Kik, Telegram, WeChat, and Line; office and team chat services such as Slack, Microsoft Teams, and many more; traditional channels such as the web chat, SMS, and voice calls; and smart speakers such as Amazon Echo and Google Home. Choose the channel based on your users and the requirements of the project. For instance, if you are building a chatbot targeting consumers, Facebook Messenger can be the best channel because of the growing number of users who use the service already to keep in touch with friends and family. To add your chatbot to their contact list may be easier then getting them to download your app. If the user needs to interact with the bot using voice in a home or office environment, smart speaker channels can be an ideal choice. And finally, there are tools that can connect chatbots to many channels simultaneously (for example, Dialogflow integration, MS Bot Service, and Smooch.io, and so on).

Chatbot development tools

There are many tools that you can use to build chatbots without having to code even a single line: Chatfuel, ManyChat, Dialogflow, and so on. Chatfuel allows designers to create the conversational flow using visual elements. With ManyChat, you can build the flow using a visual map called the FlowBuilder. Conversational elements such as bot utterances and user response buttons can be configured using drag and drop UI elements. Dialogflow can be used to build chatbots that require advanced natural language understanding to interact with users.

On the other hand, there are scripting languages such as Artificial Intelligence Markup Language (AIML), ChatScript, and RiveScript that can used to build chatbots. These scripts will contain the conversational content and flow that then needs to be fed into an interpreter program or a rules engine to bring the chatbot to life. The interpreter decides how to progress the conversation by matching user utterances to templates in the scripts. While it is straightforward to build conversational chatbots using this approach, it becomes difficult to build transactional chatbots without generating explicit semantic representations of user utterances. PandoraBots is a popular web-based platform for building AIML chatbots.

Alternatively, there are SDK libraries that one can use to build chatbots: MS Bot Builder, BotKit, BotFuel, and so on provide SDKs in one or more programming languages to assist developers in building the core conversational management module. The ability to code the conversational manager gives developers the flexibility to mould the conversation and integrate the bot to backend tasks better than no-code and scripting platforms. Once built, the conversation manager can then be plugged into other services such as natural language understanding to understand user utterances.

Analytics

Like other digital solutions, chatbots can benefit from collecting and analyzing their usage statistics. While you can build a bespoke analytics platform from scratch, you can also use off-the-shelf toolkits that are widely available now. Many off-the-shelf analytics toolkits are available that can be plugged into a chatbot, using which incoming and outgoing messages can be logged and examined. These tools tell chatbot builders and managers the kind of conversations that actually transpire between users and the chatbot. The data will give useful information such as the conversational tasks that are popular, places where conversational experience breaks down, utterances that the bot did not understand, and the requests which the chatbots still need to scale up to. Dashbot.io, BotAnalytics, and Google's Chatbase are a few analytic toolkits that you can use to analyze your chatbot's performance.

Natural Language understanding

Chatbots can be built without having to understand utterances from the user. However, adding the natural language understanding capability is not very difficult. It is one of the hallmark features that sets chatbots apart from their digital counterparts such as websites and apps with visual elements. There are many natural language understanding modules that are available as cloud services. Major IT players like Google, Microsoft, Facebook, and IBM have created tools that you can plug into your chatbot. Google's Dialogflow, Microsoft LUIS, IBM Watson, SoundHound, and Facebook's Wit.ai are some of the NLU tools that you can try. We will explore Dialogflow (previously called Api.Ai) in some of the chapters.

Directory services

One of the challenges of building the bot is to get users to discover and use it. Chatbots are not as popular as websites and mobile apps, so a potential user may not know where to look to find the bot. Once your chatbot is deployed, you need to help users find it. There are directories that list bots in various categories. Chatbots.org is one of the oldest directory services that has been listing chatbots and virtual assistants since 2008. Other popular ones are Botlist.co, BotPages, BotFinder, and ChatBottle. These directories categorize bots in terms of purpose, sector, languages supported, countries, and so on. In addition to these, channels such as Facebook and Telegram have their own directories for the bots hosted on their channel. In the case of Facebook, you can help users find your Messenger bot using their Discover service.

Monetization

Chatbots are built for many purposes: to create awareness, to support customers after sales, to provide paid services, and many more. In addition to all these, chatbots with interesting content can engage users for a long time and can be used to make some money through targeted personalized advertising. Services such as CashBot.ai and AddyBot.com can integrate with your chatbot to send targeted advertisements and recommendations to users, and when users engage, your chatbot makes money.

The aforementioned is not an exhaustive list of tools and nor are the services listed under each type. These tools are evolving over time as chatbots are finding their niche in the market. This list is to give you an idea of how multidimensional the ecosystem is and help you explore the space and feed your creative mind.

Benefits

Conversational user interfaces bring in the best of both worlds: human-like natural interaction combined with the benefits of digital technology.

- **Availability:** Like any other automated digital technologies, conversational interfaces are low-cost and are available 24/7. It is like having someone man the web chat desk all the time so that customers always have someone to get answers from.

- **Personalized experience:** Unlike websites and smartphone apps, chatbots can provide a very personalized experience owing to the conversational nature of interaction. One-to-one conversation settings provide ample opportunity to understand and adapt to a user's goals, preferences, and constraints.
- **Low cost:** Chatbots are digital solutions and therefore provide customer support services at least ten times cheaper than humans doing the very same tasks.
- **Consistency:** Chatbots can be consistent in services, which may be hard to achieve with human operators and may be very important in certain sectors.
- **Quick response times:** Unlike human-based systems, the response time for chatbots is much quicker. Users no longer have to wait for their call to be picked up and during a conversation, the chatbot responses will be quicker than human responses, especially when human operators are tasked with more than one simultaneous chat (sometimes up to five). The ability of chatbots to handle simultaneous conversations also removes the bottleneck of limited customer support bandwidth and therefore helps businesses scale up.
- **Scale up:** Chatbots can easily scale up to handle increasing and seasonal traffic, which is not easy to do when using a battery of live advisors. Holiday season may particularly drive up demand for customer support. At such times, chatbots can be used to handle low priority and easy tasks, thereby reducing the load on live advisors—and human assistance can be used judiciously to handle high-value conversations.

Chatbots are here to stay

The conversational user interface technologies are currently one of the top trending topics in the technology business. Most big brands have started formulating their chatbot strategy within their larger AI and automation strategy. Innovations such as chatbots, smart speakers, and self-driving cars are driving such major policy decisions. The world is gearing up to bear the onslaught of automation technologies that are poised to replace humans in repetitive and structured tasks.

The recent rise of chatbots has been fueled by many factors:

- Milliennials have been steadily moving toward chat as their preferred channel to interact with brands. Customer contact surveys show that people want to use web chat channels when available, compared to other traditional channels, such as email and phone, to contact businesses.

- The growth of chat messaging apps on smartphones and other devices has surpassed the usage of social media apps such as Facebook and Twitter. Now people spend more time on messaging apps, chatting with friends, family, colleagues, and even businesses.
- Rising customer demand on chat is putting tremendous pressure on brands. The lack of skilled human resources to handle growing chat traffic is also an important contributor of the rise of chatbots.
- Availability of cognitive service tools for natural language understanding, speech recognition, speech synthesis, conversation management, analytics, and so on has made the design and development of chatbots easier than it was a few years ago.
- Opening up of messaging channels and innovative new avenues, such as smart speakers, has made delivering services over chatbots a reality. The fact that there is a growing interest in messaging apps and devices such as smart speakers presents an attractive opportunity for brands to build chatbots to take advantage of the users who are already available on these channels.

There are several surveys and statistics that show that conversational interfaces are here to stay. Through the following list, we offer some of the most compelling survey findings and predictions that show that chatbots are here for the long run:

- Gartner (`https://www.gartner.com/smarterwithgartner/gartner-top-strategic-predictions-for-2018-and-beyond/`) predicts that by 2021, brands that design their websites to include voice and visual search will increase their revenue by 30% and that more that 50% of businesses will spend more on chatbots than traditional mobile apps.
- In an Oracle survey, 80% of respondents (C-level executives) said that they are planning to introduce chatbot services by 2020, if not already [OR].
- Juniper research predicts that use of chatbots will produce annual cost savings of USD 8 billion by 2022, up from USD 20 million in 2017 [JR].
- A Hubspot survey found that about 47% of consumers are open to buying items through a chatbot and around 40% don't care whether they talk to a chatbot or a human as long as they get help easily and quickly [HB].
- Finally, according to a recent Grand View Research report, the global chatbot market is poised to reach a staggering USD 1.25 billion by 2025, growing at a CAGR of 24.3% from USD 190 million in 2016 [GVR].

Lets get started!

So are you ready to get started and build some chatbots yet? I hope I have given y introduction to the world of chatbots in this chapter. We covered historical and rec developments, classification of chatbots, their application in various sectors, their benefits, their future, and their basic architecture. Over the course of the next eight chapters, I will introduce you to several tools, techniques, and concepts that will enable you to build amazing conversational interfaces. Let the journey begin!

 The tools that we are set to explore in this book are constantly evolving, and you may be experiencing an advanced version of them when you work on the projects. Care has been taken to explain the underlying concepts in every chapter so that you will be able to work out how to proceed based on your conceptual understanding and using your better judgement, rather than just executing the instructions verbatim. For the latest information on developments, refer to the documentation tools that are referenced at the end of each chapter.

References

- [Stoptober] https://www.marketingweek.com/2016/09/20/stoptober-uses-facebook-messenger-bot-to-help-people-quit-smoking/
- [Yeshi] https://www.akqa.com/work/lokai/walk-with-yeshi/
- [Emily] https://medium.com/life-folder/introducing-emily-the-chatbot-that-talks-about-death-97b390119cce
- [SPIXII] https://www.insly.com/en/blog/chatbot-is-the-future-of-automated-insurance/
- [OR] http://uk.businessinsider.com/80-of-businesses-want-chatbots-by-2020-2016-12
- [JR] https://www.juniperresearch.com/researchstore/innovation-disruption/chatbots/retail-ecommerce-banking-healthcare
- [HB] https://research.hubspot.com/reports/artificial-intelligence-is-here
- [GVR] http://www.grandviewresearch.com/industry-analysis/chatbot-market

2
Tour Guide for Your City

Having got a taste of chatbots and their brief history, in this chapter we'll get our hands dirty by building your first chatbot. We will build a chatbot that will act as a city tour guide for the user. We will use popular tourist conversations, such as learning about the city, figuring out things to do, and searching for places to eat as example tasks. We will explore how to use the various tools in the toolkit to build a chatbot capable of performing these conversational tasks.

Let us explore a popular tool, Chatfuel, and learn how to build a chatbot from scratch. **Chatfuel** is a tool that enables you to build a chatbot without having to code at all. It is a web-based tool with a GUI editor that allows the user to build a chatbot in a modular fashion. In addition to building chatbots, it also enables developers to monitor and manage the bot's performance using management and analytics tools.

In this chapter, we will explore the building blocks of a chatbot. We will then build a tour guide chatbot from scratch and deploy it on Facebook Messenger. We will explore various features provided by Chatfuel to extend the capabilities of the chatbot such as backend integrations and broadcasting messages. Finally, we will take a brief look at the analytics suite.

By the end of this chapter, you will be able to:

- Understand the basics of Chatfuel
- Understand the concept of conversational flow and navigation
- Understand the building blocks: blocks, cards, plugins, and attributes
- Manage contexts using key-value pairs and handle user utterances
- Build chatbots and integrate webhooks for backend processing
- Integrate the chatbot on Facebook Messenger

Getting started

Let's get started. To create an account with Chatfuel, go to `https://chatfuel.com`:

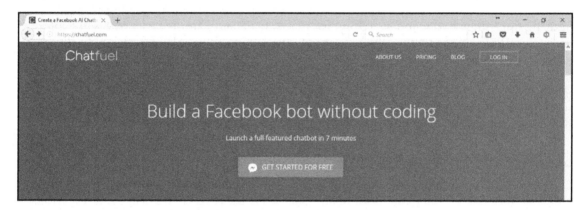

Click **GET STARTED FOR FREE**. Remember, the Chatfuel toolkit is currently free to use. This will lead you to one of the following two options:

- If you are logged into Facebook, it will ask for permission to link your Chatfuel account to your Facebook account
- If you are not logged in, it will ask you to log into Facebook first before asking for permission

Chatfuel links to Facebook to deploy bots. So it requires permission to use your Facebook account:

Authorize Chatfuel to receive information about you and to be your Pages manager:

That's it! You are all set to build your very first bot:

Building your first bot

Chatfuel bots can be published on two deployment platforms: Facebook Messenger and Telegram. Let us build a chatbot for Facebook Messenger first. In order to do that, we need to create a Facebook Page. Every chatbot on Facebook Messenger needs to be attached to a page. Here is how we can build a Facebook Page:

1. Go to `https://www.facebook.com/pages/create/`.
2. Click the category appropriate to the page content. In our case, we will use **Brand or Product** and choose **App Page**.
3. Give the page a name. In our case, let's use `Get_Around_Edinburgh`. Note that Facebook does not make it easy to change page names. So choose wisely.
4. Once the page is created, you will see Chatfuel asking for permission to connect to the page:

5. Click **CONNECT TO PAGE**. You will be taken to the bot editor.

6. The name of the bot is set to **My First Bot**. It has a Messenger URL, which you can see by the side of the name. Messenger URLs start with **m.me**. You might notice that the bot also comes with a **Welcome message** that is built in. On the left, you see the *main menu* with a number of options, with the **Build** option selected by default. We will explore other options in later sections:

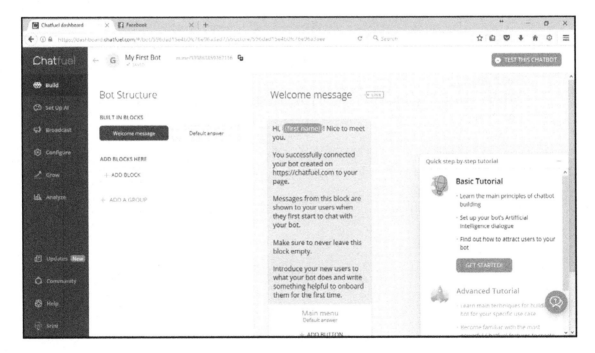

7. Click the Messenger URL to start your first conversation with the bot. This will open Facebook Messenger in your browser tab:

8. To start the conversation, click the **Get Started** button at the bottom of the chat window.
9. There you go! Your conversation has just started. The bot has sent you a welcome message:

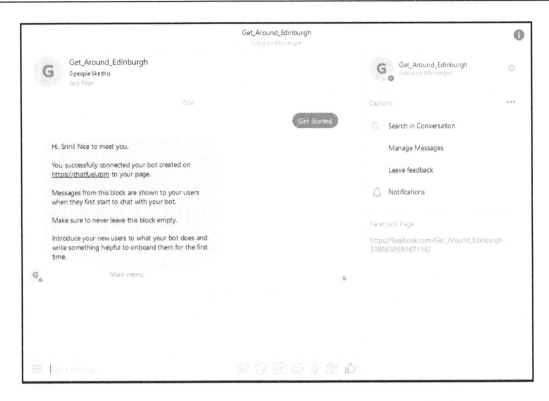

Notice how it greets you with your name. It is because you have given the bot access to your info on Facebook.

Now that you have built your first bot and had a conversation with it, give yourself a pat on your back. Welcome to the world of chatbots!

Basic building blocks

Before we move on to build our bot, let's look at the basic building blocks:

- Blocks
- Cards
- Buttons
- Plugins
- Attributes

Blocks

Go back to the editor and look at the **Bot Structure** tab. Under **Bot Structure**, you will find two types of blocks—built-in and user-defined. **Welcome message** and **Default answer** are the two built-in blocks. We will be building user-defined blocks to implement the conversation capability of the chatbot. Each block can be thought of as a response segment of the chatbot. Each block can contain one or more *cards*.

Cards

Cards are constructs that are used to send messages to the deployment platform. There are many types of cards. Text cards are the basic type of cards; they carry text messages and optional buttons. Other cards include images, quick replies (button arrays), lists, and gallery. We will investigate each of these later.

Buttons

Most cards have buttons. Buttons are used to provide users with response options. Users can respond to the chatbot's questions and requests by clicking the buttons. This is an alternative approach to letting users key in their requests and responses using natural language text.

Plugins

Plugins are parts of blocks where the chatbot is required to carry out special tasks instead of just responding to the user. For instance, you can use a plugin to send an email to yourself with all the information the chatbot got from the user. We will have a look at a number of plugins later.

Attributes

Attributes are variables in programmer's parlance. These are placeholders where we can store data temporarily during the conversation. There are attributes that are predefined and there are those that are user-defined. In this case, users actually means developers. These can be used to steer the conversation one way or the other. Or they can be used to collect data from the user for further processing in a backend module.

Default blocks

There are two blocks that are predefined—**Welcome message** and **Default message**. **Welcome message** comes along with a default card with the welcome text in it. The welcome block is triggered when the user first encounters the chatbot. On Facebook Messenger, this is triggered when the user hits the **Get Started** button. The default answer block is triggered when the bot does not know how to handle a user's input message. Try saying `hello` to the bot on Facebook Messenger and see how it responds:

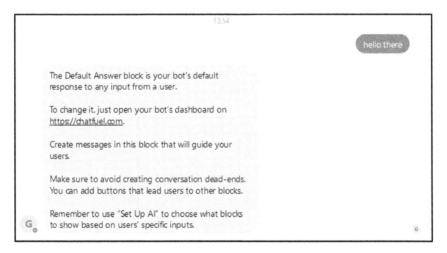

Next steps

Now that we have brushed up on the basics, let's start building our bot:

1. On the welcome block, click the default text and edit it. Hovering the mouse around the block can reveal options such as deleting the card, rearranging the order of the cards, and adding new cards between existing cards. Delete the **Main menu** button:

2. Add a **Text** card. Let's add a follow-up text card and ask the user a question.
3. Add buttons for user responses. Click **ADD BUTTON** and type in the name of the button. Ignore block names for now. Since they are incomplete, they will appear in red. Remember, you can add up to three buttons to a text card:

4. Button responses need to be tied to blocks so that when users hit a button the chatbot would know what to do or say. Let's add a few blocks. To add a new block, click **ADD BLOCK** in the **Bot Structure** tab. This creates a new untitled block. On the right side, fill in the name of the block. Repeat the same for each block you want to build:

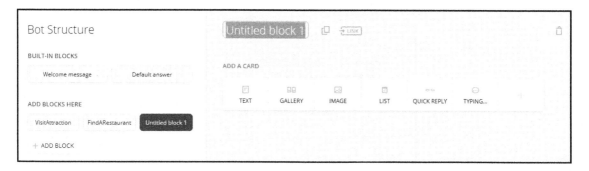

5. Now, go back to the buttons and specify block names to connect to. Click the button, choose **Blocks**, and provide the name of the block:

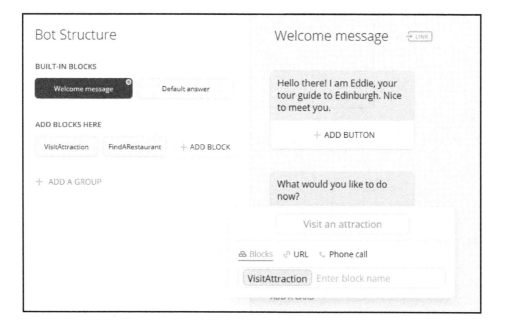

6. For each block, you created, add content by adding appropriate cards. Remember, each block can have more than one card. Each card will appear as a response, one after another:

Repeat the preceding steps to add more blocks and connect them to buttons of other blocks. When you are done, you can test it by clicking the **TEST THIS CHATBOT** button in the top-right corner of the editor. You should now see the new welcome message with buttons for responses. Go on and click one of them to have a conversation:

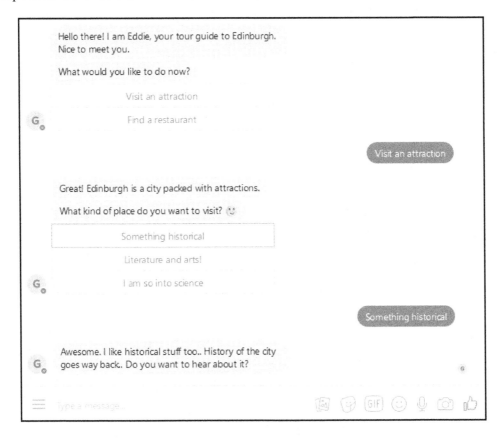

Great! You now have a bot with a conversational flow.

More cards

Besides text, there are other types of cards that can be used to deliver content. These cards are also specific to the delivery platform. Only some platforms, such as Facebook Messenger, support advanced cards such as carousels. Let's examine the types of cards available to us.

Image

To add an image card, click the **Image** icon under **ADD A CARD**. Click **Upload Image**, and choose an image file:

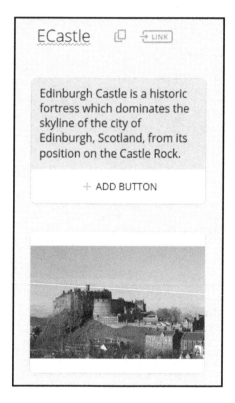

Audio

You can send audio files over chat that can be instantly played by the user. To send an audio file, click the + icon at the end of **ADD A CARD** menu. Choose **Audio** and provide the URL of the audio file. Formats such as MP3, WAV, and OGG are supported:

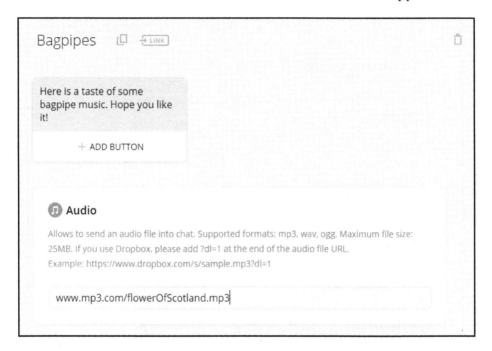

Video

Adding a video card is similar to that of the audio card. Click the **+** icon, choose **Video**, and specify the URL of the video file. Only MP4 format is supported and the maximum size of the video is limited to 25 MB. This is how it appears in the chat:

Quick replies

Quick replies is an array of buttons displayed horizontally. These can be used to obtain answers from the user in the same way as the buttons that are attached to text cards. The difference is that here you can have up to 10 buttons and they are not attached to a card. The buttons will also disappear once the user clicks one of them or types their request/response instead of clicking the buttons. This is extremely useful when you either have more than three response options or options that should not linger around after the turn as they will lose context.

To add an array of quick replies buttons, click **Quick Reply**, add the button names. For each button, you can specify the block it needs to lead to. If the responses are to be treated as answers, they can be stored as user attributes as well. We will examine user attributes further:

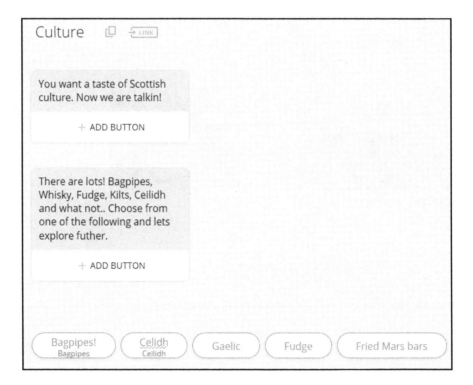

Gallery

Gallery is a type of card that allows us to create a rich experience in presenting content. Instead of just an array of buttons as quick replies, the same content can be presented in an enriched manner with images and text descriptions. To add a gallery card, click **Gallery** under **ADD A CARD** tab. A gallery card can be considered a card with a number of minicards within.

Proceed to add an image, title, subtitle, optional URL, and buttons (up to three max) for the default minicard. Once finished, add more minicards by clicking the + icon on the right:

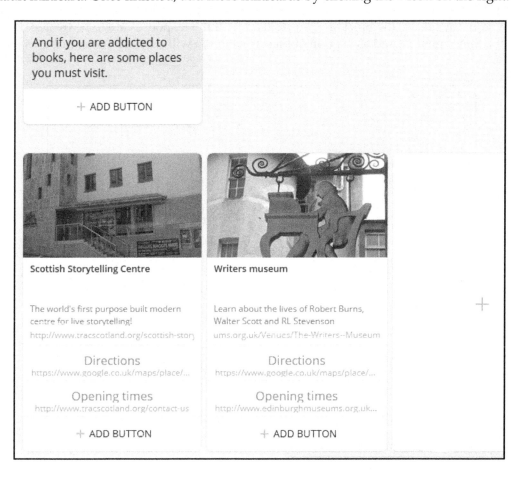

List

The list card is very similar to that of the gallery card in terms of content. It provides a way to present rich content to the user with images and URLs. However, unlike the gallery card, the layout of items is vertical. To add a list card, click the **List** icon in the **ADD A CARD** tab.

Add a cover image, title, URL, subtitle, and call to action button, and create a group header. Repeat the same for every item on the list. In fact, the top element need not be a group header and could instead just be the first element in the list displayed prominently with an image background:

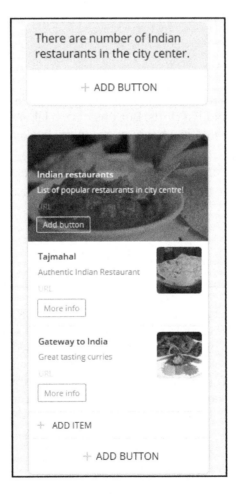

In the example shown, we have a group header with the title **Indian restaurants**. However, if you don't want to have a header, you can simply use the spot for the first item in the list. A list card has a minimum of two items and a maximum of four. You can also add an optional button at the end of the list, say for instance, to provide a "more" option to request more items.

Navigation

How can the user and the chatbot navigate through the conversation? How do they respond to each other and move the conversation forward? In this section, we will examine the devices to facilitate conversation flow.

Buttons

Buttons are a way to let users respond to the chatbot in an unambiguous manner. You can add buttons to text, gallery, and list cards. Buttons have a label and a payload. The label is what the user gets to see. Payload is what happens in the backend when the user clicks the button:

A button can take one of four types of payloads: next block, URL, phone number, or share. The next block is identified by the name of the block. This will tell the chatbot which block to execute when the button is pressed. The URL can be specified, if the chatbot is to open a web page on the embedded web browser. Since the browser is embedded, the size of the window can also be specified. The phone number can be specified, if the chatbot is to make a voice call to someone (for example, call to reserve a table). And finally, the **Share** option can be used in cards such as lists and galleries to share the card with other contacts of the user.

Go to block cards

Buttons can be used to navigate the user from one block to another, however, the user has to push the button to enable navigation. However, there may be circumstances where the navigation needs to happen automatically. For instance, if the chatbot is giving the user step-by-step instructions on how to do something, it can be built by putting all the cards (one step of information per card) in one block. However, it might be a good idea to put them in different blocks for the sake of modularity. In such a case, we need to provide the user a *next step* button to move on to the next step.

In Chatfuel, we can use the **Go to Block** card to address this problem. A **Go to Block** card can be placed at the end of any block to take the chatbot to another block. Once the chatbot executes all the cards in a block, it moves to another block automatically without any user intervention. Using **Go to Block** cards, we can build the chatbot in a modular fashion. To add a **Go to Block** card at the end of a block, choose **ADD A CARD**, click the + icon and choose **Go to Block** card. Fill in the block name for redirection:

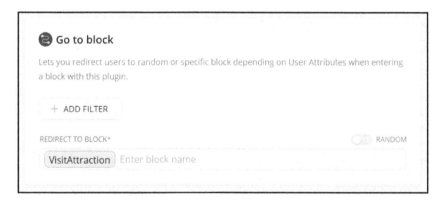

Redirections can also be made random and conditional. By choosing the random option, we can make the chatbot choose one of the mentioned blocks randomly. This adds a bit of uncertainty to the conversation. However, this needs to be used very carefully because the context of the conversation may get tricky to maintain.

Conditional redirections can be done if there is a need to check the context before the redirection is done. Let's revisit this option after we discuss context.

Managing context

In any conversation, the context of conversation needs to be managed. Context can be maintained by creating a local cache where the information transferred between the two dialogue partners can be stored. For instance, the user may tell the chatbot their food preferences, and this information can be stored in context for future reference if not used immediately. Another instance is in a conversation where the user is asking questions about a story. These questions may be incomplete and may need to be interpreted in terms of the information available in the context.

In this section, we will explore how context can be recorded and utilized during the conversation in Chatfuel. Let's take the task of finding a restaurant as part of your tour guide chatbot. The conversation between the chatbot and the user might go as follows:

```
User : Find a restaurant
Bot  : Ok. Where?
User : City center.
Bot  : Ok. Any cuisine that you fancy?
User : Indian
Bot  : Ok. Let me see... I found a few Indian restaurants in the city
center.
Here they are.
```

In the preceding conversation, up until the last bot utterance, the bot needs to save the information locally. When it has gathered all the information it needs, it can go off and search the database with appropriate parameters. Notice that it also needs to use that information in generating utterances dynamically. Let's explore how to do these two—dynamically generating utterances and searching the database.

First, we need to build the conversational flow to take the user through the conversation just as we discussed in the *Next steps* section. Let's assume that the user clicks the **Find_a_restaurant** button on the welcome block. Let's build the basic blocks with text messages and buttons to navigate through the conversation:

User input cards

As you can imagine, building the blocks for every cuisine and location combination can become a laborious task. Let's try to build the same functionality in another way—forms. In order to use forms, the u*ser input* card needs to be used. Let's create a new block called `Restaurant_search` and to it, let's add a **User Input** card. To add a **User Input** card, click **ADD A CARD**, click the **+** icon, and select the **User Input** card.

Add all the questions you want to ask the user under **MESSAGE TO USER**. The answers to each of these questions can be saved to variables. Name the variables against every question. These variables are always denoted with double curly brackets (for example, `{{restaurant_location}}`):

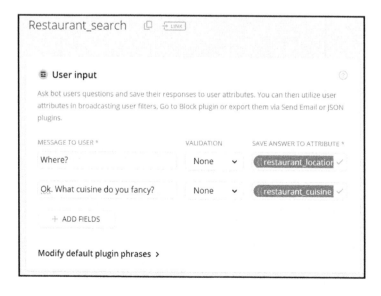

Information provided by the user can also be validated before acceptance. In case the required information is a phone number, email address, or a number, these can be validated by choosing the appropriate format of the input information. After the user input card, let's add a **Go to Block** card to redirect the flow to the results page:

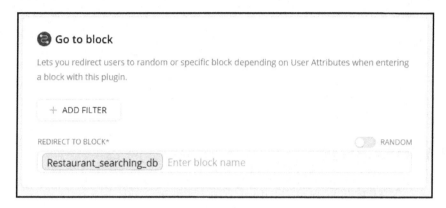

And add a block where we present the results. As you can see here, the variables holding information can be used in chatbot utterances. These will be dynamically replaced from the context when the conversation is happening:

The following screenshot shows the conversation so far on Messenger:

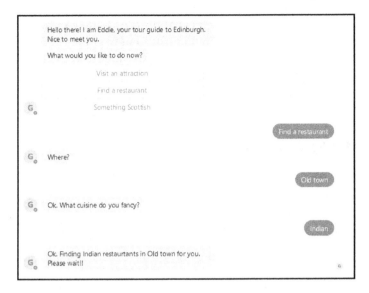

Setting user attributes

In addition to the user input cards, there is also another way to save information in context. This can be done by using the *set up user attribute* card. Using this card, you can set context-specific information at any point during the conversation. Let's take a look at how to do it. To add this card, choose **ADD A CARD**, click the **+** icon, and choose the **Set Up User Attribute** card:

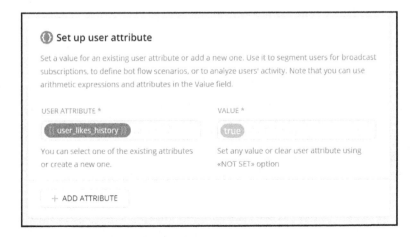

The preceding screenshot shows the `user-likes-history` variable being set to `true` when the user asked for historical attractions. This information can later be used to drive the conversation (as used in the **Go to Block** card) or to provide recommendations. Variables that are already in the context can be reset to new values or no value at all. To clear the value of a variable, use the special **NOT SET** value from the drop-down menu that appears as soon as you try to fill in a value for the variable. Also, you can set/reset more than one variable in a card.

Default contextual variables

Besides defining your own contextual variables, you can also use a list of predefined variables. The information contained in these variables include the following:

- Information that is obtained from the deployment platform (that is, Facebook) including the user's name, gender, time zone, and locale
- Contextual information—last pushed button, last visited block name, and so on

To get a full list of variables, create a new text card and type {{. This will open the drop-down menu with a list of variables you can choose from. This list will also include the variables created by you:

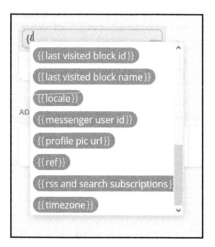

As with the developer-defined variables, these built-in variables can also be used in text messages and in conditional redirections using the **Go to Block** cards.

Understanding natural language

So far, we have seen how the conversational flow happens using buttons. In each case, the user has to press a button or type in information to fill in a slot, which makes the conversation progress. However, it is possible to have users initiate conversation and navigate using **natural language (NL)** input as well in Chatfuel. In this section, we will explore how to make the chatbot understand the user's natural language inputs and take action.

Default block

Alongside the **Welcome message** block, there is a **Default answer** block. This block is used by the chatbot as response to any input from the user that it does not understand. Go ahead and change the contents of the block as follows:

Now test the bot by typing in a question to the chatbot on Messenger. You can see how the default message gets used:

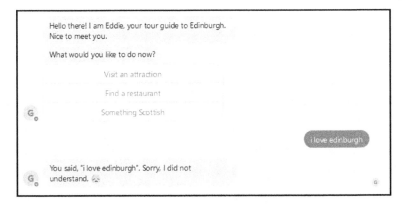

Let us now explore how to handle NL input so that users don't end up with this default response. To set up the chatbot to understand NL inputs, find and click the **Set Up AI** option in the menu on the far left of the page. This is where we will specify NL input templates and their corresponding chatbot responses:

Click **ADD AI RULE**. You will see two fields. Type user utterances and bot responses in the respective fields:

Bot responses can either be text or blocks. By providing block names, the chatbot can be redirected to appropriate blocks when the user chooses to type responses rather than push buttons. After having added a few rules, go back to Messenger and try the bot with the NL inputs:

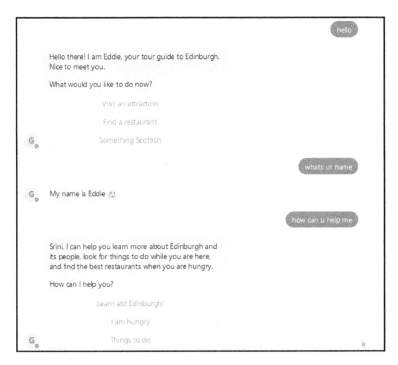

You can also add an element of uncertainty and randomness by choosing the random flag in bot response and add more than one response. The bot would then choose one response randomly.

Backend processing

Conversational tasks usually need to be backed up by backend tasks. For instance, booking a table in a restaurant is not just a conversation, it also involves the action of booking a table. This is a backend task where the information concerning the booking is sent over to a booking server as an HTTP request. In this section, we will explore how to use the JSON API card to enable backend tasks.

Before we start using a JSON API card, we need a URL that can take a few parameters and carry out a backend task. Let's build a dummy backend service that can book a table given the restaurant name, number of people, and the time. To do this, we have to build a Node.js web app and host it on the cloud:

1. Create a directory called `Eddie-bot`. In this directory, we need three files: `index.js`, `package.json`, and `Procfile`.

2. Create the package file, `package.json`, which declares the packages necessary for the app, as shown here:

```
{
  "name": "eddie-server",
  "version": "1.0.0",
  "description": "Eddie - Chatfuel",
  "main": "index.js",
  "scripts": {
    "test": "echo \"Error: no test specified\" && exit 1"
  },
  "author": "Srini Janarthanam",
  "license": "ISC",
  "dependencies": {
    "body-parser": "^1.15.2",
    "express": "^4.14.0",
    "request": "^2.72.0"
  }
}
```

3. Create `Procfile`. `Procfile` is a special file used by our cloud service, called Heroku, to tell the application dynos what command to run to get the app started. It should contain the following code:

```
web: node index.js
```

4. Create the `index.js` file. Finally, we need the program that will process the request in the backend. Paste the following code:

```
// EddieBot webhooks

const express = require('express')
const bodyParser = require('body-parser')
const app = express()
app.set('port', (process.env.PORT || 5000))

// Process application/x-www-form-urlencoded
app.use(bodyParser.urlencoded({extended: false}))
```

```
// Process application/json
app.use(bodyParser.json())
app.use(express.static('public'))

// Spin up the server
app.listen(app.get('port'), function() {
    console.log('running on port', app.get('port'))
})

// Index route
app.get('/', function (req, res) {
    res.send('Hello world, I am EddieBot webhook.')
})

app.post('/booktable/', function (req, res) {
    console.log(JSON.stringify(req.body));
    // YOUR BOOKING CODE GOES HERE!!

    var out = {
            "messages": [
                {"text": "Thanks for your booking!"},
                {"text": "See you soon!!"}
            ]
    }
    var outString = JSON.stringify(out);
    console.log('Out:' + outString);
    res.send(outString);
})
```

In the preceding program, we have a handle called `booktable`, which we will call when the user wants to book a table at a particular restaurant. To this handle, we will send a number of parameters that are necessary to make a table booking such as restaurant name, number of people, and time. Once the booking is made, the app returns a success message to the bot, which is then forwarded to the user. In the preceding code, we are not actually making the booking. We are simply assuming that the booking is made.

5. To get this app operational, we need to push it on to a cloud server. To do so on Heroku, type the following commands in the console:

```
C:\Eddie-bot> git init
C:\Eddie-bot> git add .
C:\Eddie-bot> git commit -m "Backend Eddie Bot v1"
C:\Eddie-bot> heroku create eddie-bot-backend
C:\Eddie-bot> git push heroku master
```

The last command pushes the app onto the cloud, builds it, and executes the index.js program which starts a web server. We will learn more about how to build web apps in Node.js and Java in the subsequent chapters. Now, we can call the https://eddie-bot-backend.herokuapp.com/booktable URL, with the necessary parameters, to make a booking.

6. Now that the dummy booking server is set up, let us call it and make a booking from the chatbot. This involves creating a flow using a number of card types. Let's assume that the user clicks the **More information** button on a certain restaurant, **Tajmahal**, for example. This needs to take the user to the block where we display information about the restaurant such as cuisine, menu, and location, with an option to book a table if the user is interested. Let's, therefore, build a basic block for **Tajmahal**:

7. We need to add a couple more cards to this block. To set the context, we need to add a user attribute card where we set the name of the restaurant:

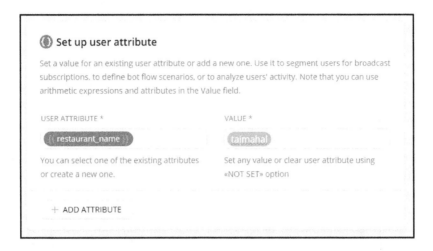

8. We then transfer the conversation to a generic table-booking block where other necessary information can be gathered. To do this, let's create a new `Table_booking_form` block:

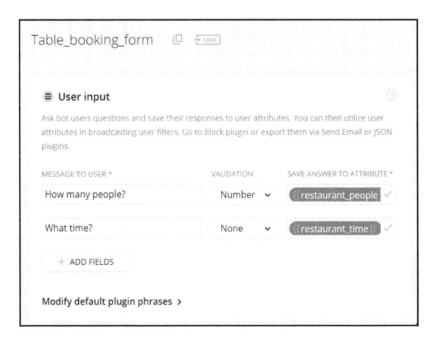

In this block, we have added a user input card where information concerning the number of people and time are sought from the user. These are stored in appropriate variables.

9. Finally, to this block, we add the **JSON API** card, which makes the chatbot call an external server for backend processing:

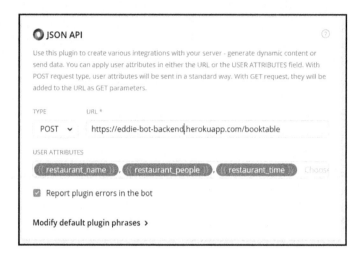

In this card, we need to mention the kind of request (**GET/POST**), the URL to call, and the parameters to send along. The response from the backend server is returned to the user.

Great! Let's test it out in Messenger:

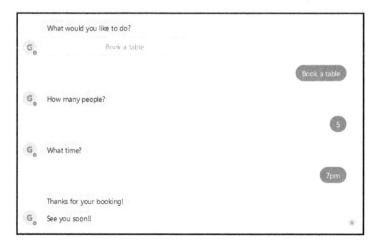

Notice how the text message returned from the backend server ends up in Messenger. The response from the backend server needs to be in a specific format. In `index.js`, we sent back a simple text message. However, other types of messages can be sent as well. For instance, the following is an example of how you can send a text block with buttons:

```
{
    "messages": [
      {
        "attachment": {
          "type": "template",
          "payload": {
            "template_type": "button",
            "text": "Here are my recommendations!",
            "buttons": [
              {
                "type": "show_block",
                "block_name": "TajMahal",
                "title": "TajMahal (5 stars)"
              },
              {
                "type": "show_block",
                "block_name": "SpicyTandoori",
                "title": "Spicy Tandoori (4 stars)"
              }
            ]
          }
        }
      }
    ]
}
```

Explore the other types of messages that you can send to create more dynamic conversational cards at `https://help.chatfuel.com/facebook-messenger/plugins/json-plugin/`.

Broadcasting

Another interesting feature provided by Chatfuel is the ability send messages to more than one user at any time. This is a facility that you can use to restart conversations with the user or send notifications periodically. To use this feature, click the **Broadcast** option in the main menu:

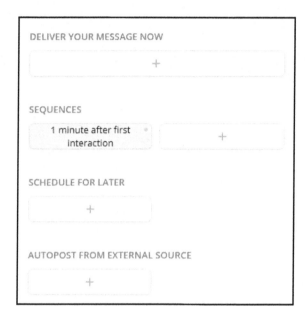

You will see four options. Let's select **DELIVER YOUR MESSAGE NOW**. There are three things to do—compose a message to send, choose users, and hit **SEND**:

Click **USER FILTER** to choose a subset of users you want to send the message to. This is done using variables and values. For instance, you can choose to send the message to all users who said that they love Indian cuisine (that is, `{{restaurant_cuisine}}` = `'Indian'`) and that they are in the Old Town (`{{restaurant_location}}` = `'Old town'`). This a message can be a discount offer at an Indian restaurant in the city:

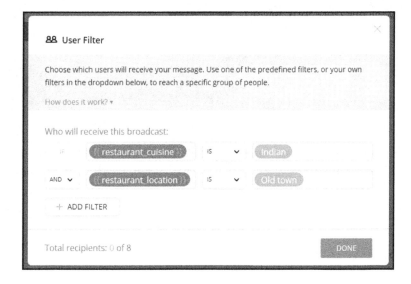

Having selected the target user group, create a block of a message and hit **SEND**. This message will be sent immediately to all the qualifying users.

You can also send messages to target user groups at scheduled times, sequence automatic messages after user interaction, and post from external sources, as well as using the broadcast feature.

Bot templates

Chatbots can be built from templates. These are basic pre-designed chatbots that can be readily edited and converted into the chatbot that you need. There are a number of templates for you to start with. To do this, go to `https://dashboard.chatfuel.com/#/bots`. Under the **TUTORIAL TEMPLATES** section, click **View All Templates**:

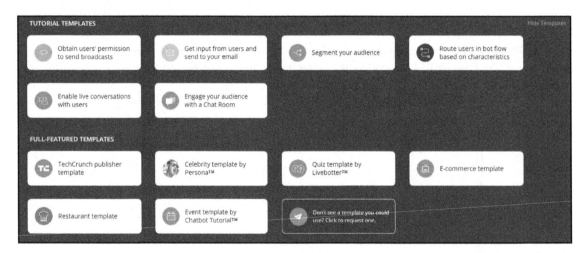

Chatfuel provides a number of templates with a variety of use cases such as restaurants, celebrity assistant, quiz, and e-commerce. Explore them further to learn how the conversation is structured and how various tools have been used to support those conversations.

Analytics

Chatfuel also provides analytics on your chatbot. To access the analytics, go to your chatbot's dashboard and click **Analyze** in the main menu. The analytics page summarizes the bot's usage statistics in terms of user growth, user activity, and user retention. It also highlights usage patterns, such as the blocks that are popular with users and issues faced by AI in terms of understanding users' language utterances. Finally, it also tells you where in the world your users are coming from.

Summary

Congratulations! In this chapter, we embarked on a journey toward building awesome chatbots. I hope, using Chatfuel, you have created your very first bot. Using tour guiding as the use case, we explored a variety of chatbot design and development topics along the way—conversation flow design, blocks, types of message content, navigating through the conversational flow, understanding basic natural language utterances, and many more. We have also learned the various building blocks provided by Chatfuel to build, monitor, and manage chatbots.

In the following chapters, we will explore using a variety of other use cases and more advanced topics in building chatbots, such as understanding nuances in natural language utterances and managing more complex conversational contexts.

References

Chatfuel documentation: `http://docs.chatfuel.com/`

3
Let's Talk Weather

Facebook Messenger is one of the most popular globally-available messaging platforms. You can access it using your Facebook account. Messenger is available separately to Facebook in the form of a website (`http://messenger.com` and `http://m.me`) and as a smartphone app. This makes it extremely accessible. Facebook has more than 1 billion global users and all of these social media users have access to Messenger as well; this staggering number is also growing every day. This makes it a popular choice for chatbot developers as a deployment platform. In addition to the number of users, the company is investing hugely in making it a place for chatbots to thrive. Its recent features, such as the **Discover** tab and SDK upgrade, serve as testimony to their commitment.

In this chapter, we will design and implement a chatbot that can talk about the weather. We will build a chatbot and integrate it with a backend service that can provide us with real-time weather information. We will then go on to integrate the chatbot in Facebook Messenger. And finally, have a look at the exclusive features of Messenger that can be used to make the chatbot more attractive and engaging.

By the end of this chapter, you will be able to:

- Design conversational tasks to talk about the weather
- Create backend integrations using the OpenWeatherMap API,
- Build a chatbot in Java 8 and Node.js and host it on the cloud using Heroku
- Understand Facebook Messenger SDK and types of message templates
- Integrate the chatbot in Messenger

Conversational tasks

Let's first figure out the tasks that we want the chatbot to perform. I would think that a chatbot capable of talking about the weather should be able to do it along the following lines:

- Weather now
- Weather today
- Weather this week
- Weather this weekend
- Weather in the future

All the mentioned reports are based on a geographical location. This piece of information could be provided in many formats. Most people would provide a city/town name, or a ZIP code. But given the fact that mobile devices have GPS capability, and messaging apps allow for location sharing, another way of locating the user could be using LatLong (latitude and longitude) coordinates. Let's account for all these variations. In addition to these tasks and input types, we need to consider requests for clarifications that the chatbot must be capable of if the input location information is ambiguous.

Conversational design

Now that we have identified the tasks that our chatbot needs to do, let's go on and design the conversational flow. Conversational flow is the basic layout of how the interaction will happen between the user and the bot.

Let's scribble down a few simple imagined conversations between the user and our weather bot.

Example 1:

```
User: Hi
Bot: Hi there! I am WeatherMan, your weather bot. What would you like to
know? Current weather or forecast?
User: current weather
Bot: Ok. Which city?
User: London, GB
Bot: Ok. Weather now in London, GB. Temperature is 10 degrees Celsius.
Clear Skies.
User: Thanks.
Bot: No problem! :)
```

Let's make another one that is slightly more complex.

Example 2:

```
User: Hi there
Bot: Hi there! I am WeatherMan, your weather bot. What would you like to
know? Current weather or forecast?
User: Forecast
Bot: Ok. When? Tomorrow or this weekend?
User: Tomorrow
Bot: Ok. Which city?
User: Edinburgh
Bot: Edinburgh, US or Edinburgh, GB?
User: Edinburgh, GB
Bot: Ok. Weather tomorrow in Edinburgh, GB. Temperature is 12 degrees
Celsius. Cloudy.
```

Well within the domain of weather talk, more complex conversations are possible. However, we will work with the preceding examples to show how you can build a chatbot and deploy it on Facebook Messenger in principle. Let us deal with more complex utterances and conversations later.

Backend tasks

Before we move on to implementing the chatbot, let us take a look at the source of information for weather data, *OpenWeatherMap* (https://openweathermap.org). OpenWeatherMap is a cloud service serving weather info about 200,000+ cities across the globe. It has both current and forecast data as well as historical data. It has both free and paid services. Navigate to the website, type your city name, and give it a try.

Getting weather data

Let us now set up an account in OpenWeatherMap service to obtain weather data.

Getting the API key

Unlike the last chapter, where we created content for the chatbot manually, we will be using this data live from the service endpoint. In order to do this, we need to sign up to this. To sign up, navigate to https://home.openweathermap.org/ and create a new account.

To get started with the data, we will have to subscribe to the appropriate API service. To do this, navigate through the website by clicking the **API** option on the main menu on the home page:

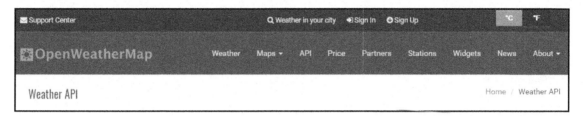

On the API page, you will see the listing on all the API services that are available. Let's start with the basic one: **Current weather data**. Click **Subscribe**:

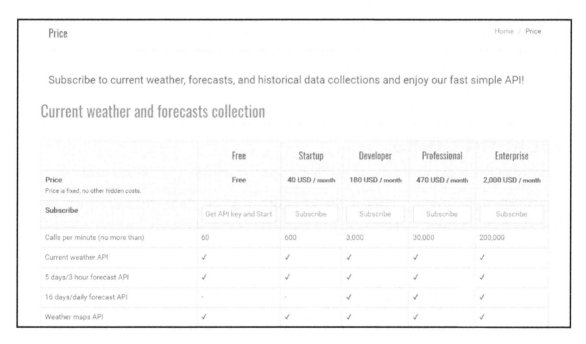

Click **Get API key and Start**. This will take you to the appid page (`https://openweathermap.org/appid`) where you can find documentation on the API (that is, how to use the key and its limitations).

To get your key, you need to go further. Navigate to the **API keys** page: `https://home.openweathermap.org/api_keys`. You will find a default key. If you don't, create one:

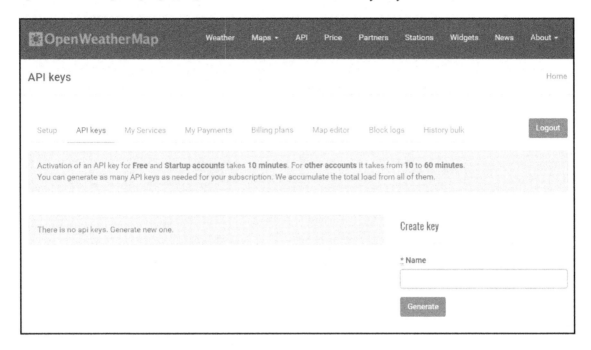

Now that we have our key, let's give it a try!

Trying your key

We have to construct the URL to get the data we need. Here is a basic one:

```
http://api.openweathermap.org/data/2.5/forecast?id=<CITY_CODE>&APPID=<YOUR_
API_KEY>
```

To get your city code, navigate to the following URL:

```
https://openweathermap.org/find?q=
```

Type **Your city name** and click **Search**. On the results page, grab your city code from the URL:

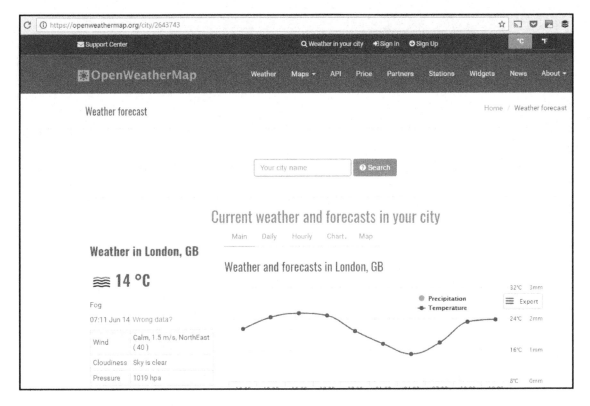

For instance, the city code for *London, GB* is **2643743**.

Replace <YOUR_API_KEY> with your key and try the URL on a web browser. You will get a JSON object with current and forecast weather information, similar to the following one:

```
{
    "cod": "200",
    "message": 0.003,
    "cnt": 37,
    "list": [ … ], // 37 items
    "city": {
        "id": 2643743,
        "name": "London",
        "coord": {
            "lat": 51.5085,
            "lon": -0.1258
        },
        "country": "GB"
    }
}
```

The list key with 37 items can be expanded, in that you will find current and forecast information for every three hours starting from the current time:

```
"list": [
    {
        "dt": 1497430800,
        "main": { … }, // 8 items
        "weather": [
            {
                "id": 800,
                "main": "Clear",
                "description": "clear sky",
                "icon": "01d"
            }
        ],
        "clouds": { … }, // 1 item
        "wind": { … }, // 2 items
        "sys": { … }, // 1 item
        "dt_txt": "2017-06-14 09:00:00"
    },
    { … }, // 7 items
    { … }, // 7 items
```

Brilliant! We now have a data source to plug into our chatbot.

Building the backend interface

Let us now try some code! We are now going to build a module in Java that can access the weather data from our data source in real time. We will then plug this module into the chatbot for the conversation manager to use:

1. Open Eclipse.
2. Create a new Maven project.
3. Choose **Create a simple project**.
4. Provide the location of the project and hit **Next**.
5. On the next page, type **Group Id**, **Artifact Id**, **Name**, and **Description**. Click **Finish**.

We now have a blank Maven project ready. Before we move on to developing the backend code, let's add a few dependency packages to our project. Find the POM file (pom.xml) and add the following Maven dependencies:

```xml
<dependencies>
    <!--https://mvnrepository.com/artifact/com.google.code.gson/gson-->
    <dependency>
      <groupId>com.google.code.gson</groupId>
      <artifactId>gson</artifactId>
      <version>2.8.0</version>
    </dependency>
    <!--
https://mvnrepository.com/artifact/org.apache.httpcomponents/httpclient-->
    <dependency>
      <groupId>org.apache.httpcomponents</groupId>
      <artifactId>httpclient</artifactId>
      <version>4.5.3</version>
    </dependency>
</dependencies>
```

We may need other dependencies later. But for the backend code, these packages will suffice. Let's now create a Java class, Weather.java, to access weather data. The following code shows the basic structure of the class:

```java
package weatherman.weather;

import com.google.gson.JsonObject;

public class Weather {
  public static void main(String[] args) {
  }
```

```
    public Weather(){}

    public JsonObject getWeather(String cityCode){ return null; }
    public JsonObject getCurrentWeather(String cityName){ return null; }
}
```

We will now add the necessary code to get the actual data from OpenWeatherMaps service:

```
package weatherman.weather;

import java.io.IOException;

import org.apache.http.HttpResponse;
import org.apache.http.client.ClientProtocolException;
import org.apache.http.client.HttpClient;
import org.apache.http.client.methods.HttpGet;
import org.apache.http.impl.client.HttpClientBuilder;
import org.apache.http.util.EntityUtils;

import com.google.gson.JsonObject;
import com.google.gson.JsonParser;

public class Weather {

  //put your api key here
  String apiKey = <Your API key>;

  public static void main(String[] args) {
     try {
         (new Weather()).getWeather("2643743");
     } catch (ClientProtocolException e) {
       e.printStackTrace();
     } catch (IOException e) {
       e.printStackTrace();
     }
  }

  public Weather(){}

  public JsonObject getWeather(String cityCode)
             throws ClientProtocolException, IOException {

     //step 1: Prepare the url
     String url = "http://api.openweathermap.org/data/2.5/forecast?id="
        + cityCode + "&APPID=" + apiKey ;

     //step 2: Create a HTTP client
     HttpClient httpclient = HttpClientBuilder.create().build();
```

```
    //step 3: Create a HTTPGet object and execute the url
    HttpGet httpGet = new HttpGet(url);
    HttpResponse response = httpclient.execute(httpGet);

    //step 4: Process the result
    JsonObject json = null;
    int statusCode = response.getStatusLine().getStatusCode();
    if (statusCode == 200) {
        String response_string = EntityUtils.toString(response.getEntity());
        json = (new JsonParser()).parse(response_string).getAsJsonObject();
        Gson gson = new GsonBuilder().setPrettyPrinting().create();
        String prettyJson = gson.toJson(json);
        System.out.println(prettyJson);
    }
    return json;
  }

}
```

In the `main` method, we have instantiated a `Weather` object to get current weather for London, GB (`2643743`). Run the preceding code and you will get the following result in the console:

```
 Problems  @ Javadoc   Declaration   Search  Console   Progress
<terminated> Weather [Java Application] C:\Program Files\Java\jre1.8.0_66\bin\javaw.exe (7 Dec 2017, 10:32:24)
{
  "cod": "200",
  "message": 0.0409,
  "cnt": 40,
  "list": [
    {
      "dt": 1512648000,
      "main": {
        "temp": 284.77,
        "temp_min": 284.77,
        "temp_max": 285.379,
        "pressure": 1010.65,
        "sea_level": 1018.28,
        "grnd_level": 1010.65,
        "humidity": 99,
        "temp_kf": -0.61
      },
      "weather": [
        {
          "id": 500,
```

The result is in the form of a JSON object that we can use to respond to weather inquiries. In the *list* item, there are 36 items. Each of those items provides weather data, such as average temperature (`temp`), minimum temperature (`temp_min`), and maximum temperature (`temp_max`) at a particular time (`dt` being the timestamp). Let's now implement two methods, `getWeatherAtTime()` and `getWeatherReport()`, to generate a short weather report:

```
public String getWeatherReport(String cityCode, Integer i)
                throws ClientProtocolException, IOException{

    JsonObject currentWeather = null;
    if (cityCode != null){
        currentWeather = getWeatherAtTime(cityCode, i);
    }

    String weatherReport = null;
    if (currentWeather != null){
        JsonObject weather = currentWeather.get("weather")
                .getAsJsonArray().get(0).getAsJsonObject();
        Double avgTemp = Double.valueOf(currentWeather.get("main")
        .getAsJsonObject().get("temp").getAsString()) - 273.15;
        String avgTempSt = String.valueOf(avgTemp).split("\\.")[0];
        weatherReport = "The temperature is " + avgTempSt +
                        " degrees Celsius. "
                        + weather.get("description").getAsString() + ".";
    }
    System.out.println(weatherReport);
    return weatherReport;
}

public JsonObject getWeatherAtTime(String cityCode, Integer i)
                throws ClientProtocolException, IOException{

    JsonObject json = getWeather(cityCode);
    JsonArray list = json.get("list").getAsJsonArray();
    JsonObject weatherAtTime = list.get(i).getAsJsonObject();
    return weatherAtTime;
}
```

You might have noticed that the `getWeatherReport()` needs two parameters—city code and time. Time is passed as an integer with `0` being the current time, `1` being the next slot, and so on. Calling the `getWeatherReport()` method from `main` with the name of the city and time as parameters will result in a short textual weather report like the following one:

```
Temperature is 297.8 degrees . clear sky.
```

Obviously, given the richness of the data source, we can extend the number of backend tasks.

Implementing the chatbot

Now that we have the backend tasks ready, let's focus on the chatbot itself. In general, the chatbot will take the user's utterances as input and respond with utterances of its own. However, since we are building a chatbot for Facebook Messenger, our chatbot will mostly take input in the form of button presses and respond using both utterances and visually appealing cards.

Let's start by implementing the Chatbot.java class. We will begin by working out an algorithm to process and respond to users' utterances:

1. Process user input.
2. Update context.
3. Identify bot intent.
4. Generate bot utterance and output structure.
5. Respond.

This one is a very simple algorithm to start with. First, user input, in the form of utterances or button presses is processed. Then the context of the conversation is updated. In the next step, we identify what the bot needs to say. Once that is determined, we figure out how to say it and respond. Let us start by implementing the basic structure based on the mentioned algorithm:

```
package weatherman.chatbot;

import com.google.gson.JsonObject;

public class Chatbot {
    JsonObject context;

    public static void main(String[] args){}

    public Chatbot(){
        context = new JsonObject();
    }

    public JsonObject process(JsonObject userInput){

        //step1: process user input
```

```
    JsonObject userAction = processUserInput(userInput);

    //step2: update context
    updateContext(userAction);

    //step3: identify bot intent
    identifyBotIntent();

    //step4: structure output
    JsonObject out = getBotOutput();

    return out;
  }
}
```

We will now modify the `main()` method to simulate a chat window where the user can type in their requests and responses and have a chat with the bot:

```
public static void main(String[] args){
    Chatbot c = new Chatbot();
    Scanner scanner = new Scanner(System.in);
    String userUtterance;

    do {
       System.out.print("User:");
       userUtterance = scanner.nextLine();
       //end the conversation
       if (userUtterance.equals("QUIT")){ break; }

       JsonObject userInput = new JsonObject();
       userInput.add("userUtterance", new JsonPrimitive(userUtterance));
       JsonObject botOutput = c.process(userInput);
       String botUtterance = "";
       if (botOutput != null && botOutput.has("botUtterance")) {
          botUtterance = botOutput.get("botUtterance").getAsString();
       }
       System.out.println("Bot:" + botUtterance);

    } while (true);
  }
```

Now, let us focus on the chatbot itself. We will first build a module to understand users' utterances. We are going to build a very simple module using rules and *regular expressions* to translate user utterances into user intents.

> ***An intent*** *is a formal unambiguous representation of what the user or the bot says. It conveys the meaning behind an utterance or a gesture.*

Let us first figure out an initial list of user intents for the tasks we have based on the example conversations that we have created:

- greet
- request_current_weather
- inform_city
- thank

The greet intent represents the many different greetings that the user may use. We will, therefore, translate a number of utterances such as hi, hi there, hello, and hello there into the greet intent. Similarly, the thank intent represents all ways the user might thank the bot. The request_current_weather intent is used to represent the utterances where the user is requesting current weather info and the inform_city intent is where they mention the name of the city:

```
public JsonObject processUserInput(JsonObject userInput){
    String userUtterance = null;
    JsonObject userAction = new JsonObject();

    //default case
    userAction.add("userIntent", new JsonPrimitive(""));
    if (userInput.has("userUtterance")){
        userUtterance = userInput.get("userUtterance").getAsString();
        userUtterance = userUtterance.replaceAll("%2C", ",");
    }
    if (userUtterance.matches("(hi|hello)( there)?")){
        userAction.add("userIntent", new JsonPrimitive("greet"));
    }
    else if (userUtterance.matches("(thanks)|(thank you)")){
        userAction.add("userIntent", new JsonPrimitive("thank"));
    }
    else if (userUtterance.matches("current weather")||
            userUtterance.matches("weather now")){
        userAction.add("userIntent", new
        JsonPrimitive("request_current_weather"));
    }
    else {
        //contextual processing
        String currentTask = context.get("currentTask").getAsString();
        String botIntent = context.get("botIntent").getAsString();
        if (currentTask.equals("requestWeather") &&
```

```
                    botIntent.equals("requestPlace")){
        userAction.add("userIntent", new
        JsonPrimitive("inform_city"));
        userAction.add("cityName", new JsonPrimitive(userUtterance));
    }
  }
  return userAction;
}
```

In the preceding code, we derive the user's intent from the utterance. Some intents have associated parameters as well. For instance, the `inform_city` intent has an associated `cityName` parameter which represents the name of the city for which the user is seeking a weather report. Interestingly, the `inform_city` intent is also an intent that we derive from context. Because, when asked for city information, the user merely mentions the name of the city. So anything typed in will be reported as a city name and will need to be validated later. Intent and its associated parameters are boxed up as a JSON object `userAction`. Let us move on to updating the context:

```
public void updateContext(JsonObject userAction){
    //copy userIntent
    context.add("userIntent", userAction.get("userIntent"));
    //
    String userIntent = context.get("userIntent").getAsString();
    if (userIntent.equals("greet")){
      context.add("currentTask", new JsonPrimitive("greetUser"));
    } else if (userIntent.equals("request_current_weather")){
      context.add("currentTask", new JsonPrimitive("requestWeather"));
      context.add("timeOfWeather", new JsonPrimitive("current"));
      context.add("placeOfWeather", new JsonPrimitive("unknown"));
      context.add("placeName", new JsonPrimitive("unknown"));
    } else if (userIntent.equals("inform_city")){
      String cityName = userAction.get("cityName").getAsString();
      JsonObject cityInfo = weather.getCityCode(cityName);
      if (!cityInfo.get("cityCode").isJsonNull()){
        context.add("placeOfWeather", cityInfo.get("cityCode"));
        context.add("placeName", cityInfo.get("cityName"));
      }
    } else if (userIntent.equals("thank")){
      context.add("currentTask", new JsonPrimitive("thankUser"));
    }
}
```

In the preceding code, we updated the context of the conversation using the input from the user. Here, the user input is translated into tasks and parameters. The idea behind context is the same as how humans keep the context of conversation while talking to someone. The `currentTask` variable represents the current task of the chatbot. Intents such as `greet`, `thank`, and `request_current_weather` will set this variable. Each task will have a number of parameters that need to be filled in. For instance, the `requestWeather` task has two slots: time and place. They need to be filled before the bot can get the weather report. If the user asks for current weather, the time is set to `current`, but the place is still unknown. Next step: identify the bot's intent!

Having updated the context, the chatbot's intent needs to be determined. For some tasks, such as greeting and thanking the user, bot intents are quite straightforward. For other complex tasks, the intents are determined based on the slots that need to be filled and the response from backend tasks. We have the following intents for the bot:

- `greetUser`
- `thankUser`
- `requestPlace`
- `informWeather`

`greetUser` and `thankUser` are used to greet and thank users. `requestPlace` is used when the bot needs to know the place of the weather report. `informWeather` is used when the bot has successfully retrieved a report from the backend service that we have built in the previous section:

```
public void identifyBotIntent(){
    String currentTask = context.get("currentTask").getAsString();
    if (currentTask.equals("greetUser")){
        context.add("botIntent", new JsonPrimitive("greetUser"));
    } else if (currentTask.equals("thankUser")){
        context.add("botIntent", new JsonPrimitive("thankUser"));
    } else if (currentTask.equals("requestWeather")){
        if
        (context.get("placeOfWeather").getAsString().equals("unknown")){
            context.add("botIntent", new JsonPrimitive("requestPlace"));
        }
        else {
            Integer time = -1;
            if
            (context.get("timeOfWeather").getAsString().equals("current")){
                time = 0;
            }
            String weatherReport = null;
```

```
    try {
      weatherReport = weather.getWeatherReport(
        context.get("placeOfWeather").getAsString(), time);
    }
    catch (ClientProtocolException e) {
      e.printStackTrace();
    } catch (IOException e) {
      e.printStackTrace();
    }
    if (weatherReport != null){
      context.add("weatherReport", new
                  JsonPrimitive(weatherReport));
      context.add("botIntent", new JsonPrimitive("informWeather"));
    }
  }
} else {
  context.add("botIntent", null);
}
}
```

In the preceding code, notice how the bot decides what to do when the `currentTask` is `requestWeather`. It decides to ask for the place when it is not known. And when both the time and place are known, it fetches the report and updates the context. Next, the bot's intent needs to be translated into an utterance:

```
public JsonObject getBotOutput(){
    JsonObject out = new JsonObject();
    String botIntent = context.get("botIntent").getAsString();
    String botUtterance = "";

    if (botIntent.equals("greetUser")){
      botUtterance = "Hi there! I am WeatherMan, your weather bot! "
        + "What would you like to know? Current weather or forecast?";
    } else if (botIntent.equals("thankUser")){
      botUtterance = "Thanks for talking to me! Have a great day!!";
    } else if (botIntent.equals("requestPlace")){
      botUtterance = "Ok. Which city?";
    } else if (botIntent.equals("informWeather")){
      String timeDescription =
        getTimeDescription(context.get("timeOfWeather").getAsString());
      String placeDescription = getPlaceDescription();
      String weatherReport = context.get("weatherReport").getAsString();
      botUtterance = "Ok. Weather " + timeDescription + " in " +
        placeDescription + ". " +  weatherReport;
    }
    out.add("botIntent", context.get("botIntent"));
    out.add("botUtterance", new JsonPrimitive(botUtterance));
```

```
        return out;
    }

    private String getPlaceDescription() {
        return context.get("placeName").getAsString();
    }
    private String getTimeDescription(String timeOfWeather) {
        if (timeOfWeather.equals("current")){
            return "now";
        }
        return null;
    }
}
```

Now that the bot's intent and utterance are identified, let us execute the `main` method and have some fun! Run the `Chatbot` class by pressing *Ctrl + F11*. On the console, you will be prompted to start the conversation. Have a look at the following example conversation:

```
User:hi there
Bot:Hi there! I am WeatherMan, your weather bot! What would you like to
know? Current weather or forecast?
User:current weather
Bot:Ok. Which city?
User:London,GB
Bot:Ok. Weather now in London,GB. The temperature is 291.72 degrees
Farenheit. broken clouds.
User:thanks
Bot:Thanks for talking to me! Have a great day!!
User:QUIT
```

As you may have noticed, there are a lot of unfinished tasks here. For instance, the city name should be typed in the same format (`<cityname, countrycode>`) as it is in our weather database. This is not ideal. The user should be able to say `in London` and still get answers. We will get back to this in the next chapter, where we will look at how to handle utterances where users may call the same entity with different names. But first, let us get this code to work in Facebook Messenger.

Creating a chatbot web service

Our next step is to make the chatbot available as a web service. This is so that platforms, such as Facebook Messenger, can access the chatbot without having to actually host them on their own servers. In order to make the chatbot available as a web service, the chatbot code needs to be packaged as a web server and hosted on a cloud platform. We will use the Java Spark library to wrap the chatbot code as a web server and the Heroku cloud platform to host it:

1. We need to add the Spark dependency to the POM file:

```
<!-- https://mvnrepository.com/artifact/com.sparkjava/spark-core -
->
<dependency>
    <groupId>com.sparkjava</groupId>
    <artifactId>spark-core</artifactId>
    <version>2.0.0</version>
</dependency>
```

2. Implement a Java class called `WebServer.java`. Make sure to place it in the default package:

```
public class WebServer {
    public static void main(String[] args) {
        Spark.setPort(getHerokuAssignedPort());
        Spark.staticFileLocation("/public");
        final Chatbot bot = new Chatbot();

        get("/", (req, res) -> "Hello World! I am WeatherMan,
        the weather bot!!");

        //post handle for WeatherMan chatbot
        post("/bot", new Route() {
            public Object handle(Request request, Response response) {
                String body = request.body();
                System.out.println("body: " + body);
                String splitChar = "&";
                String keyValueSplitter = "=";
                String[] params = body.split(splitChar);
                String userUtterance = "null";
                for (int i=0; i < params.length; i++){
                    String[] sv = params[i].split(keyValueSplitter);
                    if (sv[0].equals("userUtterance")){
                        if (sv.length > 0){
                            userUtterance = sv[1];
                        } else {
```

```
                            userUtterance = "";
                        }
                        userUtterance = userUtterance.replaceAll("%20",
                        "");
                        userUtterance = userUtterance.replaceAll("%3A",
                        ":");
                    }
                }
                if (!userUtterance.equals("null")){
                    System.out.println("User says:" + userUtterance);
                    JsonObject userInput = new JsonObject();
                    userInput.add("userUtterance", new
                    JsonPrimitive(userUtterance));
                    String botResponse = bot.processFB(userInput);
                    System.out.println("Bot says:" + botResponse);
                    if (botResponse != null) {
                        return botResponse;
                    }
                } else {
                  return null;
                }
                response.status(400);
                return new ResponseError("Error! POST not handled.");
            }
        }, json());

        after((req, res) -> { res.type("application/json"); });

        exception(IllegalArgumentException.class, (e, req, res) -> {
            res.status(400);
            res.body(toJson(new ResponseError(e)));
        });
    }

    static int getHerokuAssignedPort() {
        ProcessBuilder processBuilder = new ProcessBuilder();
        if (processBuilder.environment().get("PORT") != null) {
            return
Integer.parseInt(processBuilder.environment().get("PORT"));
        }
        return 4567;
        //return default port if heroku-port isn't set (i.e. on
        //localhost)
    }
}
```

3. Implement the web server helper classes. `WebServer.java` imports classes from Spark and Gson packages. It also needs two helper classes, `JSONUtil.java` and `ResponseError.java`. The `JSONUtil` helper class helps `WebServer` turn the response format into JSON:

```
package weatherman.web.utils;

import com.google.gson.Gson;
import spark.ResponseTransformer;

public class JSONUtil {
    public static String toJson(Object object) {
        return new Gson().toJson(object);
    }
    public static ResponseTransformer json() {
        return JSONUtil::toJson;
    }
}
```

The `ResponseError` class helps the `WebServer` class to report errors in a specific format that may occur during web service:

```
package weatherman.web.utils;

public class ResponseError {
    private String errorType;
    public ResponseError(String message, String... args) {
        this.errorType = String.format(message, args);
    }
    public ResponseError(Exception e) {
        this.errorType = e.getMessage();
    }
    public String getMessage() {
        return this.errorType;
    }
}
```

4. Change the Java compiler to 1.8. The `pom.xml` file tells Heroku which compiler to use when building the project in the cloud. Since we are using Lambda expressions, we need to set the compiler to Java 1.8. To do this, add the following code (the `build` element) in the `pom.xml` file just after the `dependencies` element:

```
<build>
  <plugins>
    <plugin>
```

```
            <artifactId>maven-compiler-plugin</artifactId>
            <version>3.1</version>
            <configuration>
                <source>1.8</source>
                <target>1.8</target>
            </configuration>
            <executions>
                <execution>
                    <id>default-compile</id>
                    <phase>compile</phase>
                    <goals>
                        <goal>compile</goal>
                    </goals>
                </execution>
                <execution>
                    <id>default-testCompile</id>
                    <phase>test-compile</phase>
                    <goals>
                        <goal>testCompile</goal>
                    </goals>
                </execution>
            </executions>
        </plugin>
    </plugins>
</build>
```

Save the `pom.xml` file. Right-click the project name, select **Maven**, and then **Update Project** on the menu. Click **OK** in the dialog box. This will update the Maven settings.

5. Add `Procfile`. `Procfile` is a Heroku artifact. In this file, we tell Heroku which program to run after building the project. Implement `Procfile`:

```
web: java -cp target/classes:target/dependency/* WebServer
```

The preceding line informs Heroku to run the `WebServer` class in the *default* package on a web dyno.

The name of the file should be `Procfile` and not `Procfile.txt` or `ProcFile`.

6. Push it onto the cloud. Now that we have created our first version of the chatbot and wrapped it as a web server, let us push it onto the cloud and make it available as a web service. From the console window, where your `Weatherman` project is, execute the following commands:

```
> git init
> git add .
> git commit -m "chatbot for weather v1"
```

By executing the preceding commands, we are creating and storing the project files in a local GIT repository. Let us now create a Heroku app to hold our web app:

```
> heroku create weatherman-bot
```

You will see the results of this command as in the following screenshot. It says that we have created a Heroku app named `weatherman-bot` and its URL is `https://weatherman-bot.herokuapp.com`:

Finally, we will push the code into Heroku and also invoke it as a web service. To do this, execute the following command:

```
> git push heroku master
```

You will see the following messages, which means the code has been pushed, compiled successfully, and launched as well:

Now that we have successfully created the chatbot as a web service, we need to get this bot to talk to users in Facebook Messenger.

Publishing on Facebook Messenger

To publish a custom built chatbot on Facebook, you need to follow these steps.

Creating a Facebook Page

You need a Facebook Page that can hold the chatbot. To create a Facebook Page, you need a Facebook account. If you don't have one, go ahead and create one at www.facebook.com.

Once you are logged in to Facebook, you should be able to create any number of pages. To create a page, follow these steps:

1. On the left, there is a menu with three tabs: **SHORTCUTS**, **EXPLORE**, and **CREATE**. Under **CREATE**, click **Page**:

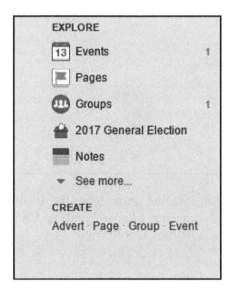

2. A Facebook Page can be created as a public profile to represent businesses, brands, celebrities, public causes, and so on. You will see the following menu:

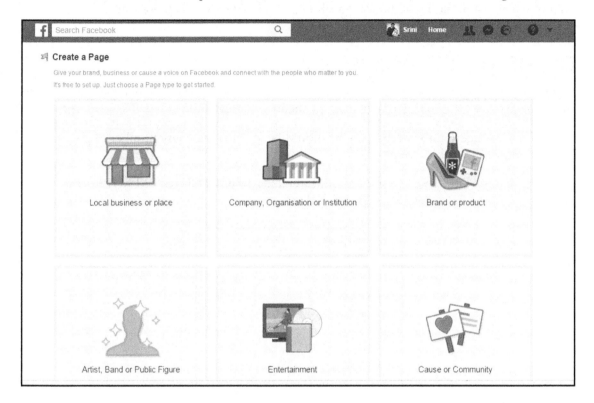

Choose **Artist, Band or Public Figure**. Since we are building a chatbot, let us create it as a fictional character. Choose **Fictional Character** from the drop-down menu, give it a name, and click **Get Started**:

3. We have now created a page. Let us go ahead and configure it:

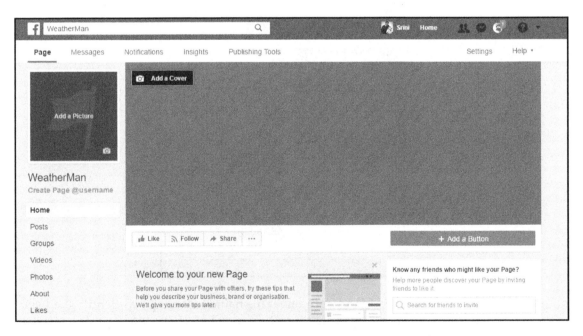

fb_new_blank_page

Bookmark your page. Add a profile image by clicking **Add a Picture** and a banner image by clicking **Add a Cover** (always use pictures that you have a copyright to).

Don't worry if you accidentally closed your browser and hadn't bookmarked your page. You can see all your pages listed at `https://www.facebook.com/bookmarks/pages`.

You should now be able to make your very first post on the page.

Creating a username

Having created the page, let us do two more things before we move on: add a description of the page and create a username.

1. To create a username, click **Create Page @username** right below the profile picture:

2. You will be prompted for a **Username**. This name will uniquely identify the page and makes the URL easy to remember. You may have to try a few names as the one you have in mind might already be taken:

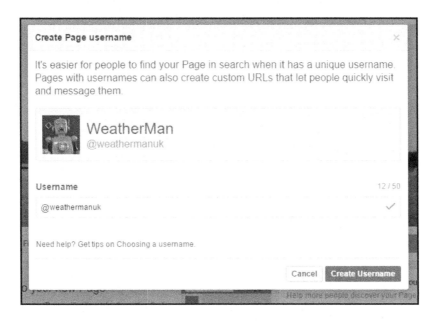

3. Finally, when it has been created, you will be notified of the new page and the Messenger URL:

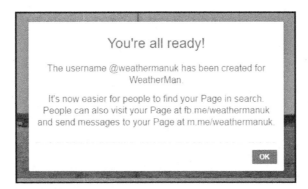

Creating a Facebook App

You need to create a Facebook App that can connect to the Facebook Page we just created. A Facebook App can be created on Facebook's developer portal. Follow the steps:

1. Navigate your browser to `https://developers.facebook.com`.

2. Click the **MyApps** button in the top-right corner (next to your profile icon).
3. Click **Add A New App**.
4. Fill in the display name of the app and your contact email and click **Create App ID**:

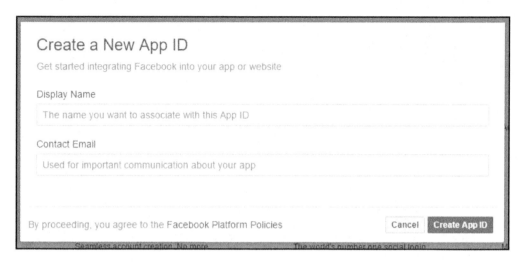

5. Having created the app shell, we need to add products to it. In our case, since we are building a chatbot, we need to add a **Messenger** product to the app:

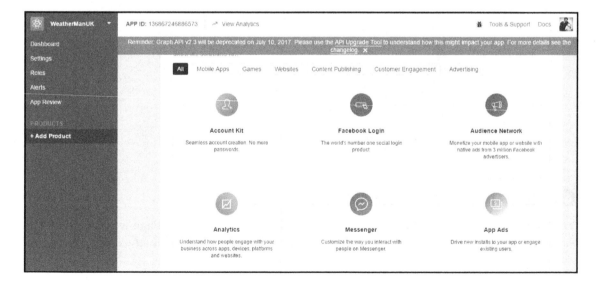

6. Hover your mouse over **Messenger** and click **Set Up**. This will add Messenger to the app and take you to the **Settings** page. Scroll down the page to **Token Generation** tab. This is where we link the app to the page that we created.

7. Click **Select A Page** and select the page you want the app to be linked to. This will open an authentication dialog box where you will have to allow the app to access the page. Click **Continue as X**, where **X** is your first name. Do not worry about the warnings for now:

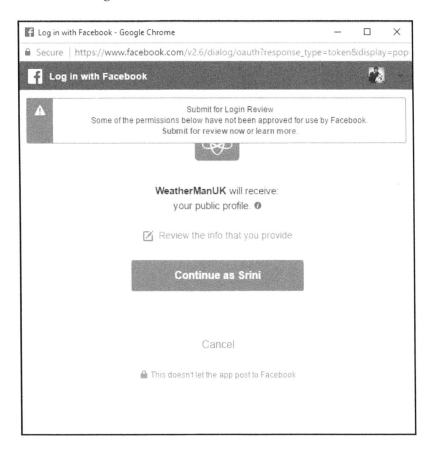

8. On the next page, click **OK** to finish the process. This will automatically close the dialog box:

9. You will now see that the page is assigned a token called the **Page Access Token**. Copy it and keep it aside.

10. We will have to set up the webhook to finish this process but we will have to do it a bit later.

Creating a Facebook interface web app

In this step, we will create an interface that will allow our chatbot to talk to the Facebook App. In the previous section, we created a Facebook App. This app will have to talk to the interface we will be building in this section. Info about this module will have to go into the webhook settings that we have left unfinished in the previous section. We will create a new project to hold this interface app. Let us call it `weatherman-fbmi`. In your console, create a separate directory (`weatherman-fbmi`) to hold this project. In this directory, we will create the following three files:

- `index.js`
- `package.json`
- `Procfile`

`index.js` is a Node.js program that acts as a web server to send and receive messages to and from our Facebook App:

```
'use strict';
const express = require('express')
const bodyParser = require('body-parser')
const request = require('request')

const app = express()

// set your weatherman fb page access token
const token = '<YourFBPageAccesToken>';

const botServerUrl = 'https://weatherman-bot.herokuapp.com/bot';

app.set('port', (process.env.PORT || 5000))

// Process application/x-www-form-urlencoded
app.use(bodyParser.urlencoded({extended: false}))

// Process application/json
app.use(bodyParser.json())

app.use(express.static('public'))

// Index route
app.get('/', function (req, res) {
    res.send('Hello world, I am Weatherman!.')
})

// Spin up the server
```

```
app.listen(app.get('port'), function() {
    console.log('running on port', app.get('port'))
})
```

You will have to replace <YourFBPageAccesToken> with the page access token that you got from Step 9 of the *Creating a Facebook App* section. You may also have to replace the botServerURL to your own.

The preceding code is enough to spin up the server when pushed onto Heroku. But we need the server to actually create a bridge between our Facebook App and our chatbot. We will now implement necessary routes to the previous web server. Add the following code to index.js:

```
// for Facebook verification
app.get('/webhook/', function (req, res) {
    if (req.query['hub.verify_token'] === 'iam-weatherman-bot') {
        res.send(req.query['hub.challenge'])
    }
    res.send('Error, wrong token')
})

//FBM webhook
app.post('/webhook/', function (req, res) {
    console.log(JSON.stringify(req.body));
    let messaging_events = req.body.entry[0].messaging
    for (let i = 0; i < messaging_events.length; i++) {
        let event = req.body.entry[0].messaging[i]
        let sender = event.sender.id
        let recipient = event.recipient.id
        let time = req.body.entry[0].time

        // we call the chatbot here..
        if (event.message && event.message.text) {
            let text = event.message.text
            //send it to the bot
            request({
                url: botServerUrl,
                method: 'POST',
                form: {
                    'userUtterance':text
                }
            }, function (error, response, body) {
                //response is from the bot
                if (!error && response.statusCode == 200) {
                    // Print out the response body
                    body = body.substring(1,body.length-1);
                    body = body.replace(/\\/g, '')
```

```
                    let botOut = JSON.parse(body)
                    if (botOut.botUtterance != null){
                        sendTextMessage(sender, botOut.botUtterance)
                    }
                } else {
                    sendTextMessage(sender, 'Error!')
                }
            }); //request ends
        }
    }
    res.sendStatus(200)
})

function sendTextMessage(sender, text) {
    if (text != 'null'){
        let messageData = { 'text':text }
        request({
            url: 'https://graph.facebook.com/v2.6/me/messages',
            qs: {access_token:token},
            method: 'POST',
            json: {
                recipient: {id:sender},
                message: messageData,
            }
        }, function(error, response, body) {
            if (error) {
                console.log('Error sending messages: ', error)
            } else if (response.body.error) {
                console.log('Error: ', response.body.error)
            }
        })
    }
}
```

The preceding code creates a POST route called webhook that will be called by the Facebook App with the user's utterances. This will be sent to the chatbot using its URL (botServerURL) as another POST request. The bot's response is sent back to Messenger in the sendTextMessage() method. There are other message formats that can be used to send richer responses from the bot. We will take a look at them in section X.

Let us create the `package.json` file to tell Heroku the packages that are needed for `index.js`. Create the `package.json` file in your text editor with the following JSON:

```
{
 "name": "weatherman-bot-server",
 "version": "1.0.0",
 "description": "Weatherman bot fbmi server",
 "main": "index.js",
 "scripts": {
  "test": "echo \"Error: no test specified\" && exit 1"
 },
 "author": "Srini Janarthanam",
 "license": "ISC",
 "dependencies": {
 "body-parser": "^1.15.2",
 "express": "^4.14.0",
 "request": "^2.72.0"
 }
}
```

As a final step, we need to create a `Procfile` to tell Heroku to run `index.js`. Create `Procfile` in your text editor with the following command.

```
web: node index.js
```

Follow these steps to push the interface program onto the cloud. From the console window, where your `Weatherman` interface project is, execute the following commands to create a Heroku app and push the interface app to the cloud:

```
> git init
> git add .
> git commit -m "fbmi for weatherman v1"
> heroku create weatherman-bot-fbmi
> git push heroku master
```

You will receive a message with the app's URL in it. In my case, it is `https://weatherman-bot-fbmi.herokuapp.com`.

Connecting the Facebook App and interface app

Finally, we have to set up the webhook that we left incomplete in Step 10 when creating the Facebook App. You may have observed that we have created two routes to serve as webhooks. The `GET` route is used to verify the app and the `POST` route is used for communicating messages to and from the chatbot:

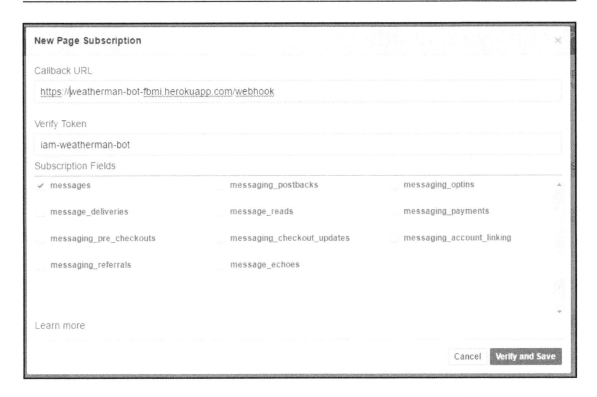

Subscribe to the **WeatherMan** Facebook Page to receive the messages sent by Messenger users on the web service:

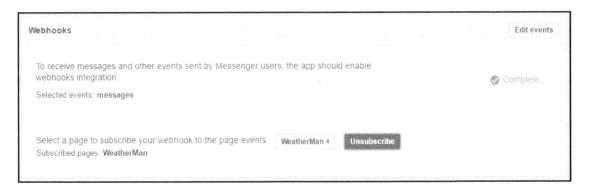

We are now ready to test the chatbot!

Testing your chatbot

Now that the chatbot is up and running, we can test it on the Facebook Page that hosts it. A username for the page was created in the *Creating a username* section. Navigate to `https://m.me/weathermanuk` on a web browser. This will open Facebook Messenger, where you can chat with our **WeatherMan** bot. Go ahead and say `hi there`:

Adding more testers

You might notice that only you have access to the chatbot. Anyone else who goes to the same URL and says `hi` will not be responded to by the chatbot. This is because the chatbot is not published yet. You can add more testers to help you with testing the chatbot. Here is how you do it:

1. Navigate your browser to `https://developers.facebook.com`.
2. Click your app.
3. On **Dashboard**, choose **Roles.**
4. Under the **Testers** tab, you can add Facebook users by mentioning their usernames.

Added users will have access to the chatbot. But remember, your bot is still unpublished:

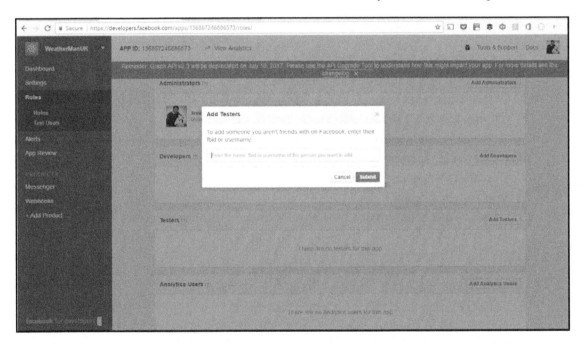

Making it public

The final step of this process is to apply to Facebook to make your chatbot public. This final step will make your chatbot available to everyone at the Messenger URL (`https://m.me/weathermanuk`).

1. On your app dashboard, click **Settings** and then **Basic** on the **Dashboard** menu.
2. Upload an icon to represent the chatbot. This has to be a 1024 x 1024 pixel image.
3. Choose a category: **Apps for Messenger**.
4. Add the URL to the privacy policy. This policy will have to tell users what happens to the user data that is collected. There are a few services that can help you create Facebook App privacy policies:
   - IUBENDA: `https://www.iubenda.com/blog/privacy-policy-facebook-app/`
   - TermsFeed: `https://termsfeed.com/blog/privacy-policy-url-facebook-app/`

5. On the **Dashboard** menu, click **App Review**.
6. Make your app public by choosing **Yes**.
7. On the **Dashboard** menu, choose **Messenger** under **PRODUCTS**.
8. On the right, find the **App Review For Messenger** tab.
9. Add **pages_messaging** to submission.
10. Go down to **Current Submission** tab.
11. Click **Edit Notes** against **pages_messaging**.
12. Select the Facebook Page that the chatbot subscribes to.
13. Choose **Your Messenger experience includes automated replies** and provide examples of interactions for what users can say and what the bot will respond with.
14. Add any other notes for the reviewer if you like. This should help the reviewer understand the chatbot and set the right expectations.
15. Click **Save**. Go back to Messenger's **Settings**. You will find the **Submit for review** button enabled. Click it for submission. If it is not enabled, you will find a list of items you will need to work on before you can submit.

You will immediately receive a message that you can view on the **Alerts** page. Click **Alerts** on the **Dashboard** menu. You will see a message stating that the app is being reviewed. The review usually takes a couple of days. Once reviewed and approved, your chatbot is ready for public use.

Congratulations on coming this far!

More Facebook message formats

In this section, we will explore other Facebook message formats besides text. In the previous example, we programmed the chatbot to send text responses back to the user. However, Facebook has more formats that can be used to provide a richer experience to the user. You can do this by changing the content of the `message` element in the `POST` request in the `sendTextMessage()` method in the `index.js` file.

Content types

Besides text, other content types such as images, audio and video clips, and files can be sent to users.

Image attachments

Images in JPEG, PNG, and GIF formats can be sent to the user using the following format for message content:

```
"message":{
    "attachment":{
      "type":"image",
      "payload":{
        "url":"https://myimagelibrary.com/ijustwannadrawsomething.jpg"
      }
    }
  }
```

Audio attachments

Audio clips can be sent to the user using the following `message` element:

```
"message":{
  "attachment":{
    "type":"audio",
    "payload":{
      "url":"https://mymp3library.com/ijustwannasing.mp3"
    }
  }
}
```

Video attachments

Video files can be sent over Messenger by specifying its URL with the following message content:

```
"message":{
  "attachment":{
    "type":"video",
    "payload":{
      "url":"https://myvideolibrary.com/ijustwannadance.mp4"
    }
  }
}
```

Files

Files can be sent to users using the following message format by specifying the URL of the file:

```
"message":{
  "attachment":{
    "type":"file",
    "payload":{
      "url":"https://myfileslibrary.com/ijustwannawrite.pdf"
    }
  }
}
```

Templates

In addition to sending simple text and other content types, Facebook provides a way to send cards. These are GUI elements that are visually appealing. There are also options for adding buttons to cards that serve as responses that users can make.

Button template

Button templates can be created using the following message format. The following message will display a card with two buttons. The labels on the buttons will be **Buy now** and **More info**. Clicking **Buy now** will send the payload (PAYLOAD_BUY) as a response message back to the bot. Clicking the **More info** button will take the user to the web page specified in an embedded web view window:

```
"message":{
  "attachment":{
    "type":"template",
    "payload":{
      "template_type":"button",
      "text":"What would you like to do now?",
      "buttons":[
        {
          "type":"postback",
          "title":"Weather this weekend",
          "payload":"PAYLOAD_WEEKEND_LONDON"
        },
        {
          "type":"Goto Website",
          "url":"https://myweather.com/london",
          "title":"More Info"
        }
      ]
    }
  }
}
```

The preceding message would render as shown in the following screenshot:

List template

List templates can be used to list a number of items in a vertical list. Using the following message format, you can make a list that is presented in a visually attractive way:

```
"message": {
    "attachment": {
        "type": "template",
        "payload": {
            "template_type": "list",
            "top_element_style": "compact",
            "elements": [
                {
                    "title": "London,GB",
                    "image_url": "https://myweather.com/london.png",
                    "subtitle": "Weather in London,GB",
                    "default_action": {
                        "type": "web_url",
                        "url": "https://myweather.com/london",
                        "messenger_extensions": true,
                        "webview_height_ratio": "tall",
                        "fallback_url": "https://myweather.com/"
                    },
                    "buttons": [
                        {
                            "title": "Info",
                            "type": "web_url",
                            "url": "https://myweather.com/london/weather",
                            "messenger_extensions": true,
                            "webview_height_ratio": "tall",
```

```
                            "fallback_url": "https://myweather.com/"
                        }
                    ]
                },
                {
                    "title": "Paris,FR",
                    "image_url": "https://myweather.com/paris.png",
                    "subtitle": "Weather in Paris,FR",
                    "default_action": {
                        "type": "web_url",
                        "url": "https://myweather.com/paris",
                        "messenger_extensions": true,
                        "webview_height_ratio": "tall",
                        "fallback_url": "https://myweather.com/"
                    },
                    "buttons": [
                        {
                            "title": "Info",
                            "type": "web_url",
                            "url": "https://myweather.com/paris/weather",
                            "messenger_extensions": true,
                            "webview_height_ratio": "tall",
                            "fallback_url": "https://myweather.com/"
                        }
                    ]
                }
            ],
             "buttons": [
                {
                    "title": "View More",
                    "type": "postback",
                    "payload": "payload"
                }
            ]
        }
    }
```

The preceding code also serves as an example of how you can use a list template in our weather chatbot. You can make a list of prominent cities or allow the user to create their own favorite cities. This list will provide shortcuts to get weather info on a list of cities. In the preceding code, this is done by adding city-centric info to the `elements` JSON array list. Each element has two URLs. One is for when the user touches the element itself and the other is for when the user clicks the `call-to-action` button.

In the preceding code, buttons are set to lead the user to a web URL rather than send payload messages to the bot. However, both can be done. You just need to change the button type. And here is how it looks on Messenger:

Generic template

The generic template is one of the first templates introduced by Facebook to create visually attractive cards. This is also called a carousel. This enables you to present a list of items as a horizontal list of cards, where the user can scroll through them and respond using buttons. Each card can have a maximum of three buttons. To create a generic template, use the following message format:

```
"message":{
    "attachment":{
      "type":"template",
      "payload":{
        "template_type":"generic",
        "elements":[
            {
              "title":"London, GB",
              "image_url":"https://myweather.com/london.png",
              "subtitle":"What's the weather in London, GB?",
              "default_action": {
                "type": "web_url",
                "url": "https://myweather.com/london",
                "messenger_extensions": true,
                "webview_height_ratio": "tall",
                "fallback_url": "https://myweather.com/"
              },
              "buttons":[
                {
                  "type":"web_url",
                  "url":"https://myweather.com/london/weather",
                  "title":"Goto Website"
                },{
                  "type":"postback",
                  "title":"Weather now",
                  "payload":"PAYLOAD_CURRENT_WEATHER_LONDON"
                }
              ]
            }
        ]
      }
    }
}
```

The preceding example has only one card. Add more to the elements list to make more cards, one for each city perhaps. Observe that the card has two buttons. One is a web view, where pushing the button labeled **Goto Website** takes you to the website with weather info on London on an embedded web browser. And the next one is a postback button, which will send as response a PAYLOAD_CURRENT_WEATHER_LONDON postback message to the chatbot:

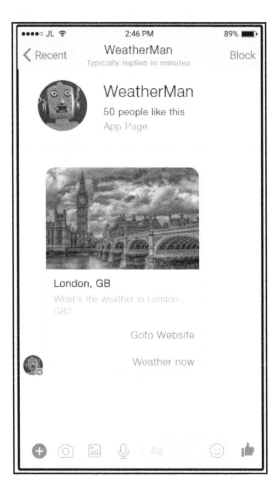

By using a combination of these elements and more, you can create magical conversational experiences for the user on Facebook Messenger. The Facebook Messenger API is rapidly evolving and new elements are being added to help developers to create amazing chatbot conversations on the platform. So keep an eye on the developments.

Summary

In this chapter, we had a look at how to build a chatbot using an external information source and integrate it with Facebook Messenger. We had a look at how to get the bot published on Messenger and exclusive features, such as buttons and templates, that can help us build a rich and engaging conversational experience for the user in Messenger.

In the next chapter, we will move away from button-based interaction and explore how to process user utterances to make the chatbot more flexible for users. We will explore a natural language understanding toolkit called Dialogflow and build a persona bot that will mimic conversations with Albert Einstein.

References

Facebook Messenger documentation: `https://developers.facebook.com/docs/messenger-platform`

4
Building a Persona Bot

In the last chapter, we built a chatbot to talk about weather information over Facebook Messenger. Although we were able to have a conversation with it, it was mainly by the use of buttons that were made available by the deployment platform. However, in order to make the chatbot sound more natural, we need to allow users to chat with the chatbot using natural language. This means that the chatbot needs to be able to process users' utterances, understand them and identify the most appropriate response to give back to the user. In this chapter, we will explore how we can process natural language inputs from the user using a tool from Google called Dialogflow (previously called API.AI) to build a chatbot that can understand natural language input from the user. We will deploy the chatbot on two platforms: web chat and Facebook Messenger. We will explore concepts in natural language such as intents, entities, and contexts, and we will discuss how to actually design and deploy a rich conversational experience using these ideas. With a basic understanding of these concepts, we will design and build a persona bot modeled on the world's favorite physicist, Albert Einstein.

By the end of this chapter, you will be able to:

- Understand the basics of Dialogflow
- Understand concepts such as intents, entities, and contexts
- Create a Dialogflow agent
- Integrate the Dialogflow agent to web chat and Facebook Messenger
- Extend the agent's capabilities using webhooks

Introducing Dialogflow

Dialogflow (previously called API.AI) is conversational agent building platform from Google. It is a web-based platform that can be accessed from any web browser. The tool has evolved over time from what was built as an answer to *Apple Siri* for the Android platform. It was called *SpeakToIt*, an Android app that created Siri-like conversational experiences on any Android smartphone. The AI and natural language technology that powered the SpeakToIt app was opened up to developers as API.AI in 2015.

API.AI enabled developers to create conversational experiences by providing them tools to undertake two kinds of tasks: understand and generate natural language utterances and manage the conversation. While there are many competing tools to API.AI that are available in the market, we chose API.AI because it was one of the first, is very mature and constantly evolving, and is easy to use and integrate within other services.

Setting up Dialogflow

First, let us create a developer account on API.AI (now called as Dialogflow).

1. Go to `https://api.ai/`:

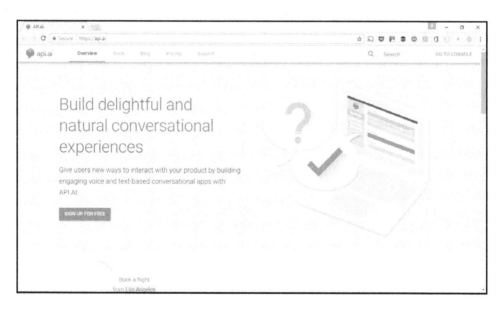

2. Click **GO TO CONSOLE** on the top-right corner.
3. Sign in. You may need to use your Google account to sign in.

Creating a basic agent

Let us create our first agent on Dialogflow. Let us start with a basic one and then add more complex features:

1. To create a new agent, click the drop-down menu on the left on the home page (api.ai) and click **Create new agent**.
2. Fill in the form on the right. Give it a name and description. Choose a time zone and click **CREATE**.
3. This will take you to the page with the intents listing. You will notice that there are two intents already: **Default Fallback Intent** and **Default Welcome Intent**.
4. Let's add your first intent. Intent is what the user or bot wants to convey using utterances or button presses. An intent is a symbolic representation of an utterance. We need intents because there are many ways to ask for the same thing. The process of identifying intents is to map the many ways unambiguously to an intent. For instance, the user could ask to know the weather in their city using the following utterances:

```
"hows the weather in london"
"whats the weather like in london"
"weather in london"
"is it sunny outside just now"
```

In the preceding utterances, the user is asking for a weather report in the city of London. In some of these utterances, they also mention time (that is, now). In others, it is implicit. The first step of our algorithm is to map these many utterances into a single intent: `request_weather_report`.

The **Intent name** corresponds to users' intents. So name them from the user's perspective. Let's add a `user_greet` intent that corresponds to the act of greeting the chatbot by the user. To add an intent, click the **CREATE INTENT** button.

5. You will see the following page where you can create a new intent:

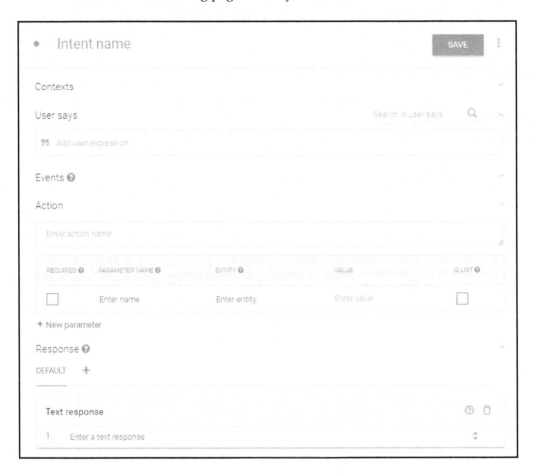

Give the intent a name (for example, user_greet).

6. Add sample user utterances in the **User says** text field. These are sample utterances that will help the agent identify the user's intent. Let's add a few greeting utterances that the user might say to our chatbot:

```
hello
hello there
Hi there Albert
hello doctor
good day doctor
```

7. Ignore the **Events** tab for the moment and move on to the **Action** tab. Add a name to identify the system intent here (for example, `bot_greet` to represent chatbot's greeting to the user).

8. In the **Response** tab, add the bot's response to the user. This is the actual utterance that the bot will send to the user. Let's add the following utterance in the **Text response** field. You can add more responses so that the agent can randomly pick one to make it less repetitive and boring:

   ```
   Hi there. I am Albert. Nice to meet you!
   ```

   You can also add up to 10 additional responses by clicking the **ADD MESSAGE CONTENT**.

9. Click **SAVE** button in the top-right corner to save the intent. You have created your very first intent for the agent.

10. Test it by using the simulator on the right side of the page. In the **Try it now** box, type `hello` and press *Enter*:

You will see the chatbot recognizing your typed utterance and responding appropriately.

11. Now go on and add a few more intents by repeating steps 5 through 10. To create a new intent, click the **+** sign beside the **Intents** option in the menu on the left:

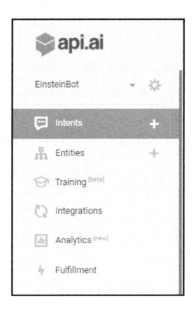

Think about what kind of information users will ask the chatbot and make a list. These will become user intents. The following is a sample list to get you started:

- `request_name`
- `request_birth_info`
- `request_parents_names`
- `request_first_job_experience`
- `request_info_on_hobbies`
- `request_info_patent_job`
- `request_info_lecturer_job_bern`

Of course, this list can be endless. So go on and have fun.

Once you have put in the sufficient number of facts in the mentioned format, you can test the chatbot on the simulator as explained in step 10.

Deploying the chatbot

Now that we have a chatbot, let us get it published on a platform where users can actually use it. Dialogflow enables you to integrate the chatbot (that is, agent) with many platforms. Click **Integrations** to see all the platforms that are available:

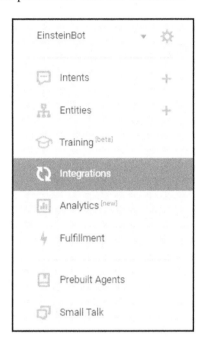

In this section, we will explore two platform integrations: website and Facebook. We will explore more in later sections:

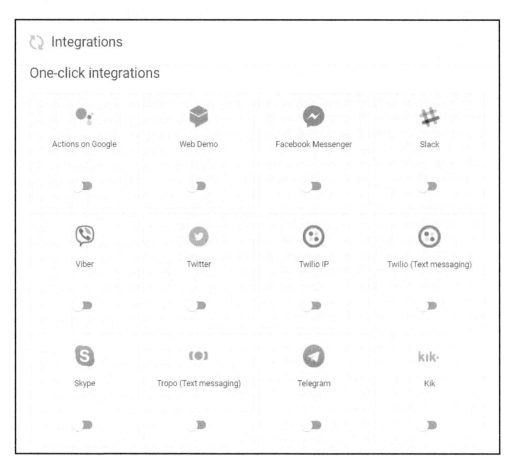

Website integration

Website integration allows you to put that chatbot on a website. The user can interact with the chatbot on the website just as they would with a live chat agent.

1. On the **Integrations** page, find the **Web Demo** platform and slide the switch from off to on.

2. Click **Web Demo** to open the following settings dialog box:

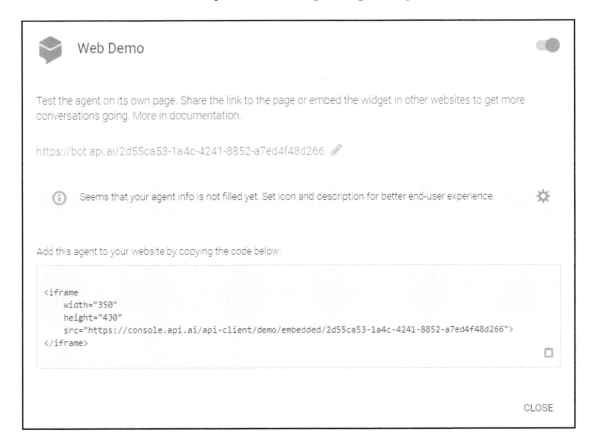

3. Click the **bot.dialogflow.com** URL to open the sample webpage where you can find the bot on a chat widget embedded on the page. Try having a chat with it:

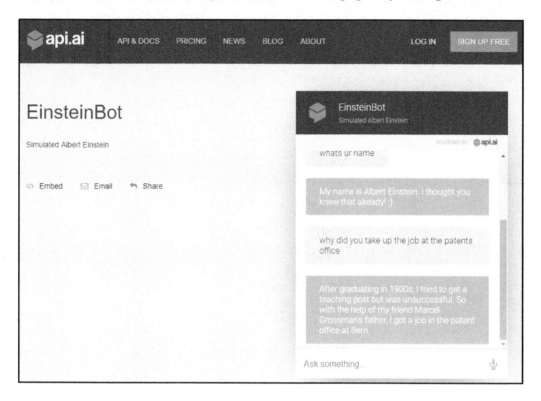

You can share the bot privately by email or on social media by clicking the **Email** and **Share** option.

4. The chat widget can also be embedded in any website by using the iframe embed code found in the settings dialog box. Copy and paste the code into an HTML page and try it out in a web browser:

```
<iframe
    width="350"
    height="430"
    src="https://console.api.ai/api-client/demo/embedded/
        2d55ca53-1a4c-4241-8852-a7ed4f48d266">
</iframe>
```

Facebook integration

In order to publish the API.AI chatbot on Facebook Messenger, we need a Facebook Page to start with. We also need a Facebook Messenger app that subscribes to the page. The steps to create a Facebook Page and a Facebook Messenger app are presented in detail in the section titled *Publishing on Facebook Messenger* in `Chapter 3`, *Let's Talk Weather* . Let's discuss the further steps here:

1. Having created a Facebook Messenger app, get its **Page Access Token**. You can get this on the app's **Messenger Settings** tab:

2. In the same tab, click **Set up Webhooks**. A dialog box called **New Page Subscription** will open. Keep it open in one browser tab.

3. In another browser tab, from the **Integrations** page of API.AI, click **Facebook Messenger**:

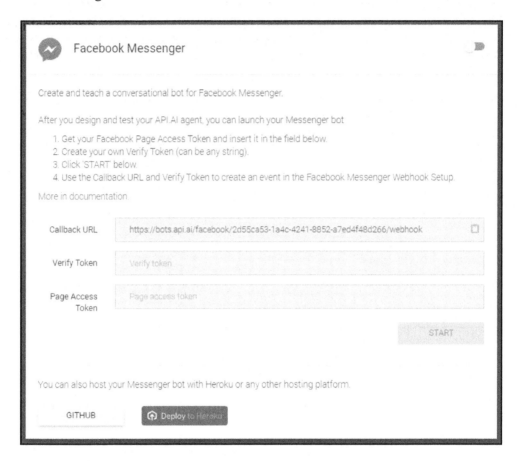

4. Copy the URL in the **Callback URL** text field. This is the URL of the API.AI agent to call from the Messenger app. Paste this in the **Callback URL** text field of the **New Page Subscription** dialog box on the Facebook Messenger app.

5. Type in a verification token. It can be anything as long as it matches the one on the other side. Let's type in `iam-einstein-bot`.

6. Subscribe to **messages** and **messaging_postbacks** in the **Subscription Fields** section. And wait! Don't click **Verify and Save** just yet:

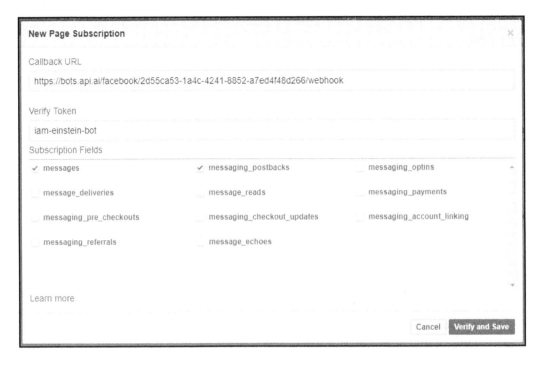

7. In the API.AI browser tab, you will have the integrations settings open. Slide the switch to on from the off position on the top-right corner.

8. This will allow you to edit the settings. Type the **Verify Token**. This has to be the same as the one used in the Facebook Messenger App settings in step 5.

9. Paste the **Page Access Token** and click **START**.

10. Now go back to the Facebook Messenger app and click **Verify and Save**. This will connect the app to the agent (chatbot).

11. Now on the Facebook Messenger settings page, under **Webhooks**, select the correct Facebook page that the app needs to subscribe to and hit **Subscribe**:

You should now be able to open the Facebook page, click **Send Message**, and have a chat with the chatbot:

Brilliant! Now you have successfully created a chatbot in API.AI and deployed it on two platforms: web and Facebook Messenger. In addition to these platforms, API.AI enables integration of your agent with several popular messaging platforms such as Slack, Skype, Cisco Spark, Viber, Kik, Telegram, and even Twitter.

Context

So far, our chatbot answers questions in one shot. The user asks a question and the chatbot answers. What if there are questions that require more conversation? What if the chatbot needs to ask to follow up questions before it can actually answer the user's question? Such tasks require conversational context.

Let us examine the following conversation:

```
User : Why did you take the job at the patents office?
Bot  : After graduating, I tried to get a teaching post but was
unsuccessful.
So with the help of my friend Marcel Grossman's father, I got a job in the
patent office at Bern.
User : When did you get the job?
```

The user's second question relates to the first question and the answer from the chatbot. It is not an independent question. The words `the job` could mean any job that Einstein might have had during his lifetime but according to the context, it is clear what the user is talking about. The chatbot, therefore, needs to take this into account to understand what the user actually means.

In API.AI, we can enable agents to keep a record of conversational context using the **Contexts** tab while creating intents. Each intent has to specify input and output contexts. Input context specifies the context in which the intent will be considered. The output context is what is set when the intent is matched and successfully executed with a response utterance.

To successfully execute the preceding conversation, the agent needs to record contextual information in the output context for the `request_info_patent_job` intent where the question about Einstein's patents office job gets answered. This will then serve as input context for follow-up questions such as, "When did you get the job?" or, "How much did the job pay?" and many more.

Here is how you can do that:

1. Open the `request_info_patent_job` intent. Click the **Contexts** tab. You will see the tab expand as shown in the following screenshot:

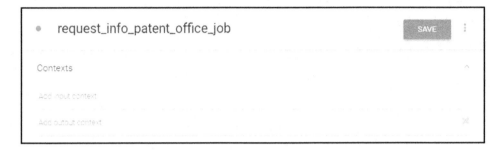

2. Type the name of the *contextual item* you want the agent to keep in the output context field. Since we want the agent to know that the user's question is about the patents office job, let us type in the name of the contextual item (that is, `patents-office-job`) in the output context:

Attached to each contextual item is the lifespan of the context. It is set to **5** by default. This ticks down by one to zero with each incoming user utterance. When it reaches zero, it will automatically be erased from the context of the conversation.

3. We have specified the output context for the intent. So if the agent recognizes this intent from user's utterance, it will respond appropriately and also set the output context. Let us try this on the simulator:

The preceding screenshot shows how the context is now changed from nothing to **patents-office-job**. Every new utterance from the user will now be processed in this context.

4. In order to use context, contextual items need to be specified as input context in subsequent user intents. Let's try this out by creating a new `request_info_poffice_joining` user intent. This intent is will be recognized when the user asks `when did you start your job in the patents office` or something similar. But even if the user asks `when did you start the job` where there is no mention of the patents office, we should be able to recognize it during the conversation about the patents office job. In order to do that, we will mention what the conversation is about in the input context:

In the preceding screenshot, you can see the way the `patents-office-job` contextual item is mentioned in the input contexts field. So, an utterance such as `when did you start` in the context of `patents-office-job` will be recognized as `request_info_poffice_joining`. The same utterance in other contexts will not be recognized as a `request_info_poffice_joining` intent:

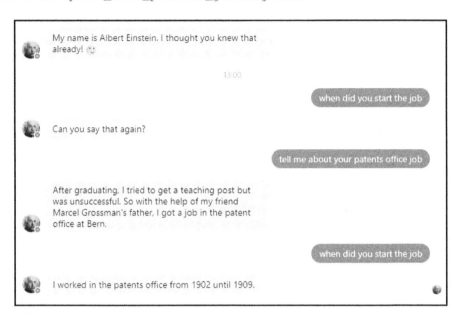

The preceding screenshot shows how the same utterance at different points of conversation yields different results because the agent is now processing inputs from the user contextually.

The lifespan of the contextual item in the output context can be increased or decreased. In case the contextual item is no longer needed, it can be deleted by setting the lifespan to zero. This can be a useful hack when the user thanks the bot after finishing a task. In such a case, the chatbot can be made to reset the conversational context.

More contextual items can be added both in input and output fields as necessary. This may be useful in creating more complex conversations. While using contextual items to drive conversation is a good idea, we recommend the use of a contextual item called `global` to create and manage global contextual items wherein `global` parameters can be stored and used. This item will be available to all intents in its input and passed on to the output context as well.

Entities

Entities add another layer of complexity to natural language conversations making the chatbot more powerful and flexible. Any object of interest in the chatbot's conversations with users can be considered an entity. For instance, in a chatbot dispensing weather information, cities and towns can be considered as entities. Other entities of interest would be the kind of information the user wants: temperature, the possibility of rain, wind speed, and so on. In the case of temperature, the metric that is used, either Fahrenheit or Celsius, can also be treated as entities.

Entities can be organized in terms of parameter names and values. For instance, in the weather domain, you can append to request city-specific weather reports in the following way:

```
intent = request_weather
city_name = london_gb
```

The preceding format is equivalent to the user asking, "What's the weather like in London?" So instead of using one intent per city (for example, `request_weather_london`), we can better organize user requests in terms of intents and entities. This also makes recognizing user intents more manageable.

Let's have a look at a couple of other examples:

```
intent = change_metric
metric = celsius
```

The preceding example represents utterances such as, "How much is that in Celsius?" and, "Can you report in Celsius scale, please."

In the case of the Einstein bot, we can represent his major works, such as Special Theory of Relativity, General Theory of Relativity, and Brownian Movement as entities. Such entities can be used in related intents such as `request_info_on_work` and `request_publications`. Take, for instance, the following intent specification:

```
intent = request_info_on_work
work = special_theory_of_relativity
```

The preceding intent could mean that the user is saying, "Tell me about your work on the special theory of relativity" or something similar.

In order to make use of entities, we need to enumerate them in the agent. To do this, follow the following steps:

1. Click the **Entities** option in the main menu. You will find this underneath the **Intents** option that was used to create user intents:

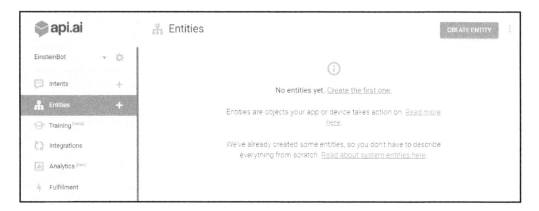

2. Click **CREATE ENTITY**.
3. Give it a type name. In the weather domain, London, Paris, or New York may be actual entities but they can be grouped under a type name called **City**. In the case of the Einstein bot, let's name it Work as the entities are actually his work.

4. There is a table with two columns. On the left, you will have to fill in a reference value for the entity and on the right, you will list the synonyms of the entity. To explain this, let us go back to the city example. Each city will have a reference value (for example, `newyork-us`) to represent it internally in an unambiguous manner. Each reference value can be expressed in terms of words or phrases in natural language. In this case, `newyork-us` can be called "the big apple," "new york city," "the city of new york," and so on. These need to be listed as *synonyms*. For our bot, let us add three of Einstein's works—Special theory of relativity, General theory of relativity, and Theory of Brownian Movement. For each of these works, let us also add synonyms:

Work		SAVE	

Define synonyms ❓   ☐ Allow automated expansion

special-theory	special theory of relativity, special theory
general-theory	general theory, general theory of relativity
brownian-movement-theory	brownian motion, theory of brownian motion, theory of brownian movement, brownian movement, brownian movement theory, Enter synonym

Click here to edit entry

+ Add a row

5. Having created the entities, let us now put them to use by creating an intent that would use them. Let us create an intent called `request_info_on_work`:

Observe in the preceding screenshot how the words **special theory of relativity** are highlighted. This is done automatically by the API.AI editor based on the entity list we created. It identifies entities in example utterances that we provide for every intent. It then adds those identified entities to the parameter list:

6. Try this in the simulator and observe the output from the agent. As shown in the preceding screenshot, you will see that the agent has picked up the name of the work and has created a parameter with the name (that is, `Work`) and value (that is, **general-theory**). In the value field, you will find the reference value of the entity no matter what synonym was used in the utterance.

Now, having extracted the parameters and values, let's figure out how to use them in the response utterance. The parameter can be referenced in the response utterances using the `$` notation. In this case, the reference value of the `Work` parameter can be obtained by using `$Work`. Try the `Sure. I will tell you all about $Work. But later! :)` response utterance and see what happens:

7. Since our reference values have a hyphen in them, they really don't suit the utterances. So we can try using the synonym that the user used. To do this, change $Work to $Work.original. Save the intent and try the simulator:

8. Try a similar but partially-specified utterance, such as tell me about your work. This maps to the intent but does not have the required parameter. How will the agent deal with this utterance? If you try it, you will see that the intent has been recognized but the response is empty. This is because the agent is not able to find the value for $Work.original.

    In order to make sure that the agent gets a value for the Work parameter, you have to make the parameter a required parameter. You do this by checking the **REQUIRED** checkbox for the parameter. Click **Define prompts** in order to give the agent a prompt to use in case the user forgot to mention the value of the parameter in their utterance:

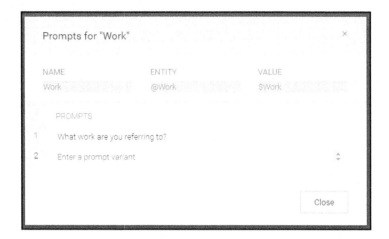

Click **SAVE** after you have defined the entities, made them required, and defined the prompts:

9. Try the simulator once again with the `tell me about your work` utterance. You will find the agent asking you back with the response prompt to name the work. Following this, the agent will respond appropriately:

10. Entities can be stored in context and be used across utterances. In order to do this, let us add a `talk_about_work` contextual item in the output context of the `request_info_on_work` intent. Let us also add another `request_info_on_work_now` intent with `talk_about_work` as the input context:

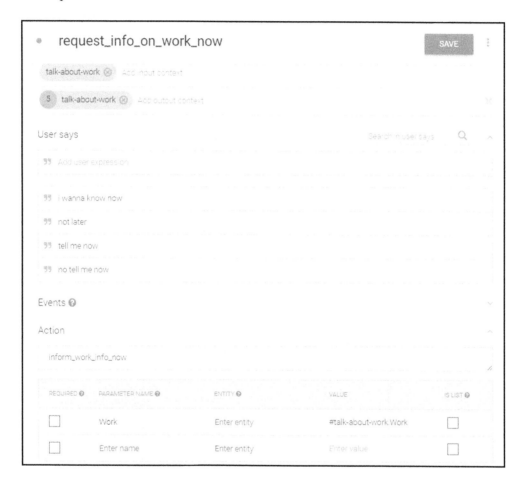

The entities get passed from one intent to another via the contextual items. We can access the entities from previous conversation turns by using the # notation. For instance, observe how we populate the value of the `Work` parameter using the `#talk-about-work.Work` value. This can then be used in the response utterance as `$Work` (for example, `Alright. I will tell you about $Work`):

We will see how to use entities to perform advanced processing in the backend toward the end of the chapter.

System entities

In addition to entities that we create (that is, *developer entities*) using the preceding approach, there are also predefined *system entities*. These have been designed to capture entities that are common to most domains and conversational tasks. Concepts such as dates, personal names, city names, country names, email addresses, and phone numbers can be recognized in user utterances using system entities:

The preceding screenshot shows how you can access them by using the `@sys` qualifier when providing sample utterances. For instance, you want to get the user's email address. For this, you can set up a user intent in the context of the conversation such as `inform_user_email`. This user instance should have sample utterances, such as "bluewhale@bmail.com" or "its bluewhale@bmail.com," where the user provides the chatbot with their email. You will notice that the email address gets recognized as `@sys.email`. If it doesn't get automatically recognized, you can specify that it is an email by selecting it and choosing `@sys.email`. This tells the agent that all utterances with valid email addresses are to be recognized as the `inform_user_email` intent:

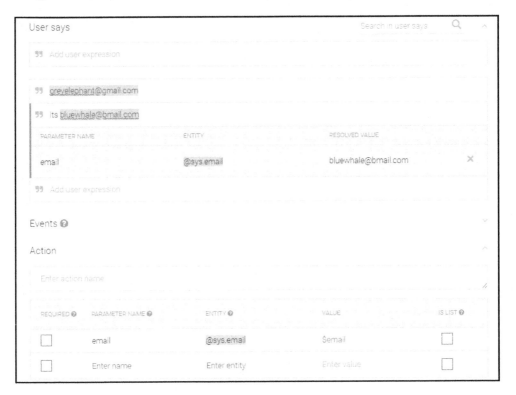

Once recognized, the entity will be passed on as a parameter to be appended to the intent. System entities such as `@sys.geo-city` and `@sys.geo-country` can be used to recognize city names and country names in user utterances without having to specify all the names as developer entities.

In order to recognize composite elements in natural language utterances such as the mention of quantities (weight, length, and so on), we can use composite system entities. `@sys.unit-weight:unit-weight` can be used to recognize utterances such as *10 kg*, *15 kilos*, and *20 kilograms*. These will be resolved into the following parameter for further action:

```
{"amount":10,"unit":"kg"}
```

Entity types cannot be directly specified in sample utterances. For instance, `its @sys.email` cannot be specified as a sample utterance. Instead, it needs to be provided as a template. To provide example templates to intents, switch the double quotes to `@` sign.

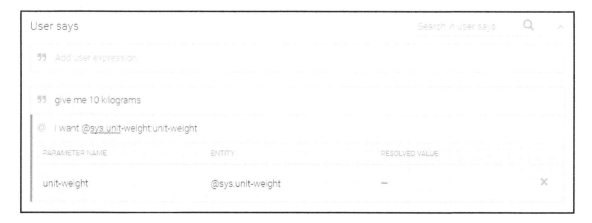

In the preceding screenshot, observe that there is a sample utterance (that is, **give me 10 kilograms**) and a sample template **i want @sys.unit-weight:unit-weight**. Explore system entities further to see how you can use predefined entities in your chatbot.

More info on system entities can be found at `https://api.ai/docs/reference/system-entities`.

Rich response formats

In addition to text responses, you can also provide rich message types such as cards, carousels, and those we used in Chapter 2, *Tour Guide for Your City*, when building our Facebook Messenger bot for weather. The type of response that we can add to the agent depends on the integrations it is enabled for. Each integration enables a different set of response types.

Since we have integrated Facebook Messenger with the Einstein bot, we can add message content specific to the platform. To do this, follow these steps:

1. Choose any user intent for which you want to add rich response formats.
2. Scroll down to the **Response** tab:

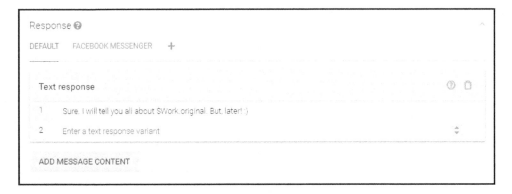

3. Alongside **DEFAULT**, there will be a tab for integrations that have been enabled (for example, **FACEBOOK MESSENGER**). If you don't see your integration, you can add it by clicking the + menu.
4. Under each integration, you will see the following:

5. If you want the default response(s) to appear first on the integration platform, turn that switch on.
6. Click **ADD MESSAGE CONTENT** and choose the type of response. In case of Facebook Messenger integration, you will find response types such as text message, image, card, quick replies, and custom payload.
7. Enter the response format specific information.

The following is an example of card type response for Facebook Messenger integration:

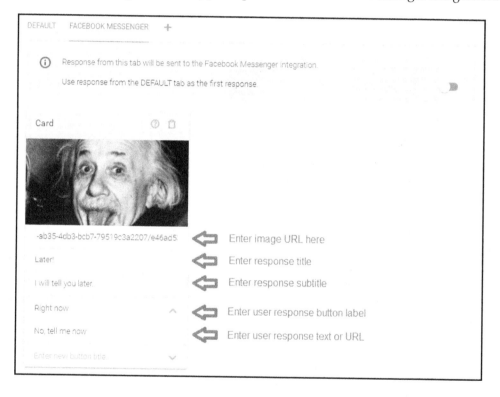

And here is how it appears on Facebook Messenger:

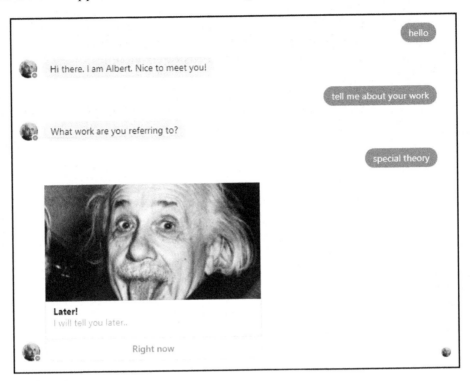

Clicking the **Right now** button will send a **No, tell me now** text message back to the agent as the user's response to the bot.

Now that you've got an idea of how to make your responses richer, go ahead and have a play with different formats available for your integration.

Importing and exporting agents

All agents in API.AI can be exported and backed up. This option also allows you to move the agent from one API.AI account to another.

Exporting, restoring, and importing agents

Here is how you can export an agent.

1. Click the Settings icon next to the agent's name on the left menu.
2. Click **Export and Import**:

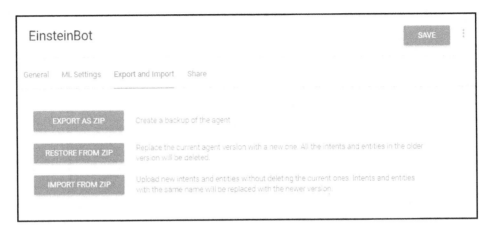

3. Click **EXPORT AS ZIP.**

The downloaded ZIP file will be organized in terms of the agent settings, entities, and intents in JSON file format. The following is the format of the JSON of the agent settings for our Einstein bot:

```
{
 "description": "Simulated Albert Einstein",
 "language": "en",
 "googleAssistant": {
   "googleAssistantCompatible": false,
   "project": "einsteinbot-dce04",
   "welcomeIntentSignInRequired": false,
   "startIntents": [],
   "systemIntents": [],
   "endIntentIds": [],
   "oAuthLinking": {
     "required": false,
     "grantType": "AUTH_CODE_GRANT"
   },
   "voiceType": "MALE_1",
   "capabilities": [],
   "protocolVersion": "V2"
```

```
  },
  "defaultTimezone": "Africa/Casablanca",
  "webhook": {
    "available": false,
    "useForDomains": false
  },
  "isPrivate": true,
  "customClassifierMode": "use.after",
  "mlMinConfidence": 0.3
  }
```

You can also restore an agent from a backup file using the **RESTORE FROM ZIP** option. All the intents and entities will be deleted and restored from the ZIP file:

In case, you want to extend your agent from a ZIP file, it can be done using the **IMPORT** option. This allows you to add extra intents and entities to an existing agent. All entities and intents in the agent with the same names as those in the file will be replaced by the ones in the ZIP file.

Exporting and importing intents and entities

Intents and entities can be exported separately and one at a time without having to export the agent entirely. This can be done by clicking the cloud_download icon listed against each intent and entity:

Here is an example intent downloaded from the Einstein bot:

```
{
  "userSays": [
    {
      "id": "aa492d7b-6119-4d4c-a626-03aea6868882",
      "data": [
        {
          "text": "what was your job at the patent office"
        }
      ],
      "isTemplate": false,
      "count": 0
    },
    {
      "id": "f8a43750-c215-4750-aac8-1a0f977611d8",
      "data": [
        {
          "text": "why did you take up the job at the patent office"
        }
      ],
      "isTemplate": false,
      "count": 0
    },
    {
      "id": "2b48f3e6-7949-4cf6-b25c-ebb4691e4812",
      "data": [
        {
          "text": "what did you do at the patent office"
        }
      ],
      "isTemplate": false,
      "count": 0
    }
  ],
```

```json
    "id": "38b83408-16ae-4b05-b841-187b7205e116",
    "name": "request_info_patent_office_job",
    "auto": true,
    "contexts": [],
    "responses": [
      {
         "resetContexts": false,
         "action": "inform_patent_office_job",
         "affectedContexts": [
           {
             "name": "patents-office-job",
             "parameters": {},
             "lifespan": 5
           }
         ],
         "parameters": [],
         "messages": [
         {
         "type": 0,
         "speech": "After graduating, I tried to get a teaching post
         but was unsuccessful. So with the help of my friend Marcel
         Grossman\u0027s father, I got a job in the patent office at Bern."
         }
        ]
      }
    ],
    "priority": 500000,
    "webhookUsed": false,
    "webhookForSlotFilling": false,
    "fallbackIntent": false,
    "events": []
}
```

Intents can also be uploaded using specifications in the JSON format shown earlier. To do this, create the JSON file, click more options in the **Intents** tab, and click **Upload Intent**:

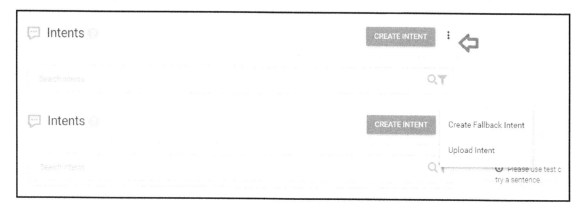

When prompted, provide the intent file in JSON format, as shown here:

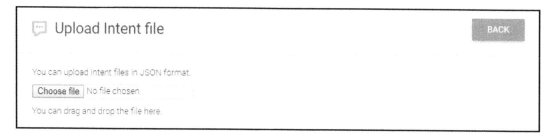

Here is an entity file from the Einstein bot (from the `Work` entity type). The name of the entity type is `Work` and each entity is entered as an entry with reference values and synonyms:

```
{
  "id": "9ed80101-6ecc-4006-bf7f-7c49bcbc03ef",
  "name": "Work",
  "isOverridable": true,
  "entries": [
    {
    "value": "special-theory",
    "synonyms": [
      "special theory of relativity",
      "special theory"
    ]
    },
    {
```

```
      "value": "general-theory",
      "synonyms": [
        "general theory",
        "general theory of relativity"
      ]
      },
      {
      "value": "brownian-movement-theory",
      "synonyms": [
        "brownian motion",
        "theory of brownian motion",
        "theory of brownian movement",
        "brownian movement",
        "brownian movement theory"
      ]
      }
  ],
  "isEnum": false,
  "automatedExpansion": false
}
```

New entity types can be added to the agent by creating them in the preceding format and uploading them. The same approach can be used to edit existing entities:

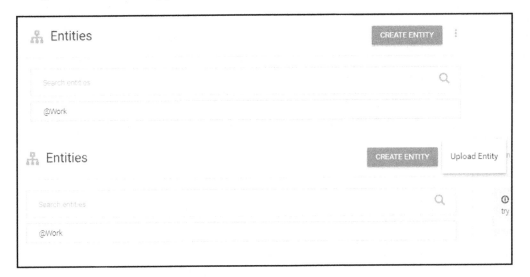

Fulfillments

Although you can build complete agents in API.AI, you still need to use external sources for backend tasks that the chatbot is supposed to perform. Backend tasks are the tasks that the chatbot will perform behind the scenes while having a conversation with the user. These can range from making a record of the conversation in the CRM, to identifying a lead, to querying the database for information requested by the user. This is called **fulfillment**.

An example of fulfillment in a travel planning chatbot would be to query the database to check and retrieve whether there are flights available for a given date, the to and from source, and destination cities. This task will be fulfilled by a web app that can be called by the chatbot once it has the necessary information to perform the query. Another instance would be when it is required to make the booking.

Let us now create a task for the Einstein bot to explore this further. Let us create a calculator module based on Einstein's world-famous equation, $E=mc^2$.

This equation calculates the amount of energy that will be generated if the mass of a system completely disappears. To do this calculation, we need to get the mass, m, of the system from the user. We will pass it on to the web app, where the amount of energy, E, generated from mass, m, is calculated. Let us have a look at an example conversation:

```
User: Hey. Can you tell me how much energy gets generated from an atom?
Bot: Yeah sure. How much does it weigh?
User: Lets say it is 2 grams.
Bot: Ok. A system that weighs 2 grams will transform into 179751036 MJ of
energy.
```

To add a webhook to the bot, do the following:

1. Create a web app that can take in parameters, do the backend task, and respond with an utterance.
2. Host it in the cloud.
3. Configure the webhook for the agent.
4. Enable webhooks in intents where they are needed.

To build and host the web app, do the following:

1. In your console, create a directory to hold this project. In this directory, we will create the following three files:

   - `index.js`
   - `package.json`
   - `Procfile`

`index.js` is a Node.js program that acts as a web app to receive parameters from the chatbot, performs a backend operation, and sends back an utterance:

```
const express = require('express')
const bodyParser = require('body-parser')
const request = require('request')

const app = express()

app.set('port', (process.env.PORT || 5000))

// Process application/x-www-form-urlencoded
app.use(bodyParser.urlencoded({extended: false}))

// Process application/json
app.use(bodyParser.json())

app.use(express.static('public'))

// Index route
app.get('/', function (req, res) {
    res.send('Hello world, I am EinsteinBot!.')
})

app.post('/emc2/', function (req, res) {
    console.log(JSON.stringify(req.body));
    var weight = req.body.result.parameters.weight;
    var m = weight.amount;
    var weight_unit = weight.unit;
    //convert weight into kg
    if (weight_unit == 'g'){
        m = m/1000.0;
    }
    var c2 = 9 * 10^16; //in m^2/s^2
    var e = m * c2;
    res.setHeader('Content-Type', 'application/json');
```

```
        var botSpeech = "Energy that the system can create is " + e
        + " Joules.";
        out = {speech: botSpeech,
                displayText: botSpeech,
                data: null};
        var outString = JSON.stringify(out);
        console.log('Out:' + outString);
        res.send(outString);
    })

    // Spin up the server
    app.listen(app.get('port'), function() {
        console.log('running on port', app.get('port'))
    })
```

emc2 is the POST handle that handles the request from the chatbot to convert mass into energy.

2. Let us create the package.json file to tell Heroku the packages that are needed for index.js. Create the package.json file in your text editor with the following JSON:

```
{
  "name": "einstein-bot-webhook",
  "version": "1.0.0",
  "description": "Einstein Bot Webhook",
  "main": "index.js",
  "scripts": {
    "test": "echo \"Error: no test specified\" && exit 1"
  },
  "author": "Srini Janarthanam",
  "license": "ISC",
  "dependencies": {
  "body-parser": "^1.15.2",
  "express": "^4.14.0",
  "request": "^2.72.0"
  }
}
```

3. As a final step, we need to create a Procfile to tell Heroku to run index.js. Create Procfile in your text editor with the following command:

```
web: node index.js
```

Perform the following steps to push the interface program onto the cloud. From the console window, where your `Weatherman` interface project is, execute the following commands to create a Heroku app and push the interface app onto the cloud:

```
> git init
> git add .
> git commit -m "webhook for einstein bot v1"
> heroku create einstein-bot
> git push heroku master
```

You will receive a message with the app's URL in it. In my case, it is `https://einstein-bot.herokuapp.com`.

To configure the webhook for the agent, do the following:

1. Click the **Fulfillment** option on the left menu.
2. Switch on the webhook. You will see the following webhook specifications form:

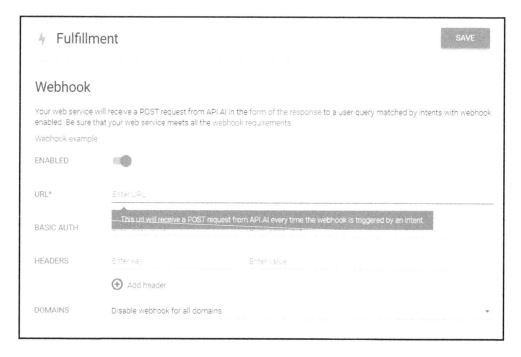

3. Fill in the URL of the web app and click **Save**. In our example, it is `https://einstein-bot.herokuapp.com/emc2/`. For now, we will not worry about the authentication and other headers.

To enable webhooks within intents, scroll all the way down on the intent page. Under the **Fulfillment** tab, click **Use webhook**. Extending from the web app designed earlier to convert mass into energy using Einstein's famous equation, let us see how it can be embedded into the agent. To do this, let us first create a `request_emc` intent, which will recognize utterances asking for the conversion (for example, "Can you convert 5 grams' mass into energy?"). This intent needs a parameter (that is, `mass`). This is specified as a system entity (`@sys.unit-weight`):

The default response should be something that can be used if the webhook fails. Enable the webhook so that the web app will be called to process and provide the agent with a response utterance:

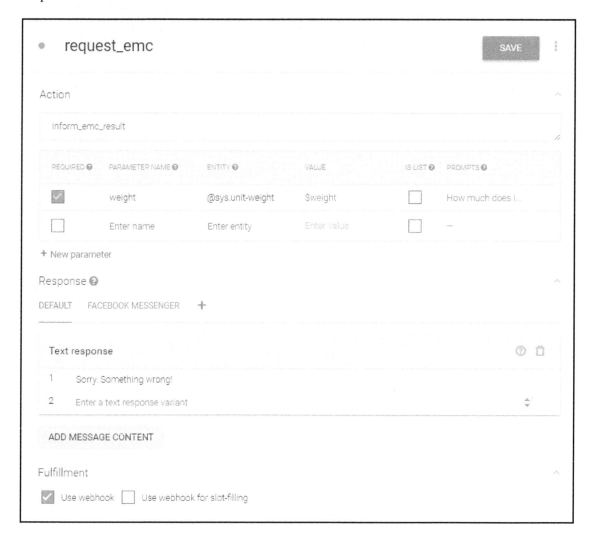

The following screenshot shows how the webhook actually works in conversation on the web chat platform:

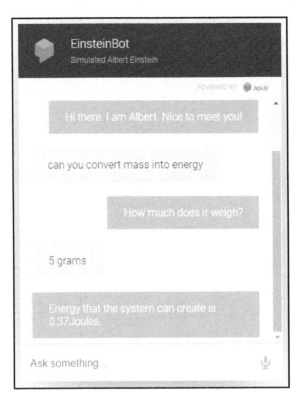

Summary

Great work! In this chapter, we have designed and built a rich conversational chatbot emulating Einstein using API.AI. Obviously, the chatbot we have built is very lean and to build one that emulates a person even to a pretty decent level would require an enormous amount of time and effort. However, this exercise has been useful to demonstrate the concepts underlying natural language understanding in conversations such as intents, entities, and contexts. We have demonstrated, with practical examples, how to perform integrations with deployment platforms such as Facebook Messenger and web chat. We have shown how backend tasks can be managed and integrated seamlessly into the conversational experience.

I would encourage you to try prebuilt agents that can be imported into any agent to enhance its conversation skills. For instance, a small talk module can be added to your agent to make it more personable without having to design and code all the intents and responses necessary for small talk. There are comparable tools from other providers. These can be explored in the same way. The structure of most of these tools is very similar. Here is the list of tools that you could explore further:

- MS LUIS
- IBM Watson
- Facebook WIT.AI
- Amazon Lex

In the next chapter, we will design and build an SMS chatbot for journey planning.

References

API.AI documentation: `https://api.ai/docs/getting-started/basics`

Facebook Messenger documentation: `https://developers.facebook.com/docs/messenger-platform`

5
Let's Catch a Train

So far, we have built chatbots and deployed them on messaging platforms such as Facebook Messenger. Facebook Messenger is currently the most popular messaging service. However, there is a messaging service that has existed for quite a long time and is still popularly used by businesses to connect with customers. **Short Messaging Service**, which is popularly abbreviated as **SMS**, is a great platform for chatbots. Businesses around the globe use this service to send thousands of notification messages to customers at various phases of their journey: marketing, sales, transactions, delivery, and so on. And the best part is that it does not require any internet data to communicate.

In this chapter, we will design and build a chatbot to help users plan their train journeys. We will use a Transport data API to obtain information about trains, their arrival and departure timings at stations, and so on, and to serve the information, build a chatbot to interact with users in natural language. We will then explore how the chatbot can be exposed to the SMS platform. We will learn to use the services of a communications API provider called Twilio. We will also learn how to plug in toolkits such as API.AI to understand user utterances and manage the conversation in an SMS chatbot.

First, let's take a look at the Transport API and the data that it has to offer. Based on the data that is available, we will then brainstorm and design some sample conversational tasks. We will then build a simple one-way SMS bot that can send timely notifications to users. And build on that to develop a two-way chatbot that sends train information to users based on their requests in natural language. We will explore how to build and integrate API.AI agents into our chatbot to understand language and drive the conversation.

By the end of this chapter, you will be able to:

- Design conversational tasks based on data
- Create backend task modules using Transport API
- Build SMS bots using Twilio
- Integrate a Dialogflow agent to understand user utterances

Exploring Transport API

To get started, let's have a look at the data source that we are going to use in this chapter. Transport API is a data service for all public transport services in the UK. If you are in a different country, you would be able to find something similar to your country. But you can still play around with this service. Transport API is a data platform for transport data providing information on live arrivals and departures, timetables, journey planning, fares, performance indicators, and commuters tweet mapping. Data is served using RESTful web services.

Creating a developer account

1. To get started, create a developer account at `https://developer.transportapi.com` and get an app key and app ID:

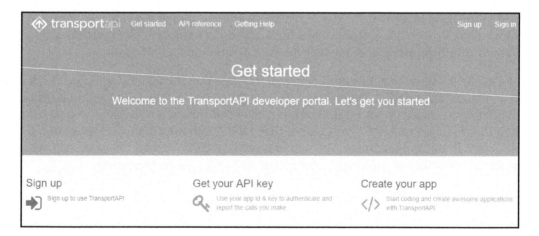

2. Let's try the following sample request. Replace YOUR_APP_ID and YOUR_APP_KEY with your app ID and key. Execute the following GET request from a web browser. At this request, we are trying to retrieve information concerning Euston train station, in London:

```
http://transportapi.com/v3/uk/places.json?query=euston&type=train_s
tation&app_id=
YOUR_APP_ID&app_key=YOUR_APP_KEY
```

The preceding request will return a JSON response with information such as the full name of the station, its latitude and longitude coordinates, and station code:

```
{
                                                              Raw    Parsed
    "request_time": "2017-08-05T07:06:08+01:00",
    "source": "Network Rail",
    "acknowledgements": "Contains information of Network Rail Infrastructure Limited. License
    http://www.networkrail.co.uk/data-feeds/terms-and-conditions/",
    "member": [
        {
            "type": "train_station",
            "name": "Edinburgh Gateway",
            "latitude": 55.940938,
            "longitude": -3.320251,
            "accuracy": 100,
            "station_code": "EGY",
            "tiploc_code": "EDINGWY"
        },
        {
            "type": "train_station",
            "name": "Edinburgh",
            "latitude": 55.952391,
            "longitude": -3.188228,
            "accuracy": 100,
            "station_code": "EDB",
            "tiploc_code": "EDINBUR"
        },
        {
            "type": "train_station",
            "name": "Edinburgh Park",
            "latitude": 55.927549,
            "longitude": -3.307664,
            "accuracy": 100,
            "station_code": "EDP",
            "tiploc_code": "EDINPRK"
        }
    ]
}
```

Exploring the dataset

Transport API provides data regarding trains, buses, the tube (subway), and many other forms of transport. To build our chatbot, let's begin with just the trains' data. In this section, let's take a look at the different kinds of data available about trains. For all requests, the base URL is `http://transportapi.com/v3/uk/`.

Train stations near you

This endpoint provides a list of train stations near a given location. The search location should be provided as a latLon coordinate, as follows:

```
http://transportapi.com/v3/uk/train/stations/near.json?lat=55.9485&lon=-3.2
021&app_id=YOUR_APP_ID&app_key=YOUR_APP_KEY
```

Response

The response we get is a list of stations near the given latLon coordinates. For each station, we get its name, location, and station code:

```
{
    "minlon": -3.4521,                              "stations": [
    "minlat": 55.6985,                                  {
    "maxlon": -2.9521,                                      "station_code": "EDB",
    "maxlat": 56.1985,                                      "atcocode": null,
    "searchlon": -3.2021,                                   "tiploc_code": "EDINBUR",
    "searchlat": 55.9485,                                   "name": "Edinburgh Waverley",
    "page": 1,                                              "mode": "train",
    "rpp": 25,                                              "longitude": -3.188228,
    "total": 54,                                            "latitude": 55.952391,
    "request_time": "2017-08-05T06:21:24+01:00",            "distance": 966
    "stations": [ … ] // 25 items                       },
}                                                       { … }, // 8 items
                                                        { … }, // 8 items
                                                        { … }, // 8 items
```

Trains in the area

Train stations can also be searched by providing a bounding box. The top-left and bottom-right coordinates of the box need to be provided. This is particularly useful if you need a list of all stations with city limits or something similar. Let's try this using the bounding box coordinates for Edinburgh:

```
http://transportapi.com/v3/uk/train/stations/bbox.json?minlon=-3.4521&minla
t=55.6985&maxlon=-2.9521&maxlat=56.1985&app_id=YOUR_APP_ID&app_key=YOUR_APP
_KEY
```

Response

The response we get is as follows:

```
{
    "minlon": -3.4521,
    "minlat": 55.6985,
    "maxlon": -2.9521,
    "maxlat": 56.1985,
    "searchlon": -3.2021,
    "searchlat": 55.9485,
    "page": 1,
    "rpp": 25,
    "total": 54,
    "request_time": "2017-08-05T06:58:20+01:00",
    "stations": [
        {
            "station_code": "EDB",
            "atcocode": null,
            "tiploc_code": "EDINBUR",
            "name": "Edinburgh Waverley",
            "mode": "train",
            "longitude": -3.188228,
            "latitude": 55.952391,
            "distance": 966
        },
        {
            "station_code": "HYM",
            "atcocode": null,
            "tiploc_code": "HAYMRKT",
            "name": "Haymarket",
            "mode": "train",
            "longitude": -3.218449,
            "latitude": 55.945806,
            "distance": 1061
        },
```

Live departures

The live status of trains arriving and departing a given station can be obtained using the following endpoint. Let's try it out for Edinburgh Waverley station, whose station code is EDB:

```
http://transportapi.com/v3/uk/train/station/EDB/live.json?&app_id=YOUR_APP_
ID&app_key=YOUR_APP_KEY
```

Response

Here is its response:

```
{                                                              Raw    Parsed
    "date": "2017-08-05",
    "time_of_day": "06:00",
    "request_time": "2017-08-05T06:49:44+01:00",
    "station_name": "Edinburgh Waverley",
    "station_code": "EDB",
  "departures": {
    "all": [
      {
          "mode": "train",
          "service": "13560015",
          "train_uid": "G83644",
          "platform": "10",
          "operator": "SR",
          "operator_name": "Scotrail",
          "aimed_departure_time": "06:07",
          "aimed_arrival_time": null,
          "aimed_pass_time": null,
          "origin_name": "Edinburgh Waverley",
          "source": "ATOC",
          "destination_name": "Milngavie",
          "category": "OO",
          "service_timetable": {
              "id": "http://transportapi.com/v3/uk/train/service/train_uid:G83644/2017-08-
              05/timetable.json?app_id=60ce46ea&app_key=251dc61414961e8ebfe110329ffa367d"
          }
      },
      {
          "mode": "train",
          "service": "22180008",
          "train_uid": "P31962",
          "platform": "7",
          "operator": "XC",
          "operator_name": "CrossCountry",
```

Station timetables

Timetables of trains arriving and departing from a given station on a given date and time can be obtained using the following endpoint. Let's get all the trains departing Edinburgh Waverley (EDB) station on 2017-08-05 at 06:00:

```
http://transportapi.com/v3/uk/train/station/EDB/2017-08-05/06:00/timetable.
json?app_id=YOUR_APP_ID&app_key=YOUR_APP_KEY
```

Response

And here is the response:

```
{                                                                    Raw    Parsed
    "date": "2017-08-05",
    "time_of_day": "06:00",
    "request_time": "2017-08-05T06:49:44+01:00",
    "station_name": "Edinburgh Waverley",
    "station_code": "EDB",
    "departures": {
        "all": [
            {
                "mode": "train",
                "service": "13560015",
                "train_uid": "G83644",
                "platform": "10",
                "operator": "SR",
                "operator_name": "Scotrail",
                "aimed_departure_time": "06:07",
                "aimed_arrival_time": null,
                "aimed_pass_time": null,
                "origin_name": "Edinburgh Waverley",
                "source": "ATOC",
                "destination_name": "Milngavie",
                "category": "00",
                "service_timetable": {
                    "id": "http://transportapi.com/v3/uk/train/service/train_uid:G83644/2017-08-
                    05/timetable.json?app_id=60ce46ea&app_key=251dc61414961e8ebfe110329ffa367d"
                }
            },
            {
                "mode": "train",
                "service": "22180008",
                "train_uid": "P31962",
                "platform": "7",
                "operator": "XC",
                "operator_name": "CrossCountry",
```

Service timetables

Timetables for each train service can be also be obtained. This data lets you see the arrival and departure times of a given train service at the various stations it calls at on a given date and time. Let's try an example out with service number, 23587103, on 2017-08-05 at 06:00:

```
http://transportapi.com/v3/uk/train/service/23587103/2017-08-05/06:00/timet
able.json?app_id=YOUR_APP_ID&app_key=YOUR_APP_KEY
```

Response

The response we get for the service timetable is as follows:

```json
{
    "service": "23587103",
    "train_uid": "G82394",
    "headcode": "",
    "toc": {
        "atoc_code": "SR"
    },
    "train_status": "P",
    "origin_name": "Markinch",
    "destination_name": "Edinburgh Waverley",
    "stop_of_interest": null,
    "date": "2017-08-05",
    "time_of_day": "06:00",
    "mode": "train",
    "request_time": "2017-08-05T06:46:22+01:00",
    "category": "OO",
    "operator": "SR",
    "operator_name": "Scotrail",
    "stops": [
        {
            "station_code": "MNC",
            "tiploc_code": "MKIN",
            "station_name": "Markinch",
            "stop_type": "LO",
            "platform": "1",
            "aimed_departure_date": "2017-08-05",
            "aimed_departure_time": "06:19",
            "aimed_arrival_date": null,
            "aimed_arrival_time": null,
            "aimed_pass_date": null,
            "aimed_pass_time": null
        },
        {
            "station_code": "GLT",
            "tiploc_code": "GLNRTHS",
            "station_name": "Glenrothes With Thornton",
```

Conversational design

Now that we have a good idea of the data we have in our hands, let's brainstorm the conversational tasks for our chatbot.

- Nearest station
- Next train
- Time of arrival
- Later trains from a station
- How do I get from A to B?

Let's start with a simple one: getting to the nearest station.

Nearest station

In order to get to the nearest station for a user, we need his/her location. This could be in the form of postcode or latLon coordinates. Platforms such as Facebook Messenger allow users to share location in the form of latLon coordinates. However, since we are going to be using the SMS platform, let's use the postcode route. The conversation for this task could go in one of the following ways:

```
User : Where is my nearest station?
Bot: Can you give me your postcode?
User : EH12 9QR
Bot: Great. Your nearest station is South Gyle.

User: What is the nearest station to EH12 9QR?
Bot: The nearest station is South Gyle.
```

Next train

In order to get information on the next train, the conversation could go the following ways:

```
User : When is the next train to Glasgow?
Bot : From which station?
User : Edinburgh Park
Bot : The next train to Glasgow Central is at 10:00.

User : Next train
Bot : From?
User : Edinburgh Park
Bot : Finding next train from Edinburgh Park. Going to?
```

```
User :  Glasgow
Bot : Next train to Glasgow Central is at 10:00.
```

Time of arrival

Sometimes users may want to know the time of arrival of the train in context at a specific station. To get information on the time of arrival, the conversation could go as follows:

```
User : What time does the train arrive at Glasgow Central?
Bot : The train will arrive in Glasgow Central at 11:00.
```

Many more conversations are possible in the domain of travel. All the preceding tasks are reactive, where the bot responds to users' requests. In contrast, proactive tasks can be designed by having the bot initiate conversations. For instance, the bot can send train times and delays/cancelled information to the user at set times during the day:

```
Bot : The 15:00 train to Edinburgh Waverley is delayed to 15:30.
User : Is there an earlier train to Haymarket?
...
```

Conversational tasks such as a list of later trains and planning your route are more complex than the preceding tasks. As we proceed, we will see how to build a chatbot that can handle a few of the mentioned tasks.

Building a simple SMS bot

Let's now build the SMS platform interface for the chatbot. To bear with the complexity, let us do this in two steps. First, let us build a bot to simply send SMS text messages to a mobile number. This could be a message concerning the status of a train arriving at a station or the next train to a certain destination from a given station. Second, we will build a two-way chatbot that can receive messages from users and respond to them appropriately. To do this, we will use a service called Twilio. Twilio is a developer platform for communications enabling developers to add messaging, voice, and video capabilities to their software. We will explore how we can build notification bots and chatbots using Twilio's messaging infrastructure.

Getting started

To get started with Twilio, perform the following steps:

1. Go to `www.twilio.com`, click **Sign Up** and register your
2. Once you have registered, go over to the console page at `www.twilio.com/console`.
3. Copy the **ACCOUNT SID** and **Account Key**. We will be using projects.

Setting up the dashboard

Let us build a bot that sends the notification to a user's mobile number. Twilio has four main products: **Programmable Chat**, **Programmable SMS**, **Programmable Voice**, and **Programmable Video**. To build a notification sender, we need to use the **Programmable SMS** service. Here are the steps:

1. On the console dashboard, select **Programmable SMS**.
2. On the **Programmable SMS Dashboard**, click **Get Started**:

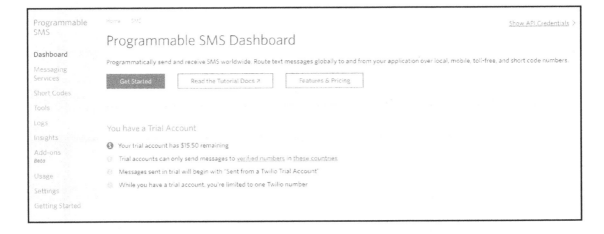

In order to send SMS messages, you need a phone number. Click **Get a number** to get one:

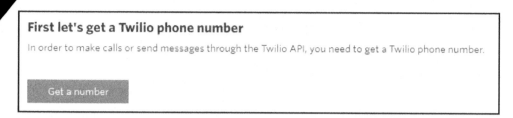

4. This will provide you with a number. You can choose to accept it by clicking **Choose this Number**. If not, pick another one. Make sure that the number has SMS capability:

5. You will receive an acknowledgment that you have been allocated the number:

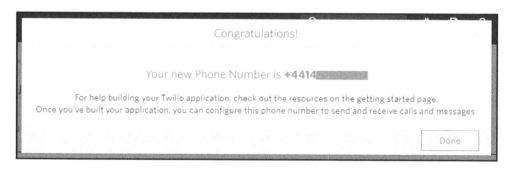

Click **Done**.

6. Are you seeing the **Send a Message** window? Why don't you send yourself a message? Send a test message to your registered cellphone number (the number that you used to verify the account):

7. Check your cellphone to see whether you have received your test message. Click **Yes** to inform Twilio that you have received your message.

Simple Message Sender

Now that we have set up the account and got a phone number, let's move ahead to create a bot to send notifications. To do this, perform the following steps:

1. Open the console window and create a directory called SMSBot.

2. In the `SMSBot` directory, create a new Node.js project using the `npm init` command, as shown here:

```
C:\Users\Srini\Documents\workspace\SMSBot>npm init
This utility will walk you through creating a package.json file.
It only covers the most common items, and tries to guess sensible defaults.

See `npm help json` for definitive documentation on these fields
and exactly what they do.

Use `npm install <pkg> --save` afterwards to install a package and
save it as a dependency in the package.json file.

Press ^C at any time to quit.
name: (SMSBot) smsbot
version: (1.0.0)
description: A simple SMS sending bot
entry point: (index.js)
test command:
git repository:
keywords:
author: Srini Janarthanam
license: (ISC)
About to write to C:\Users\Srini\Documents\workspace\SMSBot\package.json:

{
  "name": "smsbot",
  "version": "1.0.0",
  "description": "A simple SMS sending bot",
  "main": "index.js",
  "scripts": {
    "test": "echo \"Error: no test specified\" && exit 1"
  },
  "author": "Srini Janarthanam",
  "license": "ISC"
}
```

Check the directory to see the files that have been generated. You will see a file called `package.json` with meta information concerning the project.

3. We need to install the Twilio Node.js library to build our SMS bot. On the
   console, execute the `npm install twilio --save` command:

```
C:\Users\Srini\Documents\workspace\SMSBot>npm install twilio
npm WARN package.json smsbot@1.0.0 No repository field.
npm WARN package.json smsbot@1.0.0 No README data
twilio@3.6.1 node_modules\twilio
├── deprecate@1.0.0
├── scmp@0.0.3
├── rootpath@0.1.2
├── xmlbuilder@9.0.1
├── q@2.0.3 (weak-map@1.0.5, pop-iterate@1.0.1, asap@2.0.6)
├── request@2.81.0 (aws-sign2@0.6.0, tunnel-agent@0.6.0, forever-agent@0.6.1, oauth-sign@0.8.2, is-type
darray@1.0.0, caseless@0.12.0, safe-buffer@5.1.1, stringstream@0.0.5, aws4@1.6.0, isstream@0.1.2, json-
stringify-safe@5.0.1, extend@3.0.1, performance-now@0.2.0, uuid@3.1.0, qs@6.4.0, combined-stream@1.0.5,
 mime-types@2.1.16, tough-cookie@2.3.2, form-data@2.1.4, hawk@3.1.3, http-signature@1.1.1, har-validato
r@4.2.1)
├── moment@2.18.1
├── jsonwebtoken@7.4.2 (ms@2.0.0, lodash.once@4.1.1, xtend@4.0.1, jws@3.1.4, joi@6.10.1)
└── lodash@4.0.0
```

4. Let's create a new JS file called `index.js`. Add the following code to the file:

```
//Index.js - SMSBot

//Add your Account SID
var accountSid = 'your_account_sid';

//Add your Auth Token here
var authToken = 'your_auth_token';

var twilio = require('twilio');
var client = new twilio(accountSid, authToken);

//Create a message with to and from numbers
client.messages.create({
    body: 'Srini says hello',
    to: '+447888999999',
    from: '+447888999990'
})
.then((message) => console.log(message.sid));
```

In the preceding code, the `to` number must be a verified number of trial accounts.
You cannot send messages to other numbers unless you upgrade your account.
The `from` number is the Twilio number that you had obtained previously.

5. Save the file and execute it using the `node index.js` command. This should send the text message to your verified phone number.

My train notifier

Imagine a scenario where a user commutes to work every day from Edinburgh Waverley to Glasgow Queen Street. And they struggle to figure out the trains and timings as they prepare to leave every morning. Wouldn't it be great if we could provide a service that sends a list of trains from their station to their destination at some point during their morning routine?

Using the preceding Simple Message Sender module, let's build a bot that will send a list of trains from a certain station to a certain destination station. Let's add a module to get the list of trains from a given station to a certain destination:

1. Install the request library using `npm install request --save`.
2. Create a function to send SMS notifications:

```
function sendSMS(msg, userPhoneNumber){
    var twilio = require('twilio');
    var client = new twilio(accountSid, authToken);
    //Create a message with to and from numbers
    client.messages.create({
        body: msg,
        to: userPhoneNumber,
        from: '+4414XXXXXXXX' //YOUR_NUMBER
    })
    .then((message) => console.log(message.sid));
}
```

3. Create a function to get all trains departing from a given station:

```
function getTrains(sourceStation, sourceStationCode,
                                destinationStation,
                                userPhoneNumber){
    var request = require('request');
    var url = 'http://transportapi.com/v3/uk/train/station/' +
            sourceStationCode   + '/live.json?
            app_id=YOUR_APP_ID&app_key=YOUR_APP_KEY';
    request(url, function (error, response, body) {
        if (response){
            var json = JSON.parse(body);
            if (json.departures){
                //console.log('Departures:',
```

```
            //JSON.stringify(json.departures));
            var dep =
            getTrainsToDestination(destinationStation,
            json.departures.all);
            var summary = summarize(destinationStation,
                                    sourceStation, dep);
            console.log('Summary: ' + summary);
            sendSMS(summary, userPhoneNumber);
        } else {
            console.log('No Departures found!');
        }
    } else {
        console.log('error:', error); // Print the error if one
                                      // occurred
    }
  });
}
```

4. Create a function to retrieve all trains going to a certain destination station:

```
function getTrainsToDestination(destination, allDepartures){
    d = [];
    if (allDepartures){
        for (var i=0; i < allDepartures.length; i++){
            var service = allDepartures[i];
            if (service.destination_name == destination){
                d.push(service)
            }
        }
    }
    return d;
}
```

5. Create a function to call the preceding functions to send the user a notification of all trains heading to a certain destination station from the user's preferred station:

```
function summarize(destinationStation, sourceStation, departures){
    var out = '';
    if (departures.length > 0){
        out = 'Here are the departures this morning to ' +
            destinationStation
                        + ".\n";
        for (var i=0; i< departures.length; i++){
            var service = departures[i];
            var serviceSummary = service.operator_name
                        + " at " +
            service.expected_departure_time;
```

```
                    out += serviceSummary + "\n"
            }
        } else {
            out = 'There are no trains to ' + destinationStation +
                                              ' from ' +
                                    sourceStation;
        }
        return out;
    }
```

6. And set the variables and call the main module:

```
//Index.js

//Add your Account SID
var accountSid = 'your_account_sid';
//Add your Auth Token here
var authToken = 'your_auth_token';

var destinationStation = 'Glasgow Queen Street';
var userPhoneNumber = '+447888999999';
var sourceStationCode = 'EDB';
var sourceStation = 'Edinburgh Waverley';

getTrains(sourceStation, sourceStationCode, destinationStation,
userPhoneNumber);
```

7. Run it on the `node index.js` console to see whether it works. It should print the summary of trains to the destination station on the console and also send it as an SMS notification message to you:

```
C:\Users\Srini\Documents\workspace\SMSBot>node index.js
Summary: Here are the departures this morning to Glasgow Queen Street.
Scotrail at 06:45
Scotrail at 07:00
Scotrail at 07:15
Scotrail at 07:30

SM79cb0e9ed7e5499f99ec35b3c2f77681

C:\Users\Srini\Documents\workspace\SMSBot>
```

8. Check your cellphone to see whether the message has arrived:

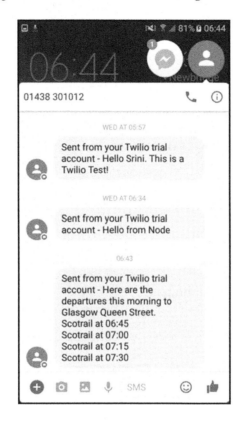

9. Congratulations! You have just created an SMS bot.

Scheduling tasks

Now that we have a bot that sends SMS notification, let us try our hand at setting it to run automatically on a daily or hourly basis. This feature will be useful to create proactive bots that initiate conversation with users at certain times of the day. To do this, follow these steps:

1. Create a `bin` directory.
2. Move the `index.js` file into the `bin` directory. Rename it as `sendTrainNotification.js`.

3. Add as the first line of code, the following shebang:

```
#!/usr/bin/env node
```

4. Go back to the project directory. We are now going to push this app into Heroku cloud.

5. Create a Git repository, add files, and commit:

```
git init
git add .
git commit -m "initial commit"
```

6. Create a Heroku app:

```
heroku create sms-notification-bot
```

7. Push the app to Heroku:

```
git push heroku master
```

We now have an app running at
`https://sms-notification-bot.herokuapp.com`.

8. Run the app locally:

```
heroku run sendTrainNotification.js
```

This should run the web app and send an SMS with train summaries to the user's phone:

```
C:\Users\Srini\Dropbox\_Book\workspace\sms-notification-bot>heroku run sendTrainNotification.js
Running sendTrainNotification.js on sms-notification-bot... up, run.6693 (Free)
Running - SMS Train Notification
Summary: Here are the departures this morning to Glasgow Queen Street.
Scotrail at 16:45
Scotrail at 17:00
Scotrail at 17:15
```

9. Now, we need to schedule the task. To do this, we need to set it up on the Heroku resources page of the app. Go to `https://dashboard.heroku.com/apps/sms-notification-bot/resources` on your browser:

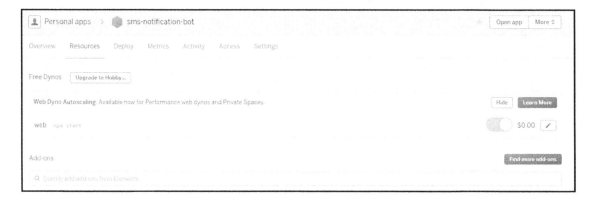

10. Type `Scheduler` in the **Add-ons** search box and choose **Heroku Scheduler**.
11. Once added, click **Heroku Scheduler**. This will take you to `https://scheduler.heroku.com/dashboard`.
12. Click **Add new job**.
13. In the textbox with **$**, type the name of the task to run (that is, `sendTrainNotification.js`). Choose **Frequency (Daily, Hourly,** or **Every 10 minutes)** and click **SAVE**:

14. Check logs on the console of Heroku logs. You should notice that the task will be running at regular set intervals and SMS are being sent to the user:

```
2017-08-13T07:07:25.867628+00:00 heroku[scheduler.4555]: Starting process with command `sendTrainNotification.js`
2017-08-13T07:07:26.517425+00:00 heroku[scheduler.4555]: State changed from starting to up
2017-08-13T07:07:28.022517+00:00 app[scheduler.4555]: Running - SMS Train Notification
2017-08-13T07:07:29.133248+00:00 app[scheduler.4555]: Summary: Here are the departures this morning to Glasgow Queen Street.
2017-08-13T07:07:29.133261+00:00 app[scheduler.4555]: Scotrail at 08:30
2017-08-13T07:07:29.133261+00:00 app[scheduler.4555]: Scotrail at 09:00
2017-08-13T07:07:29.133262+00:00 app[scheduler.4555]: Scotrail at 09:30
2017-08-13T07:07:29.133264+00:00 app[scheduler.4555]:
2017-08-13T07:07:29.133263+00:00 app[scheduler.4555]: Scotrail at 10:00
2017-08-13T07:07:29.804633+00:00 app[scheduler.4555]: SM7f6591a12f8f43eab488c7be5d5a9fbf
2017-08-13T07:07:29.892212+00:00 heroku[scheduler.4555]: State changed from up to complete
2017-08-13T07:07:29.880146+00:00 heroku[scheduler.4555]: Process exited with status 0
```

Congratulations! You have now built a proactive SMS bot.

Building a two-way chatbot

So far, we have built a bot that can send SMS notifications to users at set time intervals. Although proactive, it is only communicating one way. The user is not able to send any request to the bot to change the nature or content of the message it is sending. Let's work on that.

To build a chatbot that can communicate both ways we need to do two things: build the chatbot into the web app and modify setup configurations in Twilio. To do these, follow these steps:

1. Create an index.js file in the root directory of the project.
2. Install the express and body-parser libraries. These libraries will be used to make a web app:

   ```
   npm install body-parser --save
   npm install express --save
   ```

3. Create a web app in index.js:

   ```
   // Two-way SMS Bot

   const express = require('express')
   const bodyParser = require('body-parser')
   const twilio = require('twilio')

   const app = express()
   app.set('port', (process.env.PORT || 5000))
   ```

```
// Process application/x-www-form-urlencoded
app.use(bodyParser.urlencoded({extended: false}))

// Process application/json
app.use(bodyParser.json())

// Spin up the server
app.listen(app.get('port'), function() {
    console.log('running on port', app.get('port'))
})

// Index route
app.get('/', function (req, res) {
    res.send('Hello world, I am SMS bot.')
})

//Twilio webhook
app.post('/sms/', function (req, res) {
    var botSays = 'You said: ' + req.body.Body;
    var twiml = new twilio.TwimlResponse();
    twiml.message(botSays);
    res.writeHead(200, {'Content-Type': 'text/xml'});
    res.end(twiml.toString());
})
```

The preceding code creates a web app that looks for incoming messages from users and responds to them. The response is currently to repeat what the user has said.

4. Push it onto the cloud:

```
git add .
git commit -m webapp
git push heroku master
```

Now we have a web app on the cloud at https://sms-notification-bot. herokuapp.com/sms/ that can be called when an incoming SMS message arrives. This app will generate an appropriate chatbot response to the incoming message.

5. Go to the Twilio **Programmable SMS Dashboard** page at https://www.twilio. com/console/sms/dashboard.

6. Select **Messaging Services** on the menu and click **Create new Messaging Service**:

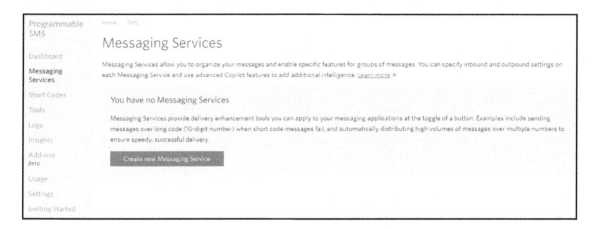

7. Give it a name and select **Chat Bot/Interactive 2-Way** as the use case:

8. This will take you to the **Configure** page with a newly-assigned service ID:

9. Under **Inbound Settings**, specify the URL of the web app we have created in the **REQUEST URL** field (that is, `https://sms-notification-bot.herokuapp.com/sms/`):

Now all the inbound messages will be routed to this web app.

10. Go back to the SMS console page at `https://www.twilio.com/console/sms/services`. Here you will notice your new messaging service listed along with the inbound request URL:

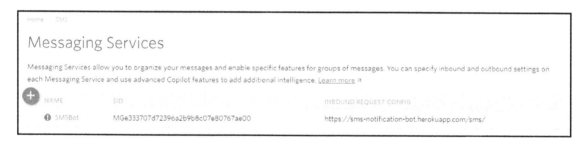

11. Click the service to attach a number to the service:

12. You can either add a new number, in which case you need to buy one or choose the number you already have. We already have one sending notifications that can be reused. Click **Add an Existing Number**.

13. Select the number by checking the box on the right and click **Add Selected**:

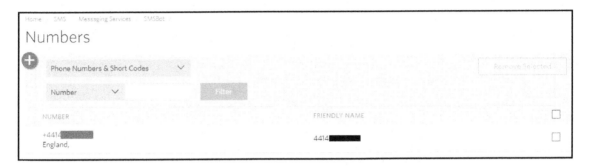

14. Once added, it will be listed on the **Numbers** page as follows:

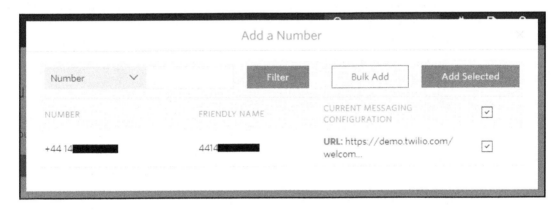

In **Advanced** settings, we can add multiple numbers for serving different geographic regions and have them respond as if the chatbot is responding over a local number.

15. The final step is to try sending an SMS message to the number and receive a response. Send a message using any SMS app on your phone and observe the response:

Congratulations! You now have a two-way interactive chatbot.

Understanding users' utterances

Now that we have a basic two-way chatbot, let us look into how we can process user utterances, understand their requests for information, and serve them effectively. In order to process user utterances, we will use the API.AI toolkit that was introduced in Chapter 3, *Let's Talk Weather*. User utterances will be processed and converted into user intents and parameters by API.AI. These will then be used to retrieve and serve appropriate information to the user.

Creating an API.AI agent

Let's first create an API.AI agent to understand user utterances in the conversational tasks that we enumerated previously. Because we have already discussed building API.AI agents extensively in Chapter 3, *Let's Talk Weather*, the following sequence of steps is going to be brief. However, we will be interfacing with the agent in a different manner compared to how it was done in Chapter 3, *Let's Talk Weather*:

1. Go to api.ai in your web browser. Log on with your Google credentials and click **GO TO CONSOLE**.
2. Click **Create new agent.** You will find this in the bottom of the drop-down list listing all the agents created by you so far.
3. Give it a name, description, and choose time zone. Click **Save**.
4. Click **Entities**. Create new entities for stations with station codes as reference values and names and alternatives as synonyms:

5. Click **Create Intent**. Create the following two intents to begin with:

- `request_live_departures`: To request the next few departures from a given station:

Set parameter **Station** as required and define the prompts to use in case the parameter is missing in the user's utterances.

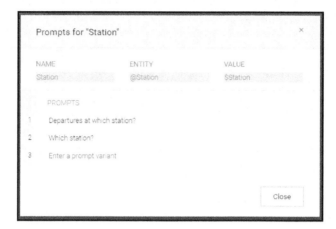

- `request_next_train`: To request the next train from a given station to a certain other station:

Set parameters **fromStation** and **toStation** as required:

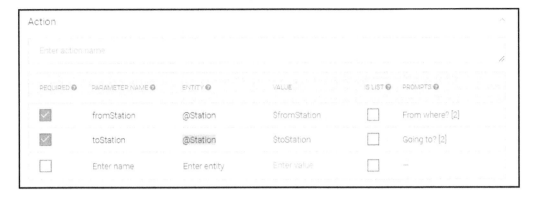

And define the prompts to use in case the parameters are missing in the user's utterances. For instance, prompts for **fromStation** are shown here:

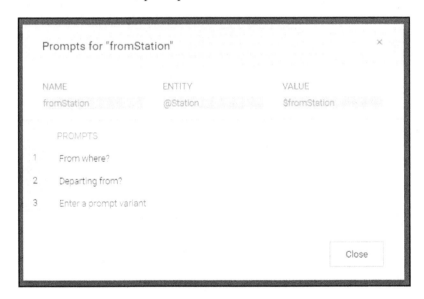

Create a Node.js interface to the API.AI agent

There are many ways to connect to an API.AI agent. We discussed some of them in `Chapter 3`, *Let's Talk Weather*. In this section, we will explore one more approach:

1. Create a Node.js program called `apiai.js` in the project root directory.
2. Install the API.AI Node.js library using the following command from the console:

    ```
    npm install apiai --save
    ```

3. Go back to agent settings (click the settings icon next to the agent's name on the drop-down list) on the web console:

4. Under the **General** tab, copy the **Developer access token:**

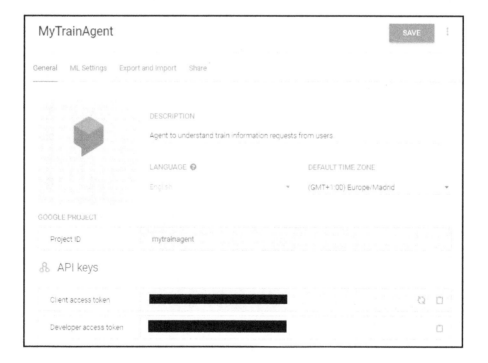

5. Go back to the Node.js program, `apiai.js`, and create a request to access the agent. Use the developer access token from the console in the code:

```
//API.AI
var apiai = require('apiai');
var apiai1 = apiai("YOUR_DEVELOPER_ACCESS_TOKEN");

var userUtterance = 'live departures from waverley';

var requestAPIAI = apiai1.textRequest(userUtterance, {
 sessionId: '12345'
});

requestAPIAI.on('response', function(response) {
 console.log(response);
});

requestAPIAI.on('error', function(error) {
 console.log(error);
});

requestAPIAI.end();
```

6. Run the program on the console using the `node apiai.js` command:

```
C:\Users\Srini\Documents\workspace\SMSBot>node apiai.js
{ id: 'a68a406c-9db3-4bc1-acf4-bd711bcac0a6',
  timestamp: '2017-08-15T05:51:31.241Z',
  lang: 'en',
  result:
   { source: 'agent',
     resolvedQuery: 'live departures from waverley',
     action: '',
     actionIncomplete: false,
     parameters: { Station: 'EDB' },
     contexts: [],
     metadata:
      { intentId: 'c35552da-b1b3-41ac-afb4-177533126c08',
        webhookUsed: 'false',
        webhookForSlotFillingUsed: 'false',
        intentName: 'request_live_departures' },
     fulfillment: { speech: '', messages: [Object] },
     score: 0.7699999809265137 },
  status: { code: 200, errorType: 'success' },
  sessionId: '12345' }
```

7. Observe the response displayed on the console. You will find the classified intent as `intentName` and associated parameters. Using these, we can fetch the appropriate information from the Transport API. And observe that there is no fulfillment speech as we did not specify any when building the intents.

8. Let's try a few more examples: change the user utterance to `show me departures` and run the code:

```
C:\Users\Srini\Documents\workspace\SMSBot>node apiai.js
{ id: 'c8ad170d-df2d-4384-b78d-727cfb394259',
  timestamp: '2017-08-15T04:50:21.052Z',
  lang: 'en',
  result:
   { source: 'agent',
     resolvedQuery: 'waverley',
     action: '',
     actionIncomplete: false,
     parameters: { Station: 'EDB' },
     contexts: [],
     metadata:
      { intentId: 'c35552da-b1b3-41ac-afb4-177533126c08',
        webhookUsed: 'false',
        webhookForSlotFillingUsed: 'false',
        intentName: 'request_live_departures' },
     fulfillment: { speech: '', messages: [Object] },
     score: 1 },
  status: { code: 200, errorType: 'success' },
  sessionId: '12345' }
```

9. Observe the difference from the previous one. In this user utterance, we haven't specified the station name. Therefore, the agent comes back with a question (in fulfillment speech): `Departures at which station?`. Also note that the `Station` parameter is empty and the `actionIncomplete` parameter is set to `true`.

10. Now change the user utterance to `waverley` and run again:

```
C:\Users\Srini\Documents\workspace\SMSBot>node apiai.js
{ id: 'c8ad170d-df2d-4384-b78d-727cfb394259',
  timestamp: '2017-08-15T04:50:21.052Z',
  lang: 'en',
  result:
   { source: 'agent',
     resolvedQuery: 'waverley',
     action: '',
     actionIncomplete: false,
     parameters: { Station: 'EDB' },
     contexts: [],
     metadata:
      { intentId: 'c35552da-b1b3-41ac-afb4-177533126c08',
        webhookUsed: 'false',
        webhookForSlotFillingUsed: 'false',
        intentName: 'request_live_departures' },
     fulfillment: { speech: '', messages: [Object] },
     score: 1 },
  status: { code: 200, errorType: 'success' },
  sessionId: '12345' }
```

11. Now examine the result again. There is no fulfillment speech and the
    `Station` parameter is set to `EDB` (which is the station code for Edinburgh
    Waverley). The `actionIncomplete` parameter is set to `false`.

What we have done so far is create a Node.js program to call an API.AI agent using its
Node.js library. We have also run and rerun the program to simulate a conversation. We
have been using the agent as a module to understand natural language utterances and
manage the conversation. Now we need to link this up to the main Node.js program
`index.js` to go fetch the results from Transform API and enable the conversation over
SMS.

Integrating API.AI agent to SMS chatbot

Now that we have an API.AI agent and a Node.js interface to interact with it, let's move on to integrate it with the two-way SMS chatbot we have been building. To do this, we need to revisit the `index.js` file which is the web app that responds to the incoming SMS messages. We will copy and rework the code from `apiai.js` to call the API.AI agent from `index.js`:

1. In the Twilio webhook, call the API.AI agent with the user's utterance. We shall also use the user's phone number as `sessionId` so that the context of the conversation is not lost:

```
//Twilio webhook
app.post('/sms/', function (req, res) {
    //send it to the bot
    var sessionId = req.body.From;
    var userUtterance = req.body.Body;
    //API.AI
    var apiai = require('apiai');
    var apiai1 = apiai("YOUR_DEVELOPER_ACCESS_TOKEN");

    var requestAPIAI = apiai1.textRequest(userUtterance, {
        sessionId: sessionId
    });

    var botSays = '';
    requestAPIAI.on('response', function(response) {
        console.log(response);
        if (response.result.actionIncomplete){
            botSays = response.result.fulfillment.speech;
            console.log('BotSays: ' + botSays);
            var twiml = new twilio.TwimlResponse();
            twiml.message(botSays);
            res.writeHead(200, {'Content-Type': 'text/xml'});
            res.end(twiml.toString());
        }
        else {
            getTrainInfo(
                response.result.metadata.intentName,
                response.result.parameters, res);
        }
    });

    requestAPIAI.on('error', function(error) {
        console.log(error);
    });
```

```
    requestAPIAI.end();
})
```

We use the `actionIncomplete` flag in API.AI agent's response to decide whether to use the agent's fulfillment speech as bot response or to call the backend module to look for train information.

2. Create a new module to get train information:

```
function getTrainInfo(intent, parameters, res){
    if (intent == 'request_live_departures'){
        return getLiveDepartures(parameters.Station, res);
    }
    else if (intent == 'request_next_train'){
        return getNextTrain(parameters.fromStation,
        parameters.toStation, res);
    }
    else {
        var botSays = 'Working on it...';
        console.log('BotSays: ' + botSays);

        var twiml = new twilio.TwimlResponse();
        twiml.message(botSays);
        res.writeHead(200, {'Content-Type': 'text/xml'});
        res.end(twiml.toString());
    }
}
```

3. Create modules to get live trains. We reuse the code from `SendTrainNotification.js` that we used to send one-way notifications:

```
function getLiveDepartures(source, res){
    var request = require('request');
    var url = 'http://transportapi.com/v3/uk/train/station/'
            + source +
              '/live.json?
            app_id=YOUR_APP_ID&app_key=YOUR_APP_KEY';
    request(url, function (error, response, body) {
        if (response){
            var json = JSON.parse(body);
            if (json.departures){
                var botSays = summarize(json.departures.all, 5);
                console.log('BotSays: ' + botSays);

                var twiml = new twilio.TwimlResponse();
                twiml.message(botSays);
                res.writeHead(200, {'Content-Type': 'text/xml'});
```

```
                    res.end(twiml.toString());
              } else {
                  var botSays = 'No Departures found!'
                  console.log('BotSays: ' + botSays);

                  var twiml = new twilio.TwimlResponse();
                  twiml.message(botSays);
                  res.writeHead(200, {'Content-Type': 'text/xml'});
                  res.end(twiml.toString());
              }
          } else {
              console.log('error:', error); // Print the error if one
                                            // occurred
              var botSays = 'Error in fetching trains info. Sorry!';
              console.log('BotSays: ' + botSays);

              var twiml = new twilio.TwimlResponse();
              twiml.message(botSays);
              res.writeHead(200, {'Content-Type': 'text/xml'});
              res.end(twiml.toString());
          }
      });
  }


  function summarize(departures, n){
      var out = '';
      if (departures.length > 0){
          out = 'Live departures:\n';
          for (var i=0; i < n; i++){
              var service = departures[i];
              var serviceSummary = service.operator_name + ":" +
                      service.destination_name + "@" +
                      service.expected_departure_time;
              out += serviceSummary + "\n";
          }
      } else {
          out = 'There are no trains from ' + source;
      }
      return out;
  }
```

And a function to get the next train from source to destination:

```
function getNextTrain(source, destination, res){
    var request = require('request');
    var url = 'http://transportapi.com/v3/uk/train/station/'
                + source + '/live.json?
                app_id=YOUR_APP_ID&app_key=YOUR_APP_KEY';
    request(url, function (error, response, body) {
        if (response){
            var json = JSON.parse(body);
            if (json.departures){
                var botSays = getNextTrainToDestination(
                                    destination,
                                json.departures.all);
                console.log('BotSays: ' + botSays);

                var twiml = new twilio.TwimlResponse();
                twiml.message(botSays);
                res.writeHead(200, {'Content-Type': 'text/xml'});
                res.end(twiml.toString());
            } else {
                var botSays = 'No Departures found!'
                console.log('BotSays: ' + botSays);

                var twiml = new twilio.TwimlResponse();
                twiml.message(botSays);
                res.writeHead(200, {'Content-Type': 'text/xml'});
                res.end(twiml.toString());
            }
        } else {
            console.log('error:', error);
            // Print the error if one
            // occurred
            var botSays = 'Error in fetching trains info. '
                            + 'Sorry!';
            console.log('BotSays: ' + botSays);

            var twiml = new twilio.TwimlResponse();
            twiml.message(botSays);
            res.writeHead(200, {'Content-Type': 'text/xml'});
            res.end(twiml.toString());
        }
    });
}
```

And a function to get the next train to destination:

```
function getNextTrainToDestination(destination, allDepartures){
    if (allDepartures){
        for (var i=0; i < allDepartures.length; i++){
            var service = allDepartures[i];
            if (service.destination_name ==
                getStationName(destination)){
                var serviceSummary = service.operator_name + ":"
                + service.destination_name + "@" +
                    service.expected_departure_time + "\n";
                return serviceSummary;
            }
        }
    }
    return null;
}

function getStationName(stationCode){
    if (stationCode == 'GLC'){
        return 'Glasgow Central';
    }
    else if (stationCode == 'EDB'){
        return 'Edinburgh';
    }
}
```

4. Save and push the revised code to Heroku.
5. Test it by sending an SMS. Try the live trains task by saying, Live departures. The bot will ask for the station name before presenting the live departures information:

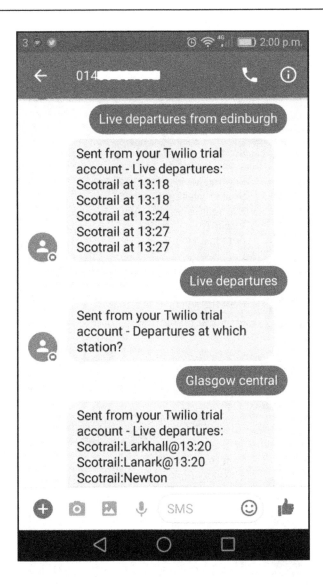

Test the next trains task by saying `Get next train`. The bot will ask for both source and destination stations before presenting the results:

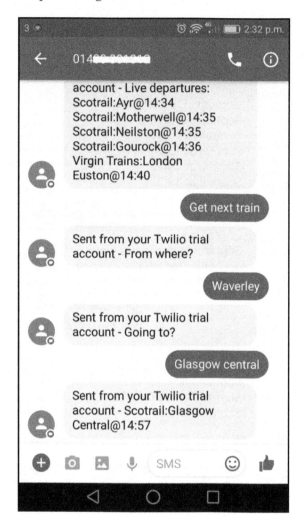

You can also try asking for the same information in other ways to test how well the API.AI agent understands the user's intent. Congratulations! You have now built a two-way SMS chatbot that understands natural language inputs.

Summary

Brilliant! I hope you had a great time exploring and building a transport chatbot providing useful information on trains to users. Besides building the chatbot, we also explored the use of Twilio communication APIs to expose the chatbot over the SMS platform. I hope you tried to chat with your bot over SMS and realized how easy it is to get useful information without internet data. We did explore a few conversational tasks and also got to implement a couple. However, you could move on to more complex tasks, such as journey planning, based on the chatbot model that we built in this chapter.

We also learned how to enable the chatbot to process natural language utterances from the user by building a Dialogflow agent and plugging it into the SMS chatbot. This is a trick you can use while building chatbots for other platforms too. You might now realize that there are many ways in which the modules can be plugged in and played with. I encourage you to try them all and design your system to suit the needs of the use case.

I hope you had fun building a chatbot for the SMS platform in this chapter. In the upcoming chapters, we will learn how to deploy chatbots in other interesting social media platforms, such as Twitter, and voice platforms, such as Alexa and Google Assistant.

References

- Twilio documentation: `https://www.twilio.com/docs/`
- Dialogflow: `https://dialogflow.com/docs/`

6
Restaurant Search

In previous chapters, we dealt with conversation management in one of the two ways—built from scratch (Chapter 3, *Let's Talk Weather*) or using GUI tools such as Dialogflow (Chapter 4, *Building a Persona Bot*) and Chatfuel (Chapter 1, *Introduction*). In Dialogflow and Chatfuel, the conversational flow was specified by the developer using visual elements (such as forms) on their custom-built web-based editor. However, it may not always be the best way to tell the system how to manage the conversation. On the other hand, we built a simple conversation manager in Java. Conversation management can get complicated in complex human-chatbot conversations. Luckily, we have got toolkits that allow us to build conversation management modules using code libraries specifically built for the purpose.

In this chapter, we are going to explore how a conversation management module can be built using an existing library—Bot Builder SDK. First, we will understand the MS Bot Framework that Bot Builder SDK is a part of. We will install the necessary software and libraries and learn to build chatbots using the SDK, test them on the emulator, and deploy them in the cloud. Next, we will learn about the rich presentation options, and the devices for which the conversational flow can be designed. We will then explore the Zomato service for restaurant data and integrate it into a chatbot built using the Bot Builder SDK. We will finally deploy it on Skype.

By the end of this chapter, you will be able to:

- Understand the basics of MS Bot Framework
- Build a chatbot with the Botbuilder Node.js library
- Register the bot with Bot Framework
- Host the bot in the cloud

- Understand message types and card types
- Manage context and conversational flow
- Integrate with the Zomoto data API
- Integrate the bot with Skype

MS Bot Framework

MS Bot Framework is a Microsoft product for chatbot development. It houses three products: Bot Builder SDK, Bot Framework Portal, and channels. Bot Builder SDK is the toolkit for building chatbots. It has libraries of classes and code that represent various elements of a conversation. These can be used in our development process to build chatbots at a faster pace than building them from scratch. The Bot Framework Portal is used to register the bot in order to manage it efficiently and there is a host of tools for analytics and diagnostics that can be used on this portal. Finally, the framework provides a unified approach to integrating with several channels.

There are a huge number of channels that you can integrate your bot with, including Skype, Facebook Messenger, Kik, Telegram, Slack, MS Teams, and Twilio. You can also create a web chat client using the portal that can be embedded on any website. In addition to the three tools, there are two other tools that are very useful during the development process: channel emulator and channel inspector.

Channel emulator

Before we begin, we need to install software called a channel emulator. We will be using this to emulate the channel (for example, Skype) to connect to the bot locally for development and testing purposes. You can chat with your bot as well as inspect the messages sent and received to identify any bugs.

To download it, go to the following page:

```
https://github.com/Microsoft/BotFramework-Emulator/releases/tag/v3.5.31
```

Download the version based on your needs and install it on your computer.

Building a bot

Let us now look at the steps to build a chatbot. Here we will use the botbuilder library and create a bot using Node.js:

1. Create a Node.js project called `foodie-bot`:

   ```
   > npm init
   ```

2. Install the two libraries that we need to use:

   ```
   > npm install botbuilder --save
   > npm install restify --save
   ```

3. Create a file named `app.js`.

4. In `app.js`, paste the following code (from the Bot Framework tutorials):

   ```
   var restify = require('restify');
   var builder = require('botbuilder');

   // Lets setup the Restify Server
   var server = restify.createServer();
   server.listen(process.env.port || process.env.PORT || 3978,
   function () {
      console.log('%s listening to %s', server.name, server.url);
   });


   // Create chat connector for communicating with the Bot Framework
   Service
   var connector = new builder.ChatConnector({
       appId: process.env.MICROSOFT_APP_ID,
       appPassword: process.env.MICROSOFT_APP_PASSWORD
   });


   // Listen for messages from users
   server.post('/foodiebot', connector.listen());

   // Echo their message back.. just parrotting!
   var bot = new builder.UniversalBot(connector, function (session) {
       session.send("You said: %s", session.message.text);
   });
   ```

Notice that there are two classes, `UniversalBot` and `ChatConnector`, that the Bot Framework's Node.js SDK provides. `UniversalBot` is the class where we define the conversation flow, while the `ChatConnector` class connects the bot to the chat channel. In the previous code, we used the `session.send()` method to send text messages to the chat channel.

5. Save the file.

6. Run the emulator. In the address bar, type the following address and connect:

    ```
    http://localhost:3978/api/messages
    ```

    At this stage, you don't have to provide an app ID or password.

7. The emulator will connect to the bot (running in `app.js`). The app will start logging messages on the console, as shown here:

    ```
    C:\Users\Srini\Dropbox\_Book\workspace\foodie-bot>node app.js
    restify listening to http://[::]:3978
    WARN: ChatConnector: receive - emulator running without security enabled.
    ChatConnector: message received.
    WARN: ChatConnector: receive - emulator running without security enabled.
    ChatConnector: message received.
    WARN: ChatConnector: receive - emulator running without security enabled.
    ```

8. In the emulator, in the following textbox, type a message to the bot and hit **SEND**. You will see that the bot repeats the message back to you:

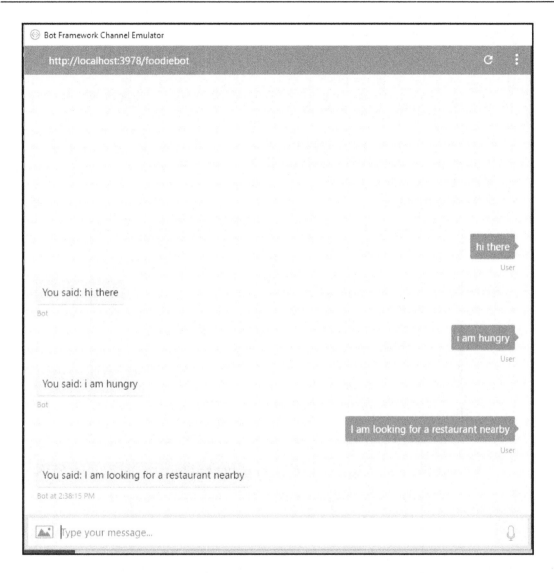

9. Congratulations! You have just created your first bot using Bot Framework.

Deploying your bot

For now, we have our bot running on a local machine and have interacted with it over the channel emulator. How about we push it further and get it talking to the user on a website. To do this, we need to register our bot in Bot Framework's very own bot directory. To get your bot registered, perform the following steps:

1. Go to the Bot Framework page at `https://dev.botframework.com`.
2. Create an account, if you don't already have one. Sign in.
3. Click the **My bots** tab.
4. Click **Create a bot**:

5. Click **Create**. Choose **Register an existing bot built using Bot Builder SDK**:

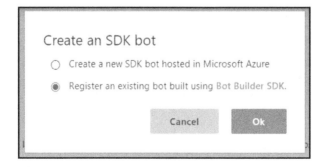

6. Scroll down to **Configuration**. Click **Create Microsoft App ID and Password**:

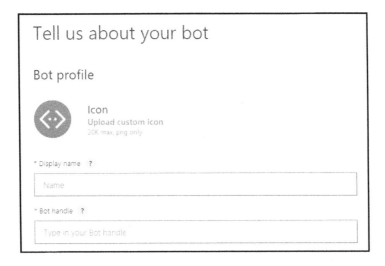

Copy the app ID and password and hang on to it.

7. Go back to app.js and replace the app ID and password variable with these new values. Save it. Alternatively, we can set these as configuration parameters.

8. We are now ready to host our bot in the cloud and link it up to the Bot Framework register. In order to do that, we need to create Procfile. Create a file called Procfile, which tells Heroku how to start the app. Here is what goes into Procfile:

```
web: node app.js
```

9. Create a Heroku web app:

```
> heroku create foodie-bot-sj
```

10. We need a Git repository to store our bot code:

```
> git init
> git add .
> git commit -m initial-commit
```

11. Finally, let's push the code:

```
> git push heroku master
```

Now we need to set the app ID and password as config variables in Heroku:

```
> heroku config:set MICROSOFT_APP_PASSWORD=<YOUR_APP_PASSWORD>
> heroku config:set MICROSOFT_APP_ID=<YOUR_APP_ID>
```

12. Having pushed the code onto the cloud, we can test it using the channel emulator. Type the URL of the bot, along with the app ID and password, and click **CONNECT**:

13. Once connected, type your message to the bot. You will see the bot parroting the messages that you send:

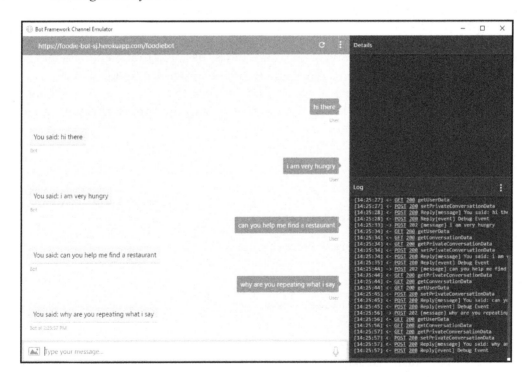

Good work! Your bot is in the cloud and ready to be deployed on Skype and other channels, but we will explore that later in the chapter.

More message types

Now that we have set up the chatbot and have the emulator to test it, let's try out more messaging options.

Sending more than one message per turn

First, we can send more than one message at a time. So when the chatbot gets its turn, it can send multiple messages using the `session.send()` method:

```
var bot = new builder.UniversalBot(connector, [
    function (session) {
        session.send('Hello there!');
        session.send('Welcome to New India restaurant!');
        });
    }
]);
```

Prompting users for information

To ask users for information, use the `builder.Prompts.text()` method, as shown here:

```
var bot = new builder.UniversalBot(connector, [
    function (session) {
        builder.Prompts.text(session, 'Hi! What is your name?');
    },
    function (session, results) {
        session.endDialog('Hello ' + results.response + '!
                        My name is FoodieBot!');
    }
]);
```

`builder.Prompts.text()` can be used to get text data such as the names of people and cities. The responses can be accessed using `results.response`. Try the preceding code by replacing the definition for the `bot` variable in the previous code for `app.js`:

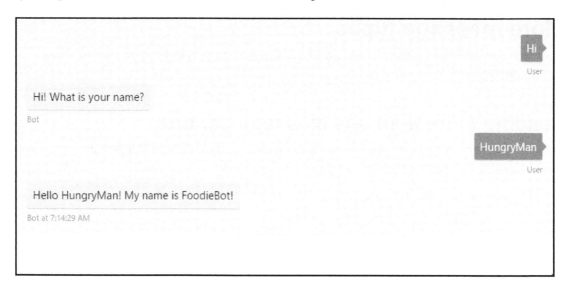

You can get numeric data using `builder.Prompts.number()`:

```
var bot = new builder.UniversalBot(connector, [
    function (session) {
        builder.Prompts.number(session, 'Booking a table!
                            For how many people?');
    },
    function (session, results) {
        session.endDialog('Ok. Looking for a table for ' +
                            results.response + ' people.');
    }
]);
```

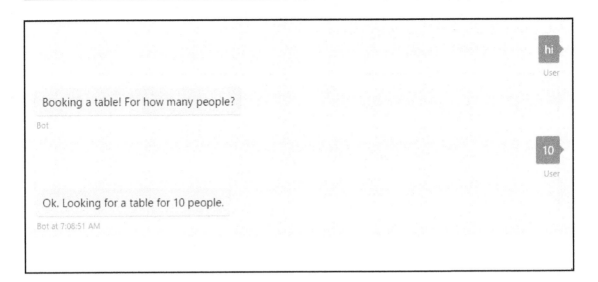

You can also ask users to choose one of the given options using the `builder.Prompts.choice()` method:

```
var bot = new builder.UniversalBot(connector, [
    function (session) {
        builder.Prompts.choice(session, 'Booking a table!
        Any specific cuisine?', ['Indian', 'Chinese', 'Italian']);
    },
    function (session, results) {
        session.endDialog('Ok. Looking for a ' +
        results.response.entity + ' restaurant.');
    }
]);
```

Notice that the label for the choice (for example, `Indian`) is stored in `results.response.entity`:

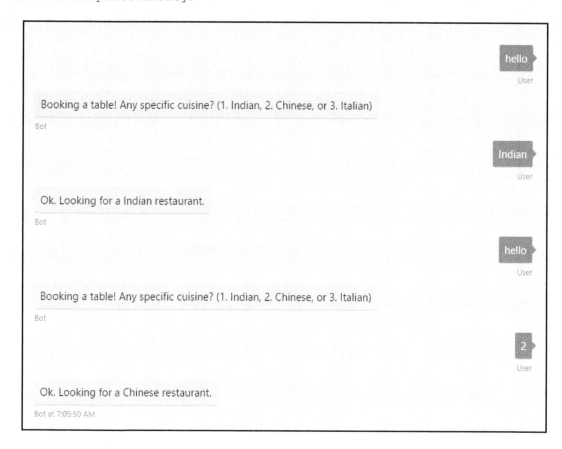

You can also provide choices in the following format, instead of an array, as shown here:

```
builder.Prompts.choice(session, 'Booking a table! Any specific cuisine?',
'Indian|Chinese|Italian');
```

You can also prompt for date and time and parse varied inputs such as `tomorrow at 2pm`, `Saturday at 8`, or `next Friday` using the `EntityRecognizer` class, as follows:

```
builder.Prompts.time(session, "So when is the party?");
....
session.dialogData.partyDate =
builder.EntityRecognizer.resolveTime([results.response]);
```

Rich messages

Now that we know how to serve messages and prompts, let's dig a little deeper to learn how to make it look more visually appealing by adding images and cards. To do this, we will use Hero card. Hero card is a template for presenting information in a rich format using images, URLs, and so on. Here is an example:

```
var bot = new builder.UniversalBot(connector, [
    function (session) {
        var msg = new builder.Message(session);
        msg.attachmentLayout(builder.AttachmentLayout.carousel)
        msg.attachments([
            new builder.HeroCard(session)
                .title("Chennai Kitchen")
                .subtitle("Authentic South Indian Restaurant")
                .text("Great tasting dosas. 5 star reviews.")
                .images([builder.CardImage.create(session,
                    'https://images.pexels.com/photos/221143/
                    pexels-photo-221143.jpeg?
                    w=940&h=650&auto=compress&cs=tinysrgb')])
                .buttons([
                    builder.CardAction.imBack(session,
                    "book_table:chennai_kitchen", "Book a table")
                ]),
            new builder.HeroCard(session)
                .title("Mumbai Tandoor")
                .subtitle("Best Indian Restaurant in town")
                .text("Amazing reviews!")
                .images([builder.CardImage.create(session,
                    'https://images.pexels.com/photos/45844/
                    spices-white-pepper-nutmeg-45844.jpeg?
                    w=940&h=650&auto=compress&cs=tinysrgb')])
                .buttons([
                    builder.CardAction.imBack(session,
                    "book_table:mumbai_tandoor", "Book a table")
                ])
        ]);
```

```
        session.send(msg)

    }
]);
```

For each Hero card, a title, subtitle, text, image, and button response can be specified. In the preceding example, the buttons have been programmed to send response messages back to the bot using the `imBack()` method. However, you can also program it to open a web page using the `openUrl()` method, as follows:

```
builder.CardAction.openUrl(session,
'https://mumbaitandoor.com/bookTable','Book a table');
```

There are other types of cards as well: Thumbnail card, Adaptive card, Audio card, and Animation card, for example. For a complete list of cards, please refer to the Bot Framework documentation at `https://docs.microsoft.com/en-us/bot-framework/nodejs/bot-builder-nodejs-send-rich-cards`.

Thumbnail cards are similar to Hero cards but smaller. You can create Thumbnail cards using the `ThumbnailCard` class, as shown here:

```
new builder.ThumbnailCard(session)
            .title("Chennai Kitchen")
            .subtitle("Authentic South Indian Restaurant")
            .text("Great tasting dosas. 5 star reviews.")
            .images([builder.CardImage.create(session,
                    'https://images.pexels.com/photos/221143/
                    pexels-photo-221143.jpeg?w=940&h=650&
                    auto=compress&cs=tinysrgb')])
            .buttons([
                builder.CardAction.imBack(session,
                "book_table:chennai_kitchen",
                "Book a table")
            ])
```

Let's run the preceding code on the emulator:

Let's create a card to show GIF images. The `AnimationCard` class can be used to display animated images:

```
new builder.AnimationCard(session)
        .title('Microsoft Bot Framework')
        .subtitle('Animation Card')
        .image(builder.CardImage.create(session,
        'https://makeYourOwnCurry.com/curryAnimation.jpeg'))
        .media([
            { url: 'http://i.giphy.com/Ki55RUbOV5njy.gif' }
        ])
```

Audio and Video cards can be used to present audio and video information:

```
//Video card
new builder.VideoCard(session)
        .title('Chicken Tikka')
        .subtitle('from Sanjeev Kapoor Khazana')
        .text('Authentic Chicken Tikka recipe by Chef
              Harpal Singh Sokhi')
        .image(builder.CardImage.create(session,
              'https://commons.wikimedia.org/wiki/
              File:Chicken_Tikka_(1).jpg'))
        .media([
            { url: 'http://fakevideourl.com/makingofchickentikka.mp4' }
        ])
        .buttons([
            builder.CardAction.imBack(session, "order:chicken_tikka",
"Order Chicken Tikka")
])

//Audio card

new builder.AudioCard(session)
    .title('Delicious Chicken Tikka')
    .subtitle('Must have at Mumbai Tandoor')
    .text('User')
    .image(builder.CardImage.create(session,
          'https://commons.wikimedia.org/wiki/
          File:Chicken_Tikka_(1).jpg'))
    .media([
        { url: 'http://fakeaudiourl.com/reviews1.wav' }
    ])
    .buttons([
     builder.CardAction.imBack(session, "order:chicken_tikka",
     "Order Chicken Tikka")
])
```

Let's see how it looks on the emulator:

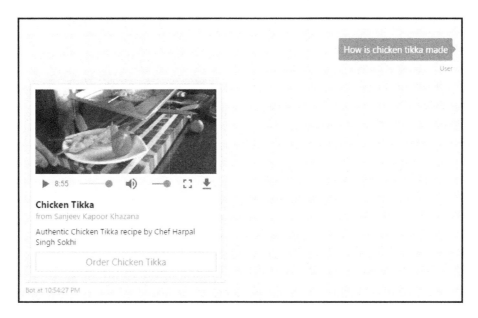

In addition to these cards, there is a special card called the Receipt card which will present information in a receipt format. It can be used to present an itemized bill with payment information, as follows:

```
new builder.ReceiptCard(session)
    .title('James White')
    .facts([
        builder.Fact.create(session, '12345', 'Order Number'),
        builder.Fact.create(session, 'VISA 2392-****',
                              'Payment Method')
    ])
    .items([
        builder.ReceiptItem.create(session, '£ 6.50', 'Chicken Tikka')
            .quantity(1),
        builder.ReceiptItem.create(session, '£ 5.00', 'Garlic Naan')
            .quantity(2)
    ])
    .tax('£ 1.15')
    .total('£ 12.65')
    .buttons([
        builder.CardAction.imBack(session, 'sendemail',
                                  'Send by email')
    ])
```

Let's run it on the emulator:

Finally, there is a card that can be used to authenticate the user by asking them to sign in. This flow can be initiated using the SignIn card:

```
new builder.SigninCard(session)
        .text('Mumbai Tandoor Login')
        .button('Login', 'https://mumbaitandoor.com/login')
        ]);
```

Clicking the SignIn card takes the user to the web page where the user can be authenticated:

Now that we have explored the cards, let's move on to implementing the conversation flow.

Conversation flow

Now that we have a setup to test the chatbot and have explored a variety of ways information can be presented to the user, let's examine the ways in which conversation flow can be managed. The basic model available to us is the waterfall model, where the conversation is composed of a sequence of steps. Let's take the example of booking a table at a restaurant where the conversation proceeds in the following way: get the time of reservation, the number of people at the table, and the name of the user:

```
// Bot Dialogs
var bot = new builder.UniversalBot(connector, [
    function (session) {
        session.send('Welcome to New India restaurant!');
        builder.Prompts.time(session, 'Table reservations.
                            What time?');
    },
    function (session, results) {
        session.dialogData.timeOfReservation =
        builder.EntityRecognizer.resolveTime([results.response]);
        builder.Prompts.number(session, "And how many people?");
    },
    function (session, results) {
        session.dialogData.numberOfPeople = results.response;
        builder.Prompts.text(session, "And your name?");
    },
    function (session, results) {
        session.dialogData.nameOnReservation = results.response;
        session.send('Great! Your reservation is booked!');
    }
]);
```

Let's try this out on the emulator:

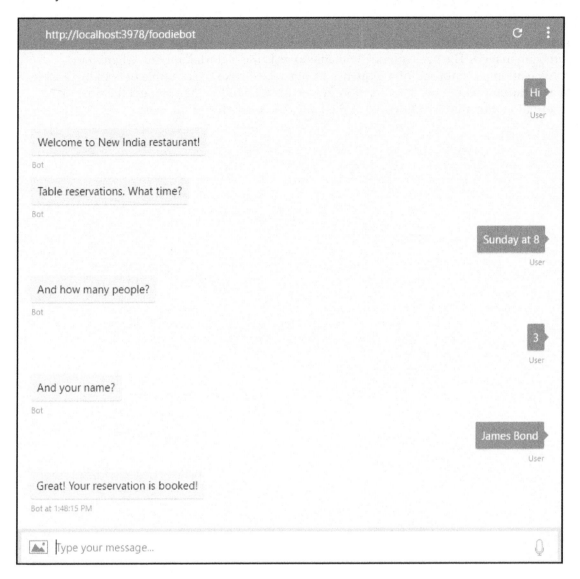

Let us dissect the code a little to understand what is happening. We start by constructing a bot using the `UniversalBot` class. As we build the bot, we specify the steps of the waterfall conversation as an array of functions. This is the root dialogue. Each function is a step in the conversation. At each step, the bot says or prompts the user with a message. In case of prompts, it expects the user to respond. The response is stored in `results.response`, which is updated to the dialogue state managed in `session.dialogData`. This assignment happens in the subsequent steps, the bot makes the next utterance or prompts for more information. As we have discussed previously, there are a variety of ways information can be prompted and verified.

It is not always possible to map out the entire conversation as an array of functions. What if there are parts of the conversation that repeat? As programmers, we handle these situations using functions and methods. A method would be a well-defined piece of code performing a specific task and can be called for whenever it is required by the `main` method or another method. Let's take, for example, the task of payment when placing an order. Whether you are at the table or ordering takeout, you will have to make payments the same way. The same set of questions will be asked: paying by card or cash, the card number, the name on the card, the CVV number, and so on. Imagine a payment dialogue between the user and the bot. Will this dialogue be used in more than one scenario? Wouldn't it be nice to keep the conversational step of the payment dialogue separate and call the process whenever a payment needs to be taken? This is what we can accomplish using the `dialog()` method.

The bot that we create using the `UniversalBot` class can be provided conversational skills to carry out a variety of tasks, such as payments and product listing, using the `dialog()` method. These can then be called upon when necessary from the root dialogue. Each `dialog()` method can be used to define a sub-dialogue, and structurally will be an independent waterfall dialogue. Let's now build a root dialogue and embed within it two sub-dialogues asking for the order and asking for payment:

```
//Main dialogue
var bot = new builder.UniversalBot(connector, [
    function (session) {
        session.send("Welcome to New India restaurant.");
        session.beginDialog('askForOrder');
    },
    function (session) {
        session.beginDialog('askForPayment');
    },
    function (session) {
        session.send('Thanks for your order!');
        session.send(`Order summary:
        ${session.conversationData.order}<br/>`+
            `Payment card number:
```

```
                ${session.conversationData.cardNumber}<br/>`);
                session.endDialog();
        }
    ]);

    // Ask for Order
    bot.dialog('askForOrder', [
        function (session) {
            builder.Prompts.text(session, 'Whats your order?');
        },
        function (session, results) {
            session.conversationData.order = results.response;
            session.endDialog();
        }
    ]);

    // Ask for payment
    bot.dialog('askForPayment', [
        function (session) {
            builder.Prompts.text(session, 'Whats the card number?');
        },
        function (session, results) {
            session.conversationData.cardNumber = results.response;
            builder.Prompts.text(session, 'Whats the CVV number?');
        },
        function (session, results) {
            session.conversationData.cardCVVNumber = results.response;
            session.send('Thanks for the payment!');
            session.endDialog();
        }
    ])
```

In the preceding code, you can see three dialogues: root, asking for the order, and asking for payment. Within the root dialogue, we use the `session.beginDialog()` to call upon the sub-dialogues:

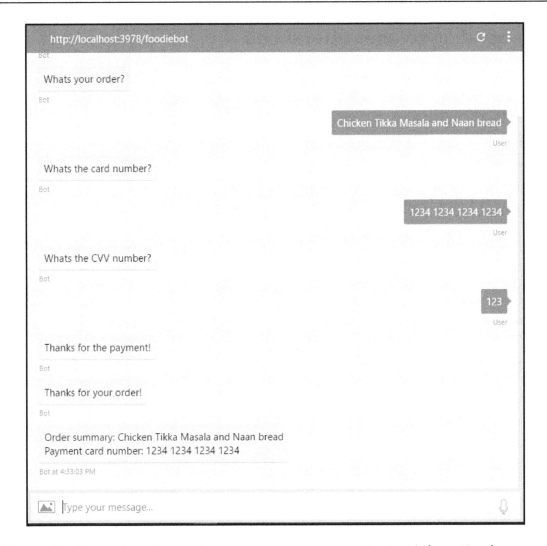

Also, notice that we have been using `session.dialogData` to store information from user utterances so far. But now, we are using `session.conversationData`. We will explore the difference between them later.

At this point, we need to understand the concept of **dialog stack**. In the beginning, the dialog stack contains the root dialogue. As sub-dialogues get called from the root, these are stacked on top of the root dialogue. Sub-dialogues can themselves call other sub-dialogues. These, in turn, get stacked over them. When a sub-dialogue is finished, the bot returns the next dialogue in the stack and continues doing so until there are no more.

Responding to user utterances

What we have now is a default conversation that starts the same way no matter what the user says. You could say `hi`, or `help`, or any other utterance and the bot would answer with a welcome message. Another way in which a conversation can get started is based on what the user says.

Let us now explore how to respond when the user says `help` in the middle of the conversation:

```
bot.dialog('help', function (session, args, next) {
    session.endDialog("Hi. I can take food orders.<br/>
                      Say 'continue' to continue?");
})
.triggerAction({
    matches: /^help$/i,
});
```

Responding to user utterances can be done by adding `triggerAction()` with utterances specified as regular expressions in the `matches` clause. Add the preceding code to `app.js` and restart the server. Now the conversation may go as follows:

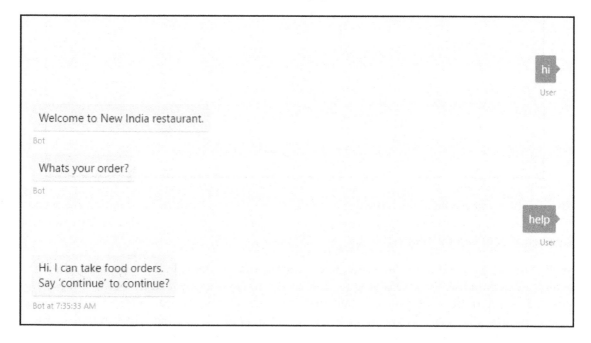

The code we added allows the bot to respond to the `help` user utterance. Notice how this overrides the current expectation of order information that the bot is waiting for.

There are two other ways of interpreting user utterances: a custom recognizer and using NLU services such as LUIS. Let us try the custom recognizer first. To your bot, attach the following recognizer:

```
bot.recognizer({
    recognize: function (context, done) {
        var intent = { score: 0.0 };
        if (context.message.text) {
            switch (context.message.text.toLowerCase()) {
                case 'help':
                    intent = { score: 1.0, intent: 'get-help' };
                    break;
                case 'goodbye':
                    intent = { score: 1.0, intent: 'say-goodbye' };
                    break;
            }
        }
        done(null, intent);
    }
});
```

And create appropriate sub-dialogues for the intents:

```
bot.dialog('help', [
    function (session) {
        session.send('I can help you look for a
                    restaurant or order a takeaway!');
        session.endDialog();
    }
]).triggerAction({
    matches: 'get-help'
});

bot.dialog('goodbye', [
    function (session) {
        session.send('Goodbye now!');
        session.endConversation();
    }
]).triggerAction({
    matches: 'say-goodbye'
});
```

While utterance patterns can be specified using the matches option for each sub-dialogue, it is even better to organize them as intents using a global recognizer for all sub-dialogues. This is to ensure that we do not have to duplicate the regular expressions. Once the intents are identified, they can be used to trigger appropriate sub-dialogues, as shown here:

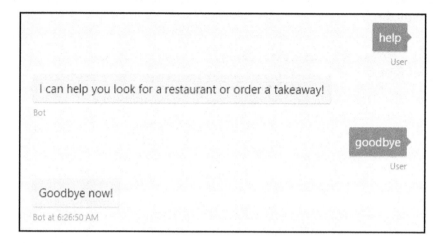

LUIS is Microsoft's natural language understanding service. It is similar to Google's API.AI and Amazon's Lex. Any of these tools can be integrated with the bot to provide NLU services if custom recognizers ,such as the preceding, are not adequate. To explore this option further, consult the official documentation at `https://docs.microsoft.com/en-us/bot-framework/nodejs/bot-builder-nodejs-recognize-intent-luis`.

Keeping context intact

Processing user utterances using sub-dialogues can take the conversation out of context:

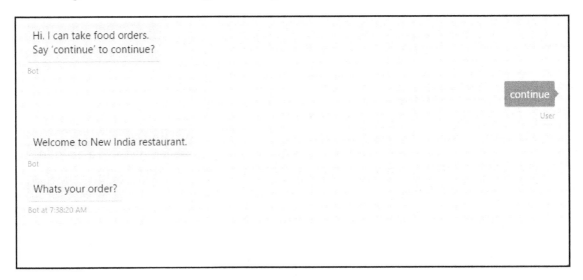

What happened to the conversation when the user typed continue, as mentioned in the help message? Does the conversation continue? No, it doesn't. The bot seems to have completely forgotten what it was doing before. This is because the dialog stack is cleared when user utterances are processed. It may be ideal to clear the stack when the user wants to change the topic of the conversation, but not when the user is asking for help.

There is a way to keep context intact even when users interrupt with questions and remarks. This can be done by adding the onSelectAction option to the sub-dialogue that gets invoked. This will keep the dialog stack intact and not clear it:

```
bot.dialog('help', function (session, args, next) {
    session.endDialog("Hi there. I can take food orders.");
})
.triggerAction({
    matches: /^help$/i,
    onSelectAction: (session, args, next) => {
        session.beginDialog(args.action, args);
    }
});
```

So it is actually part of the design decision to designate where the dialogue stack needs to be cleared and where it should not be. For instance, when the user asks for help, it is better not to clear the context as the help request could be related to the context. However, if the user seems to be switching to another task (for example, asking for a table booking when they are actually ordering food), it may be a good idea to clear the context as it is not appropriate to return to taking the food order once the table has been booked.

Context switching

However, there may be cases where the user wants to switch from one task to another. In such cases, we do not want to keep the dialog stack intact. By not using the onSelectAction option, we can wipe out dialog stack. However, it is also a good idea to let the user know that the bot is going to abandon the current task to take up the next task. This can be done using the confirmPrompt option in the triggerAction() method:

```
bot.dialog('askForOrder', [
    ...
])
.triggerAction({
    matches: /^order food$/i,
    confirmPrompt: "Your food order will be abandoned. Are you sure?"
});

// Search for a restaurant
bot.dialog('searchRestaurant', [
    function (session) {
        session.send('Searching for a restaurant!');
        builder.Prompts.text(session, 'Where?');
    },
    function (session, results) {
        session.conversationData.searchLocation = results.response;
        session.endDialog();
    }
])
    .triggerAction({
    matches: /^restaurant search$/i,
    confirmPrompt: 'Your restaurant search task
    will be abandoned. Are you sure?'
});
```

By appending the triggerAction() method to the askForOrder dialogue, we will be able to respond to user requests to order food at any point in the conversation. However, the bot will proactively prompt them that any other task being done (for example, booking a table) will be abandoned:

Notice how the confirm prompts are invoked when the user switches from one task to other.

Contextual NLU

It may also be ideal to provide help in a contextual way. For instance, provide the user with a menu when they ask for help while ordering. Let us see how utterances can be processed contextually. To do this, we need to create a `help` sub-dialogue and append it to an existing dialogue so that it can trigger when what the user says matches the template provided:

```
// Ask for Order
bot.dialog('askForOrder', [
    function (session) {
        builder.Prompts.text(session, 'Whats your order?');
    },
    function (session, results) {
        session.conversationData.order = results.response;
        session.endDialog();
    }
])
.beginDialogAction('orderHelpAction', 'orderHelp',
                   { matches: /^help$/i });

// Contextual help for ordering
bot.dialog('orderHelp', function(session, args, next) {
    var msg = "You can order for Chicken Tikka Masala,
    Paneer Butter Masala, Naan and Briyani.";
    session.endDialog(msg);
})
```

Notice how we use the `beginDialogAction()` method to link the `orderHelp` sub-dialogue. `orderHelp` gets triggered when the user says `help` during the food ordering step:

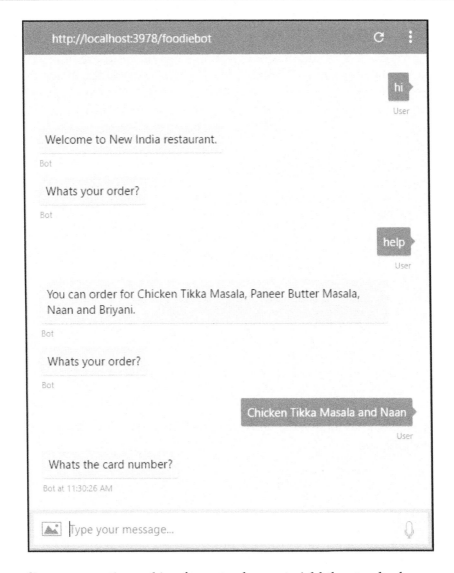

In the preceding conversation, asking for `help` does not yield the standard response. Instead, we get a contextual one.

Ending the conversation

Finally, it is a good practice to end the conversation when the tasks are finished. This is done by informing the user that the tasks are finished, clearing out the dialogue stack, and resetting the `session.conversationData` object. To do this, use the `session.endConversation()` method. So, let us rewrite our root dialogue with the `session.endConversation()` method:

```
//Main dialogue
var bot = new builder.UniversalBot(connector, [
    function (session) {
        session.send("Welcome to New India restaurant.");
        session.beginDialog('askForOrder');
    },
    function (session) {
        session.beginDialog('askForPayment');
    },
    function (session) {
        session.send('Thanks for your order!');
        session.send(`Order summary:
${session.conversationData.order}<br/>` +
            `Payment card number:
        ${session.conversationData.cardNumber}<br/>`);
        session.endConversation();
    }
]);
```

You can also set a default dialogue that gets triggered when the user says `Goodbye` and ends the conversation:

```
bot.dialog('endConversation', [
    session.endConversation("Goodbye!")
])
.endConversationAction(
    "endTasks", "Ok. Goodbye.",
    {
        matches: /^goodbye$/i,
        confirmPrompt: "Cancelling current task. Are you sure?"
    }
);
```

Now let's have a look at how we can store the context of the conversation.

Conversational state

The state of the conversation can be stored in the form of key/value pairs. There are four data stores that are available to do this. These are housed within the `session` object:

- `dialogData`: Remember, the conversation is divided into dialogs (the root dialogue and sub-dialogues initiated with `beginDialog()`). Within each dialog, the state can be maintained separately. This is done using `session.dialogData`, which we have used in the previous examples. It stores data pertaining to the current sub-dialogue, and each sub-dialogue has its own copy of the `dialogData`. When the dialogue finishes (that is, `endDialog()` is executed) and is removed from the dialog stack, this data is deleted.

- `conversationData`: This stores data pertaining to the whole conversation and is shared among all members (that is, users) in the conversation. It gets cleared when the conversation ends or when `endConversation()` is executed. This data can be accessed using `session.conversationData`.

- `privateConversationData`: This stores data pertaining to the whole conversation as `conversationData`, but is private to every individual member of the conversation. This is not shared with other members participating in the conversation. It gets cleared when the conversation ends or when `endConversation()` is executed. This data can be accessed using `session.privateConversationData`.

- `userData`: Private data pertaining to a user can be stored here. This is persistent across conversations. Data such as the user's name, age, gender, address, phone number, email, and payment info can be stored here and be used in conversations. This data can be accessed using `session.userData`.

So far, we have covered a number of concepts in the Bot Builder toolkit with examples worked out. We have examined how to set up a root dialogue and take the conversational flow into sub-dialogues. We have explored how to handle user utterances locally and globally, as well as the use of various data objects to store user and conversation data. Let us now proceed to building a bot with restaurant data.

Getting started with Zomato

First, we need to create an account with Zomato and get an API key:

    1. Go to `https://developers.zomato.com/api`:

    2. Click **Generate API Key**:

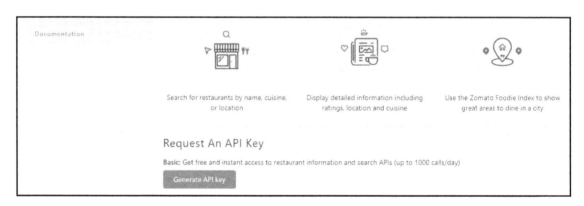

3. Sign up:

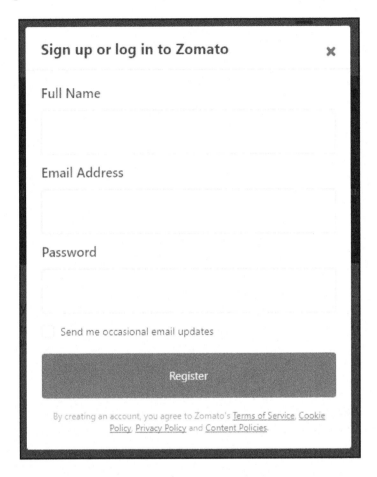

4. Confirm your email address and click **Generate API Key** again:

5. Copy the API key.

Getting data from Zomato

The base URL for fetching data is `https://developers.zomato.com/api/v2.1/`. Every query sent to the Zomato server should have the API key sent as part of the header, as follows:

```
curl -X GET --header "Accept: application/json" --header "user-key:
YOURAPIKEY" "https://developers.zomato.com/api/v2.1/categories"
```

In the preceding HTTP GET call, categories specify the handle that pulls out the various categories of restaurants that are available. Categories include delivery, takeout, and dine-in. Here is the list of handles that are available:

Handle	Description
/categories	Restaurant categories: dine-in, takeout, delivery, and many more.
/cities	Get info about the cities across the globe. Get the Zomato city ID from this query to use in search queries later. Search using a name or the latitude and longitude (latLong) of the city.
/collections	Get a list of restaurants given the city ID or latLong coordinates.
/cuisines	Get a list of cuisines in the city.
/establishments	Get a list of restaurant categories that are available in the city.
/locations	Get the location ID to search for. These are IDs at different scales: city, subzone, zone, landmark, and so on. This will be used to search for restaurants.
/search	Search for restaurants in a given location ID, cuisine, category, and so on.
/reviews	Get reviews of a specific restaurant.

Now that we have explored the data that Zomato has about restaurants, let's move on to building a bot using Zomato and Bot Builder SDK.

Restaurant search bot

Let us build a chatbot that can search for restaurants based on user goals and preferences. Let us begin by building Node.js modules to get data from Zomato based on user preferences. Create a file called zomato.js. Add a request module to the Node.js libraries using the following command in the console:

```
> npm install request --save
```

In `zomato.js`, add the following code to begin with:

```
var request = require('request');

var baseURL = 'https://developers.zomato.com/api/v2.1/';
var apiKey = 'YOUR_API_KEY';

var catergories = null;
var cuisines = null;

getCategories();
getCuisines(76);
```

Replace YOUR_API_KEY with your Zomato key. Let's build functions to get the list of categories and cuisines at startup. These queries need not be run when the user asks for a restaurant search because this information is pretty much static:

```
function getCuisines(cityId){
    var options = {
        uri: baseURL + 'cuisines',
        headers: {
            'user-key': apiKey
        },
        qs: {'city_id':cityId},
        method: 'GET'
        }
    var callback = function(error, response, body) {
            if (error) {
                console.log('Error sending messages: ', error)
            } else if (response.body.error) {
                console.log('Error: ', response.body.error)
            } else {
                console.log(body);
                cuisines = JSON.parse(body).cuisines;
            }
        }
    request(options,callback);
}
```

The preceding code will fetch a list of cuisines available in a particular city (identified by a Zomato city ID). Let us add the code for identifying the list of categories:

```
function getCategories(){
    var options = {
        uri: baseURL + 'categories',
        headers: {
            'user-key': apiKey
        },
        qs: {},
        method: 'GET'
    }
    var callback = function(error, response, body) {
            if (error) {
                console.log('Error sending messages: ', error)
            } else if (response.body.error) {
                console.log('Error: ', response.body.error)
            } else {
                categories = JSON.parse(body).categories;
            }
        }
    request(options,callback);
}
```

Now that we have the basic functions out of our way, let us code in the restaurant search code:

```
function getRestaurant(cuisine, location, category){
    var cuisineId = getCuisineId(cuisine);
    var categoryId = getCategoryId(category);

    var options = {
        uri: baseURL + 'locations',
        headers: {
            'user-key': apiKey
        },
        qs: {'query':location},
        method: 'GET'
    }
    var callback = function(error, response, body) {
            if (error) {
                console.log('Error sending messages: ', error)
            } else if (response.body.error) {
                console.log('Error: ', response.body.error)
            } else {
                console.log(body);
                locationInfo = JSON.parse(body).location_suggestions;
```

```
                    search(locationInfo[0], cuisineId, categoryId);
            }
        }
    request(options,callback);
}

function search(location, cuisineId, categoryId){
    var options = {
        uri: baseURL + 'search',
        headers: {
            'user-key': apiKey
        },
        qs: {'entity_id': location.entity_id,
            'entity_type': location.entity_type,
            'cuisines': [cuisineId],
            'categories': [categoryId]},
        method: 'GET'
    }
    var callback = function(error, response, body) {
            if (error) {
                console.log('Error sending messages: ', error)
            } else if (response.body.error) {
                console.log('Error: ', response.body.error)
            } else {
                console.log('Found restaurants:')
                var results = JSON.parse(body).restaurants;
                console.log(results);
            }
        }
    request(options,callback);
}
```

The preceding code will look for restaurants in a given location, cuisine, and category. For instance, you can search for a list of Indian restaurants in Newington, Edinburgh that do delivery. We now need to integrate this with the chatbot code. Let us create a separate file called index.js. Let us begin with the basics:

```
var restify = require('restify');
var builder = require('botbuilder');
var request = require('request');

var baseURL = 'https://developers.zomato.com/api/v2.1/';
var apiKey = 'YOUR_API_KEY';

var catergories = null;
var cuisines = null;
```

```
getCategories();
//setTimeout(function(){getCategoryId('Delivery')}, 10000);

getCuisines(76);
//setTimeout(function(){getCuisineId('European')}, 10000);


// Setup Restify Server
var server = restify.createServer();
server.listen(process.env.port || process.env.PORT || 3978, function () {
   console.log('%s listening to %s', server.name, server.url);
});


// Create chat connector for communicating with
// the Bot Framework Service
var connector = new builder.ChatConnector({
    appId: process.env.MICROSOFT_APP_ID,
    appPassword: process.env.MICROSOFT_APP_PASSWORD
});

// Listen for messages from users
server.post('/foodiebot', connector.listen());
```

Add the bot dialog code to carry out the restaurant search. Let us design the bot to ask for cuisine, category, and location before proceeding to the restaurant search:

```
var bot = new builder.UniversalBot(connector, [
    function (session) {
        session.send("Hi there! Hungry? Looking for a restaurant?");
        session.send("Say 'search restaurant' to start searching.");
        session.endDialog();
    }
]);

// Search for a restaurant
bot.dialog('searchRestaurant', [
    function (session) {
        session.send('Ok. Searching for a restaurant!');
        builder.Prompts.text(session, 'Where?');
    },
    function (session, results) {
        session.conversationData.searchLocation = results.response;
        builder.Prompts.text(session, 'Cuisine? Indian,
                          Italian, or anything else?');
    },
    function (session, results) {
        session.conversationData.searchCuisine = results.response;
```

```
            builder.Prompts.text(session, 'Delivery or Dine-in?');
        },
        function (session, results) {
            session.conversationData.searchCategory = results.response;
            session.send('Ok. Looking for restaurants..');
            getRestaurant(session.conversationData.searchCuisine,
                    session.conversationData.searchLocation,
                    session.conversationData.searchCategory,
                    session);
        }
    ])
    .triggerAction({
    matches: /^search restaurant$/i,
    confirmPrompt: 'Your restaurant search task will be abandoned.
                Are you sure?'
});
```

Notice that we are calling the getRestaurant() function with four parameters. Three of these are ones that we have already defined: cuisine, location, and category. To these, we have to add another: session. This passes the session pointer that can be used to send messages to the emulator when the data is ready. Notice how this changes the getRestaurant() and search() functions:

```
function getRestaurant(cuisine, location, category, session){
    var cuisineId = getCuisineId(cuisine);
    var categoryId = getCategoryId(category);
    var options = {
        uri: baseURL + 'locations',
        headers: {
            'user-key': apiKey
        },
        qs: {'query':location},
        method: 'GET'
        }
    var callback = function(error, response, body) {
            if (error) {
                console.log('Error sending messages: ', error)
            } else if (response.body.error) {
                console.log('Error: ', response.body.error)
            } else {
                console.log(body);
                locationInfo = JSON.parse(body).location_suggestions;
                search(locationInfo[0], cuisineId,
                categoryId, session);
            }
        }
    request(options,callback);
```

```
    }

function search(location, cuisineId, categoryId, session){
    var options = {
        uri: baseURL + 'search',
        headers: {
            'user-key': apiKey
        },
        qs: {'entity_id': location.entity_id,
            'entity_type': location.entity_type,
            'cuisines': [cuisineId],
            'category': categoryId},
        method: 'GET'
    }
    var callback = function(error, response, body) {
            if (error) {
                console.log('Error sending messages: ', error)
            } else if (response.body.error) {
                console.log('Error: ', response.body.error)
            } else {
                console.log('Found restaurants:')
                console.log(body);
                //var results = JSON.parse(body).restaurants;
                //console.log(results);
                var resultsCount = JSON.parse(body).results_found;
                console.log('Found:' + resultsCount);
                session.send('I have found ' + resultsCount +
                                    ' restaurants for you!');
                session.endDialog();
            }
        }
    request(options,callback);
}
```

Once the results are obtained, the bot responds using `session.send()` and ends the dialog:

Now that we have the results, let's present them in a more visually appealing way using cards. To do this, we need a function that can take the results of the search and turn them into an array of cards:

```
function presentInCards(session, results){
    var msg = new builder.Message(session);
    msg.attachmentLayout(builder.AttachmentLayout.carousel)
    var heroCardArray = [];
    var l = results.length;
    if (results.length > 10){
        l = 10;
    }
    for (var i = 0; i < l; i++){
        var r = results[i].restaurant;
        var herocard = new builder.HeroCard(session)
            .title(r.name)
            .subtitle(r.location.address)
            .text(r.user_rating.aggregate_rating)
            .images([builder.CardImage.create(session, r.thumb)])
            .buttons([
                builder.CardAction.imBack(session,
                        "book_table:" + r.id,
                        "Book a table")
            ]);
        heroCardArray.push(herocard);
    }
    msg.attachments(heroCardArray);
    return msg;
}
```

And we call this function from the `search()` function:

```
function search(location, cuisineId, categoryId, session){
    var options = {
        uri: baseURL + 'search',
        headers: {
            'user-key': apiKey
        },
        qs: {'entity_id': location.entity_id,
            'entity_type': location.entity_type,
            'cuisines': [cuisineId],
            'category': categoryId},
        method: 'GET'
    }
    var callback = function(error, response, body) {
            if (error) {
                console.log('Error sending messages: ', error)
            } else if (response.body.error) {
                console.log('Error: ', response.body.error)
            } else {
                console.log('Found restaurants:')
                console.log(body);
                var results = JSON.parse(body).restaurants;
                var msg = presentInCards(session, results);
                session.send(msg);
                session.endDialog();
            }
        }
    request(options,callback);
}
```

Here is how it looks:

Connecting to Skype

Now that we have a chatbot to search for restaurants, push it back on to Heroku cloud as before. Remember to change the `Procfile` as we need to run `index.js` and not `app.js`. Having set up the chatbot as a web app in Heroku, we are all set to deploy the bot on Skype and other channels.

1. Go to your dashboard on Bot Framework at `https://dev.botframework.com/bots`:

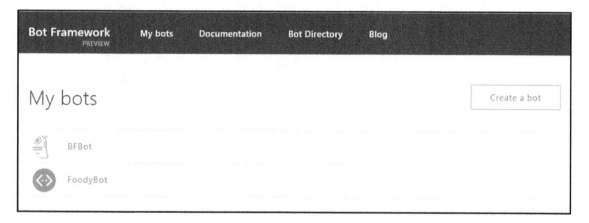

2. Choose your bot. You will see that your bot is already connected to two channels, **Skype** and **Web Chat**:

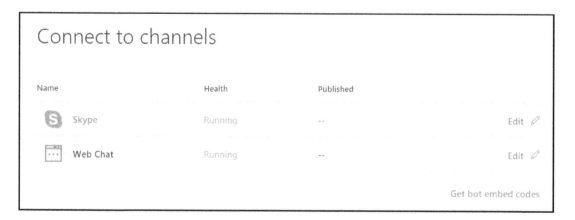

3. You will also be able to see the chat client on the right side. If you do not see one, you should be able to open it by pressing the **Test** button. This is similar to the emulator. So go on and say `Hi` to the bot:

You should be able to chat with the bot here as it is in the cloud and not on localhost.

4. Click **Skype**:

5. Click **Add to Contacts**:

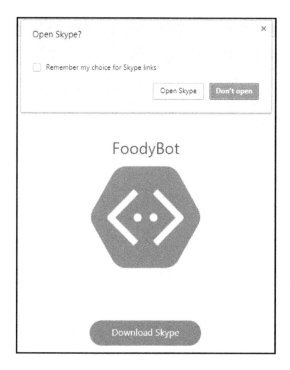

6. Click **Open Skype**:

7. Add the bot to your contacts and start chatting:

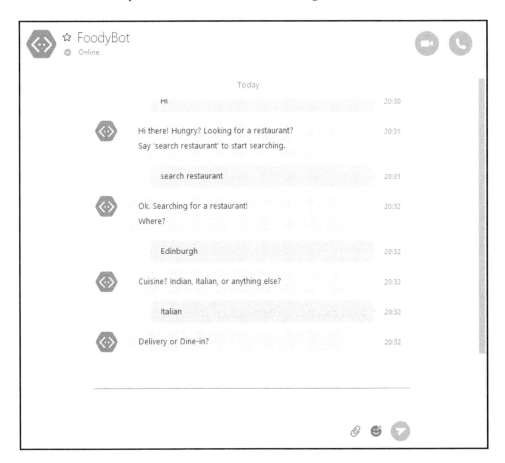

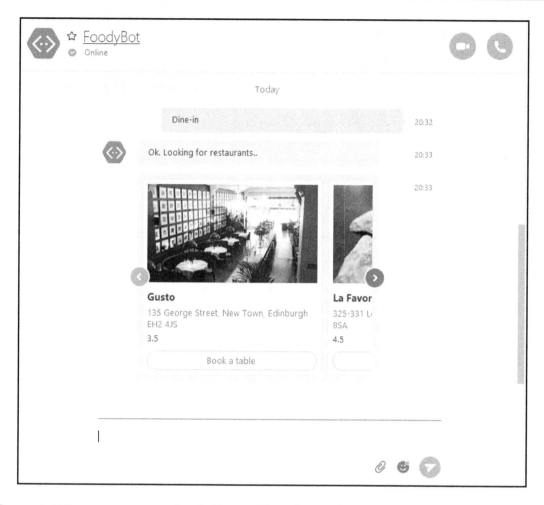

Congratulations on your new bot in Skype. Now that we have created a bot using Bot Builder SDK and deployed it on Skype, go explore all the other options that we learned about but did not get to experiment with. Add a user-profiling dialogue where the bot learns about the user's preferences. Extend the restaurant search dialogue by asking follow-up questions based on reviews, ratings, and price range once the restaurants are found and need further sorting. Try to add natural language support so that the user can switch between tasks easily.

Summary

In the previous chapters, we explored and learned about how to build a chatbot using a variety of tools. These include development environments such as Chatfuel, natural language processing tools such as API.AI, and channel-specific SDKs such as Messenger SDK. However, when it comes to coding the conversational flow to manage the conversation, we either used form-based tools or built it from scratch. However, there is a middle path. MS Bot Framework offers the Bot Builder SDK that can be used to develop conversation management modules that manage how the dialogue flows between the bot and the user. The SDK models the elements of conversations in an elegant manner allowing developers to build chatbots quickly and easily. This gives developers greater flexibility than drag-and-drop tools, and it saves time and effort compared to building the bot from scratch.

In this chapter, we learned how to built a bot with the Bot Builder SDK and deploy it on the Skype channel. In the next chapter, we will move on to more advanced bots that are drastically different from those that we have explored so far—the Twitter bot!

References

Microsoft Bot Builder Node.js documentation: `https://docs.microsoft.com/en-us/bot-framework/nodejs/bot-builder-nodejs-overview`

7
The News Bot

So far we have explored how to build chatbots and deploy them in a variety of messaging platforms such as Facebook Messenger, Skype, and even SMS. We explored the different ways that tools, such as API.AI, can be used in the context of chatbot building. In this chapter, we are going to explore how chatbots can be integrated into Twitter, a social media platform. There are many similar social media platforms, such as Facebook and LinkedIn, that cater to different contexts and markets. What we will explore in this chapter conceptually applies to all of these platforms.

Twitter is an online news and social media platform where users can post and interact with messages that are called **tweets**. It has around 328 million active monthly users worldwide, with around 317 million active monthly users tweeting around 500 million tweets every day (Statista 2017). Twitter is used by businesses as a tool for brand engagement, product announcements, and customer service.

In this chapter, we will explore how to build chatbots on Twitter so that tweets can be posted and responded to automatically and quickly. We are going to build a news bot on the Twitter platform that tweets current news on its timeline on a regular basis. It will also personalize the experience for its followers by sending them news from topics that they are interested in. We will first explore the Twitter API and build core modules for tweeting, searching, and retweeting. Then, we will explore a data source for news around the globe. We will then build a simple bot that tweets top news on its timeline. Finally, we will build a personalized news bot that listens to incoming tweets from users about the topics that they are interested in and tweets user-specific news to them.

By the end of this chapter, you will be able to:

- Understand the basics of the Twitter API
- Create a bot that listens to hashtags
- Build a Twitter bot that tweets and retweets
- Integrate NewsAPI and tweet top stories
- Integrate MongoDB to track user interests
- Build a conversational bot to get user interests and serve personalized news
- Use Heroku Scheduler to tweet personalized news at a regular frequency

Getting started with the Twitter app

To get started, let us explore the Twitter developer platform. Let us begin by building a Twitter app and later explore how we can tweet news articles to followers based on their interests:

1. Log on to Twitter at `www.twitter.com`. If you don't have an account on Twitter, create one.
2. Go to `https://apps.twitter.com/`, which is Twitter's application management dashboard.
3. Click the **Create New App** button:

Twitter Apps

You don't currently have any Twitter Apps.

Create New App

Chapter 7

4. Create an application by filling in the form providing name, description, and a website (fully-qualified URL). Read and agree to the **Developer Agreement** and hit **Create your Twitter application**:

Create an application

Application Details

Name *

MyNewsBot

Your application name. This is used to attribute the source of a tweet and in user-facing authorization screens. 32 characters max.

Description *

Personalised News Tweeter Bot

Your application description, which will be shown in user-facing authorization screens. Between 10 and 200 characters max.

Website *

http://chatbotgu.ru

Your application's publicly accessible home page, where users can go to download, make use of, or find out more information about your application. This fully-qualified URL is used in the source attribution for tweets created by your application and will be shown in user-facing authorization screens.

(If you don't have a URL yet, just put a placeholder here but remember to change it later.)

Callback URL

Where should we return after successfully authenticating? OAuth 1.0a applications should explicitly specify their oauth_callback URL on the request token step, regardless of the value given here. To restrict your application from using callbacks, leave this field blank.

[263]

5. You will now see your application dashboard. Explore the tabs:

6. Click **Keys and Access Tokens**:

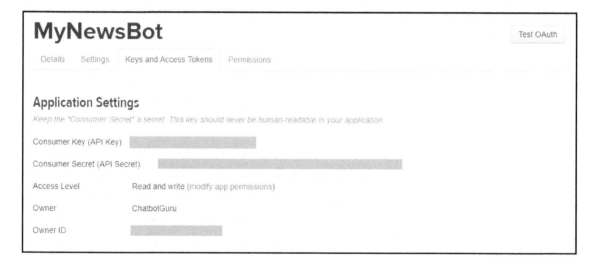

7. Copy *consumer key* and *consumer secret* and hang on to them.

8. Scroll down to **Your Access Token**:

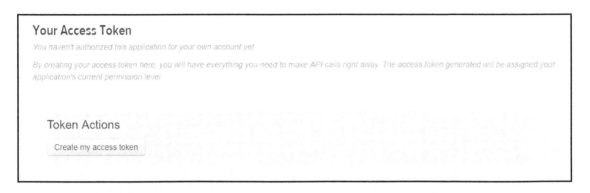

9. Click **Create my access token** to create a new token for your app:

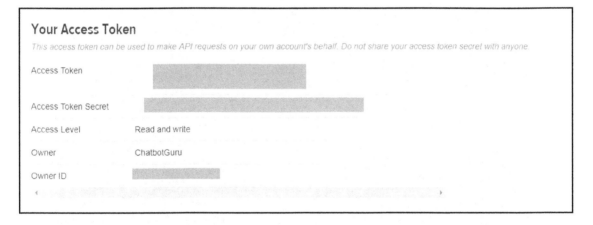

10. Copy the **Access Token** and **Access Token Secret** and hang on to them.

Now, we have all the keys and tokens we need to create a Twitter app.

Building your first Twitter bot

Let's build a simple Twitter bot. This bot will listen to tweets and pick out those that have a particular hashtag. All the tweets with a given hashtag will be printed on the console. This is a very simple bot to help us get started. In the following sections, we will explore more complex bots.

1. Go to the root directory and create a new Node.js program using `npm init`:

```
C:\Users\Srini\Dropbox\_Book\workspace\twitterbot>npm init
This utility will walk you through creating a package.json file.
It only covers the most common items, and tries to guess sensible defaults.

See `npm help json` for definitive documentation on these fields
and exactly what they do.

Use `npm install <pkg> --save` afterwards to install a package and
save it as a dependency in the package.json file.

Press ^C at any time to quit.
name: (twitterbot)
version: (1.0.0)
description: my news bot
entry point: (index.js)
test command:
git repository:
keywords:
author:
license: (ISC)
About to write to C:\Users\Srini\Dropbox\_Book\workspace\twitterbot\package.json:

{
  "name": "twitterbot",
  "version": "1.0.0",
  "description": "my news bot",
  "main": "index.js",
  "scripts": {
    "test": "echo \"Error: no test specified\" && exit 1"
  },
  "author": "",
  "license": "ISC"
}
```

2. Execute the `npm install twitter --save` command to install the Twitter Node.js library:

```
C:\Users\Srini\Dropbox\_Book\workspace\twitterbot>npm install twitter --save
npm WARN package.json twitterbot@1.0.0 No repository field.
npm WARN package.json twitterbot@1.0.0 No README data
twitter@1.7.1 node_modules\twitter
├── deep-extend@0.5.0
└── request@2.81.0 (aws-sign2@0.6.0, oauth-sign@0.8.2, forever-agent@0.6.1, tunnel-agent@0.6.
0, is-typedarray@1.0.0, caseless@0.12.0, safe-buffer@5.1.1, stringstream@0.0.5, isstream@0.1.
2, aws4@1.6.0, json-stringify-safe@5.0.1, extend@3.0.1, performance-now@0.2.0, uuid@3.1.0, qs
@6.4.0, combined-stream@1.0.5, mime-types@2.1.16, tough-cookie@2.3.2, form-data@2.1.4, hawk@3
.1.3, http-signature@1.1.1, har-validator@4.2.1)
```

Run `npm install request --save` to install the Request library as well. We will use this in the future to make HTTP GET requests to a news data source.

3. Explore your `package.json` file in the root directory:

```json
{
  "name": "twitterbot",
  "version": "1.0.0",
  "description": "my news bot",
  "main": "index.js",
  "scripts": {
    "test": "echo \"Error: no test specified\" && exit 1"
  },
  "author": "",
  "license": "ISC",
  "dependencies": {
    "request": "^2.81.0",
    "twitter": "^1.7.1"
  }
}
```

4. Create an `index.js` file with the following code:

```js
//index.js

var TwitterPackage = require('twitter');
var request = require('request');

console.log("Hello World! I am a twitter bot!");
```

```
var secret = {
 consumer_key: 'YOUR_CONSUMER_KEY',
 consumer_secret: 'YOUR_CONSUMER_SECRET',
 access_token_key: 'YOUR_ACCESS_TOKEN_KEY',
 access_token_secret: 'YOUR_ACCESS_TOKEN_SECRET'
}

var Twitter = new TwitterPackage(secret);
```

In the preceding code, put the keys and tokens you saved in their appropriate variables. We don't need the `request` package just yet, but we will later.

5. Now let's create a *hashtag listener* to listen to the tweets on a specific hashtag:

```
//Twitter stream

var hashtag = '#brexit'; //put any hashtag to listen e.g. #brexit
console.log('Listening to:' + hashtag);
Twitter.stream('statuses/filter', {track: hashtag},
function(stream) {
  stream.on('data', function(tweet) {
    console.log('Tweet:@' + tweet.user.screen_name +
                '\t' + tweet.text);
    console.log('------')
  });
  stream.on('error', function(error) {
    console.log(error);
  });
});
```

Replace #brexit with the hashtag you want to listen to. Use a popular one so that you can see the code in action.

6. Run the `index.js` file with the `node index.js` command.

7. You will see a stream of tweets from Twitter users all over the globe who used the hashtag:

```
C:\Users\Srini\Dropbox\_Book\workspace\twitterbot>node index.js
Hello World! I am a twitter bot!
Listening to:#brexit
Tweet:@belanisiya      RT @weloveeconomics: The UK economy grew faster after joining the EU but popu
lism (no facts!) made people believe the opposite.…
------
Tweet:@BazzieSmith     RT @jlivingstone100: Brexit support fading it seems -'Marketplace did not enc
ounter any farmers at the show who admitted voting for Brex…
------
Tweet:@frankietaggart   RT @brexitcountdow1: Brexit is 13850 hours away. #brexit
------
Tweet:@pm_kristin      RT @laute_europaeer: Ist nach Abschluss der #Brexit -Verhandlungen ein 2. #Re
ferendum über das Abkommen zwischen #UK und #EU notwendig?
htt…
------
Tweet:@GillianRAdams    RT @nickreeves9876: Shocking how seldom the question of Freedom of Movement i
s couched in terms of the loss of our Right to live &amp; work in…
------
Tweet:@hpw_llp  RT @TheLawSociety: What is the European Court of Justice and why does it matter? A #B
rexit Q&amp;A https://t.co/C0Vi6J0fm4 https://t.co/8ankRoV…
------
Tweet:@h1llbillies      RT @LeedsEurope: Leeds for Europe Stop Brexit Day of Action! 16 Sep - Rally,
Question Time &amp; Social with @RCorbettMEP @emmyzen &amp; mor…
------
Tweet:@KarenMc10       RT @trevdick: Britain 2017 with Brexit looming is peddling backwards to 1971.
..
Memories are not made of this...
#Brexit is Barmy https://t…
```

Congratulations! You have built your first Twitter bot. We will use the hashtag listening module later in this chapter to build a more complex bot.

Exploring the Twitter SDK

In the previous section, we explored how to listen to tweets based on hashtags. Let's now explore the Twitter SDK to understand the capabilities that we can bestow upon our Twitter bot.

Updating your status

You can also update your status on your Twitter timeline by using the following *status update* module code:

```
tweet ('I am a Twitter Bot!', null, null);

function tweet(statusMsg, screen_name, status_id){
```

```
console.log('Sending tweet to: ' + screen_name);
console.log('In response to:' + status_id);
var msg = statusMsg;
if (screen_name != null){
    msg = '@' + screen_name + ' ' + statusMsg;
}
console.log('Tweet:' + msg);
Twitter.post('statuses/update', {
        status: msg
    }, function(err, response) {
        // if there was an error while tweeting
        if (err) {
            console.log('Something went wrong while TWEETING...');
            console.log(err);
        }
        else if (response) {
            console.log('Tweeted!!!');
            console.log(response)
        }
});
}
```

Comment out the hashtag listener code and instead add the preceding status update code and run it. When run, your bot will post a tweet on your timeline:

In addition to tweeting on your timeline, you can also tweet in response to another tweet (or status update). The screen_name argument is used to create a response. tweet . screen_name is the name of the user who posted the tweet. We will explore this a bit later.

Retweet to your followers

You can retweet a tweet to your followers using the following *retweet status* code:

```
var retweetId = '899681279343570944';
retweet(retweetId);

function retweet(retweetId){
    Twitter.post('statuses/retweet/', {
        id: retweetId
    }, function(err, response) {
        if (err) {
            console.log('Something went wrong while RETWEETING...');
            console.log(err);
        }
        else if (response) {
            console.log('Retweeted!!!');
            console.log(response)
        }
    });
}
```

Searching for tweets

You can also search for recent or popular tweets with hashtags using the following *search hashtags* code:

```
search('#brexit', 'popular')
function search(hashtag, resultType){
    var params = {
        q: hashtag, // REQUIRED
        result_type: resultType,
        lang: 'en'
    }

    Twitter.get('search/tweets', params, function(err, data) {
        if (!err) {
            console.log('Found tweets: ' + data.statuses.length);
            console.log('First one: ' + data.statuses[1].text);
        }
        else {
          console.log('Something went wrong while SEARCHING...');
        }
    });
}
```

Exploring a news data service

Let's now build a bot that will tweet news articles to its followers at regular intervals. We will then extend it to be personalized by users through a conversation that happens over direct messaging with the bot. In order to build a news bot, we need a source where we can get news articles. We are going to explore a news service called NewsAPI.org in this section. NewsAPI is a service that aggregates news articles from roughly 70 newspapers around the globe.

Setting up NewsAPI

Let us set up an account with the NewsAPI data service and get the API key:

1. Go to `newsapi.org`:

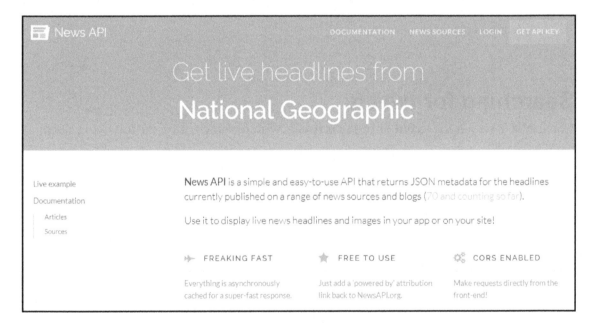

2. Click **Get API key**.
3. Register using your email.
4. Get your API key.

5. Explore the sources:
   `https://newsapi.org/v1/sources?apiKey=YOUR_API_KEY.`

There are about 70 sources from across the globe including popular ones such as BBC News, Associated Press, Bloomberg, and CNN. You might notice that each source has a category tag attached. The possible options are: business, entertainment, gaming, general, music, politics, science-and-nature, sport, and technology. You might also notice that each source also has language (`en`, `de`, `fr`) and country (`au`, `de`, `gb`, `in`, `it`, `us`) tags. The following is the information on the BBC-News source:

```
{
    "id": "bbc-news",
    "name": "BBC News",
    "description": "Use BBC News for up-to-the-minute news,
    breaking news, video, audio and feature stories.
    BBC News provides trusted World and UK news as well as
    local and regional perspectives. Also entertainment,
    business, science, technology and health news.",
    "url": "http://www.bbc.co.uk/news",
    "category": "general",
    "language": "en",
    "country": "gb",
    "urlsToLogos": {
        "small": "",
        "medium": "",
        "large": ""
    },
    "sortBysAvailable": [
        "top"
        ]
}
```

6. Get sources for a specific category, language, or country using:

   `https://newsapi.org/v1/sources?category=business&apiKey=YOUR_API_KEY`

The following is the part of the response to the preceding query asking for all sources under the business category:

```
"sources": [
    {
        "id": "bloomberg",
        "name": "Bloomberg",
        "description": "Bloomberg delivers business
```

```
                    and markets news, data, analysis, and video
                    to the world, featuring stories from Businessweek
                    and Bloomberg News.",
                    "url": "http://www.bloomberg.com",
                    "category": "business",
                    "language": "en",
                    "country": "us",
                    "urlsToLogos": {
                        "small": "",
                        "medium": "",
                        "large": ""
                    },
                    "sortBysAvailable": [
                    "top"
                    ]
            },
            {

                    "id": "business-insider",
                    "name": "Business Insider",
                    "description": "Business Insider is a fast-growing
                    business site with deep financial, media, tech, and
                    other industry verticals. Launched in 2007, the
                    site is now the largest business news site on the web.",
                    "url": "http://www.businessinsider.com",
                    "category": "business",
                    "language": "en",
                    "country": "us",
                    "urlsToLogos": {
                        "small": "",
                        "medium": "",
                        "large": ""
                    },
                    "sortBysAvailable": [
                    "top",
                    "latest"
                    ]
            },
            ...
        ]
```

7. Explore the articles:

```
https://newsapi.org/v1/articles?source=bbc-news&apiKey=YOUR_API
_KEY
```

The following is the sample response:

```
"articles": [
    {
        "author": "BBC News",
        "title": "US Navy collision: Remains found in
                hunt for missing sailors",
        "description": "Ten US sailors have been missing since Monday's
                collision with a tanker near Singapore.",
        "url": "http://www.bbc.co.uk/news/world-us-canada-41013686",
        "urlToImage":
        "https://ichef1.bbci.co.uk/news/1024/cpsprodpb/80D9/
                    production/_97458923_mediaitem97458918.jpg",
        "publishedAt": "2017-08-22T12:23:56Z"
    },
    {

        "author": "BBC News",
        "title": "Afghanistan hails Trump support in 'joint struggle'",
        "description": "President Ghani thanks Donald Trump for
                    supporting Afghanistan's battle against the
                    Taliban.",
        "url": "http://www.bbc.co.uk/news/world-asia-41012617",
        "urlToImage":
        "https://ichef.bbci.co.uk/images/ic/1024x576/p05d08pf.jpg",
        "publishedAt": "2017-08-22T11:45:49Z"
    },
    ...
]
```

For each article, the `author`, `title`, `description`, `url`, `urlToImage`,, and `publishedAt` fields are provided. Now that we have explored a source of news data that provides up-to-date news stories under various categories, let us go on to build a news bot.

Building a Twitter news bot

Now that we have explored NewsAPI, a data source for the latest news updates, and a little bit of what the Twitter API can do, let us combine them both to build a bot tweeting interesting news stories, first on its own timeline and then specifically to each of its followers:

1. Let's build a news tweeter module that tweets the top news article given the source. The following code uses the `tweet()` function we built earlier:

   ```
   topNewsTweeter('cnn', null);
   ```

```
function topNewsTweeter(newsSource, screen_name, status_id){
    request({
            url: 'https://newsapi.org/v1/articles?source='
            + newsSource +
                  '&apiKey=YOUR_API_KEY',
            method: 'GET'
        },
        function (error, response, body) {
            //response is from the bot
            if (!error && response.statusCode == 200) {
                var botResponse = JSON.parse(body);
                console.log(botResponse);
                tweetTopArticle(botResponse.articles, screen_name);
            } else {
                console.log('Sorry. No new');
            }
        });
}

function tweetTopArticle(articles, screen_name, status_id){
    var article = articles[0];
    tweet(article.title + " " + article.url, screen_name);
}
```

Run the preceding program to fetch news from CNN and post the topmost article on Twitter:

```
C:\Users\Srini\Dropbox\_Book\workspace\twitterbot>node index.js
Hello World! I am a twitter bot!
{ status: 'ok',
  source: 'cnn',
  sortBy: 'top',
  articles:
   [ { author: 'Nicole Chavez, CNN',
       title: 'Hurricane Harvey strengthens to Category 2',
       description: 'As heavy rain and gusty winds move in over Texas, coastal residents are deciding whethe
r to flee their homes or to stay put and brace for a potentially life-threatening hurricane.',
       url: 'http://www.cnn.com/2017/08/25/us/hurricane-harvey/index.html',
       urlToImage: 'http://i2.cdn.cnn.com/cnnnext/dam/assets/170825094917-01-hurricane-harvey-nws-super-teas
e.jpg',
       publishedAt: '2017-08-25T10:25:21Z' },
     { author: null,
       title: 'What Hurricane Harvey looks like from space - CNN Video',
       description: 'The International Space Station captured video of Hurricane Harvey from about 220 miles
 above the Earth.',
       url: 'http://www.cnn.com/videos/us/2017/08/25/hurricane-harvey-space-station-sje-lon-orig.cnn',
       urlToImage: 'http://i2.cdn.cnn.com/cnnnext/dam/assets/170825100553-hurricane-harvey-space-station-3-s
uper-tease.jpg',
       publishedAt: null },
```

Here is the post on Twitter:

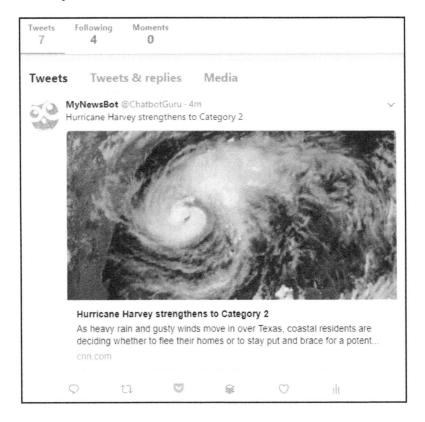

2. Now, let us build a module that tweets news stories from a randomly-chosen source in a list of sources:

```
function tweetFromRandomSource(sources, screen_name, status_id){
    var max = sources.length;
    var randomSource = sources[Math.floor(Math.random() *
                                (max + 1))];
    //topNewsTweeter(randomSource, screen_name, status_id);
}
```

3. Let's call the tweeting module after we acquire the list of sources:

```
function getAllSourcesAndTweet(){
    var sources = [];
    console.log('getting sources...')
    request({
            url: 'https://newsapi.org/v1/sources?
```

```
                    apiKey=YOUR_API_KEY',
                    method: 'GET'
            },
            function (error, response, body) {
                //response is from the bot
                if (!error && response.statusCode == 200) {
                    // Print out the response body
                    var botResponse = JSON.parse(body);
                    for (var i = 0; i < botResponse.sources.length;
                        i++){
                        console.log('adding.. ' +
                                    botResponse.sources[i].id)
                        sources.push(botResponse.sources[i].id)
                    }
                    tweetFromRandomSource(sources, null, null);
                } else {
                    console.log('Sorry. No news sources!');
                }
            });
    }
```

4. Let's create a new JS file called `tweeter.js`. In the `tweeter.js` file, call `getSourcesAndTweet()` to get the process started:

```
//tweeter.js

var TwitterPackage = require('twitter');
var request = require('request');

console.log("Hello World! I am a twitter bot!");

var secret = {
  consumer_key: 'YOUR_CONSUMER_KEY',
  consumer_secret: 'YOUR_CONSUMER_SECRET',
  access_token_key: 'YOUR_ACCESS_TOKEN_KEY',
  access_token_secret: 'YOUR_ACCESS_TOKEN_SECRET'
}

var Twitter = new TwitterPackage(secret);
getAllSourcesAndTweet();
```

5. Run the `tweeter.js` file on the console. This bot will tweet a news story every time it is called. It will choose top news stories from around 70 news sources randomly.

Building a personalized news bot

We now have a news bot that tweets news (or posts status updates) on its own timeline. We will look at how to set it to run on a regular basis in a little while. Let us now build a more interesting bot that can tweet to its followers using the news stories that they might like. In other words, let's personalize the news:

1. Let's assume that we have information about the users and their interests. Add the following to the `tweeter.js` file. For now, we are hardcoding the user interests information into the code itself. Later we will see how they can be stored and retrieved from a database:

```
var userInterests = [{'screen_name':'srinivasancj',
                               'user_interest': 'technology'}];
```

2. Create a `tweetUserSpecificNews` module that uses `userInterests` to get the category-specific sources. Call `tweetUserSpecificNews()` after `getAllSourcesAndTweet()`:

```
tweetUserSpecificNews();

function tweetUserSpecificNews(){
console.log('Tweeting personalised news');
    for (var i=0; i < userInterests.length; i++){
        var user = userInterests[i];
        var screen_name = user.screen_name;
        var interest = user.user_interest;
        var status_id = user.in_reply_to_status_id;
        //get sources
        request({
            url: 'https://newsapi.org/v1/sources?category=' +
                interest +
                        '&apiKey=YOUR_API_KEY',
            method: 'GET'
        },
        function (error, response, body) {
            if (!error && response.statusCode == 200) {
                // Print out the response body
                var botResponse = JSON.parse(body);
                console.log(botResponse);
                var sources = [];
                for (var i = 0; i < botResponse.sources.length;
                    i++)
                {
                    console.log('adding.. ' +
```

```
                                    botResponse.sources[i].id)
                        sources.push(botResponse.sources[i].id)
                    }
                    tweetFromRandomSource(sources, screen_name,
                                          status_id);
            } else {
                console.log('Sorry. No news in this category.');
            }
        });
    }
}
```

By specifying the `screen_name` of a tweet from the user, the tweets sent by the bot are treated as a response to the user's original tweet. Therefore these tweets don't end up on the bot's timeline. Instead they are sent directly to the user and therefore personalized to the user.

3. Now that we have a bot that, when run, updates its own timeline with a random news article and sends personalized news to its followers, let's make it run automatically on a regular basis, say, once an hour. To do this, we first need to create a web app and push it on to the Cloud.

4. Create a `bin` folder and move the `tweeter.js` file into the `bin` folder.

5. Rename the `tweeter.js` file to `tweeter`. And add the following code as the first line. This is to tell Heroku which interpreter program to use to run the script:

    ```
    #!/usr/bin/env node
    ```

6. In the project root directory, create a file named `Procfile` with the following code:

    ```
    web: node index.js
    ```

7. Create a local Git repository for the project, add files, and make an initial commit. Type the following command on the console:

    ```
    > git init
    > git add .
    > git commit -m initial-commit-personalised-bot
    ```

8. Create a Heroku app:

    ```
    > heroku create my-twitter-bot
    ```

9. Push the app onto Heroku Cloud:

   ```
   > git push heroku master
   ```

10. Add a Heroku Scheduler:

    ```
    > heroku addons:add scheduler
    ```

11. Open your Heroku Dashboard on a browser:

    ```
    https://dashboard.heroku.com/apps
    ```

12. Choose your Twitter bot app and open the app's dashboard.

13. In the **Overview** tab, under **Installed add-ons**, you will find the Heroku Scheduler add-on listed. Click it:

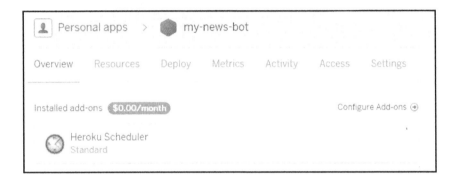

14. You will now see the scheduled tasks for the app. Since we have just created this app, you won't see any. Click **Add new job**:

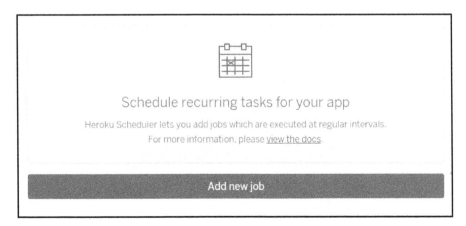

15. Type the name of the program that needs to run on a scheduled basis, in our case it is **tweeter**, and click **Save**:

16. The scheduler will now run the tweeter program on a regular basis, sending personalized news to subscribed users:

Creating a database of user interests

Now that we have a web app that runs regularly, tweeting personalized news to users, let's move on to the next obvious step, which is creating a database where the Twitter bot can pick up user information. Currently, we have hardcoded this information into the bot, which is not ideal. To create a database, let us use a MongoDB hosting service called mlab.com.

 Be aware that for legal reasons, if you decide to make the bot publicly available, you may have to inform users that the bot will store users' personal information.

To create a database for the twitter bot, follow these steps:

1. Go to `www.mlab.com`. Click **SIGN UP**:

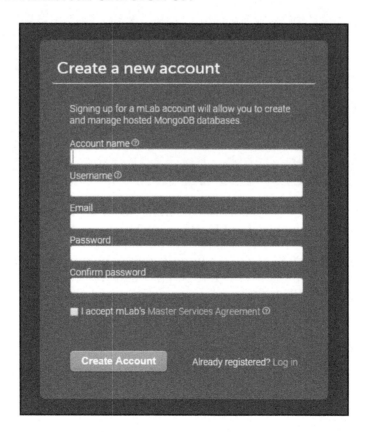

2. Fill in your details and click **Create Account**.
3. Verify your email by clicking the link that they send you. This will take you to the account dashboard:

4. We need a MongoDB deployment. So, on the dashboard, click **Create new**:

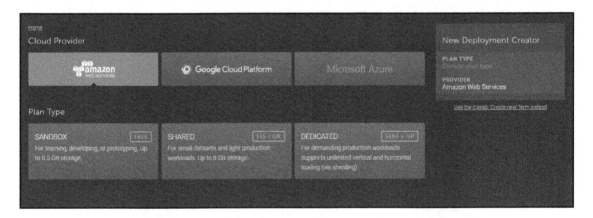

5. Choose any Cloud provider you like from the following three choices: **amazon web services**, **Google Cloud Platform**, or **Microsoft Azure**.

6. Click **SANDBOX**. Sandbox is a type of environment where you can play and practice with deployments before you move them on to production. Click **CONTINUE**:

7. Choose the AWS region and click **CONTINUE**:

8. Provide the final details, database name, and click **CONTINUE**:

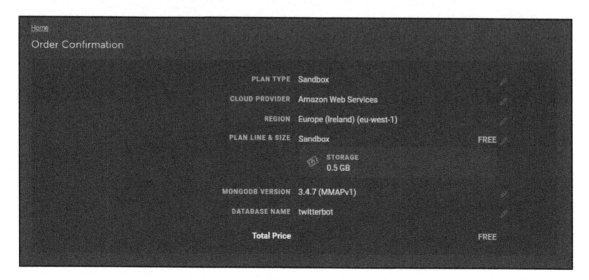

9. Check the details and click **SUBMIT ORDER** to finish:

You have now created a database called `twitterbot`, which can be used to store information concerning user interests.

10. Create a new collection by double-clicking the `twitterbot` database entry:

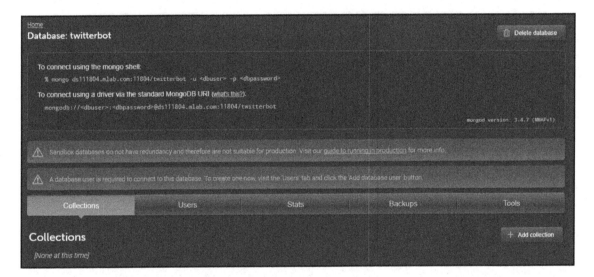

11. Click **Add collection**. Create a collection called `users`.
12. Now, in order to connect to a database, we need to define its users. To create a user, click the **Users** tab (next to **Collections**).
13. Click **Add database user**.
14. Create a new database user.

15. Get the URL of the database. It looks like this one:

```
mongodb://<dbuser>:<dbpassword>@ds111804.mlab.com:11804/twitter
bot
```

Replace `<dbuser>` and `<dbpassword>` with the user ID and password of the new database user that you just created. Hang on to this.

16. Let's add some data into the `users` collection for the Twitter bot to read. Click the **Collections** tab and then the `users` collection.

17. Click **Add document**. Type the JSON object from the `user_interests` list. Click **Create and go back**:

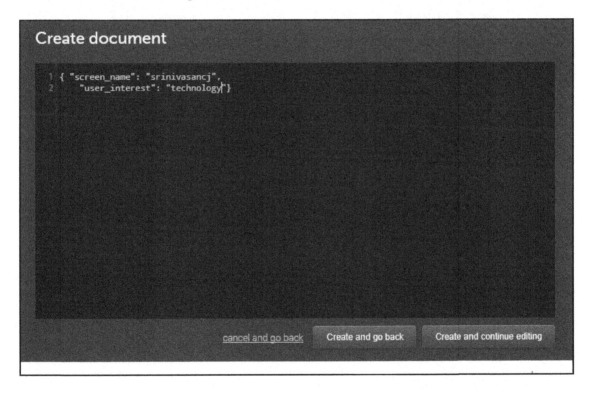

18. Now you have your documents added to the collection:

Great! Now we have a MongoDB document database in the Cloud (`Mlab.com`) to store information about user interests. Let's now figure out how to use this database to store and retrieve information on user interests with the bot.

Accessing the user interests database

In the previous section, we created a MongoDB document database where we can store user information that will be used by the Twitter bot to personalize news. In this section, we will see how to connect to the database in real time with the bot.

1. Install the `mongodb` library (version 2.2.31) using the `npm install` command:

   ```
   > npm install mongodb@2.2.31 --save
   ```

2. Test the connection by creating a Node.js program called `mongodb.js` with the following code:

   ```
   var MongoClient = require('mongodb').MongoClient;

   // Connection URL
   var url = 'YOUR_MONGO_DB_URI';
   ```

```
  // Use connect method to connect to the server
  MongoClient.connect(url, function(err, db) {
    console.log("Connected successfully to server");
    db.close();
  });
```

3. Run it to see whether the program is able to connect to your database.
4. Add a function to the `mongodb.js` program to fetch all documents in your collection:

```
function findDocuments(db, callback) {
    // Get the documents collection
    var collection = db.collection('users');
    // Find documents
    collection.find({}).toArray(function(err, docs) {
        callback(docs);
    });
}
```

5. Replace the `db.close()` call in `mongodb.js` with a call to the preceding function, as shown here:

```
var userInterests = [];

// Use connect method to connect to the server
MongoClient.connect(url, function(err, db) {
  console.log("Connected successfully to server");
  findDocuments(db, function(docs) {
      for (var i = 0; i < docs.length; i++){
          var user = {};
          user.screen_name = docs[i].screen_name;
          user.user_interest = docs[i].user_interest;
          userInterests.push(user);
      }
      db.close();
      console.log(userInterests);
  });
});
```

6. Run it to see whether it fetches the document that we put into the collection:

```
C:\Users\Srini\Dropbox\_Book\workspace\twitterbot>node mongodb.js
Connected successfully to server
[ { screen_name: 'srinivasancj', user_interest: 'technology' } ]
```

You should be able to see the document that we already stored in the `users` collection. Later we will see how to put more user data into the collection using the Twitter bot.

7. Now that we are able to successfully read user interests, let's wire this up to the bot so that it can send personalized news to users based on the information it finds in the database.

8. Open the `tweeter` program in the `bin` folder. Replace the `userInterests` variable declaration with the following:

```
var MongoClient = require('mongodb').MongoClient;
// Connection URL
var url = 'YOUR_MONGO_DB_URI';
var userInterests = [];
loadUserData();
```

9. Let's define the `loadUserData()` function that will load the user data from the document database:

```
function loadUserData(){
    // Use connect method to connect to the server
    MongoClient.connect(url, function(err, db) {
      console.log("Connected successfully to server");

      findDocuments(db, function(docs) {
        //console.log("Found the following records");
        for (var i = 0; i < docs.length; i++){
            var user = {};
            user.screen_name = docs[i].screen_name;
            user.user_interest = docs[i].user_interest;
            userInterests.push(user);
        }
        db.close();
        console.log(userInterests);
        //tweet to those followers who have
        //expressed interest in specific categories
        tweetUserSpecificNews();
      });
    });
}
```

10. Notice how `tweetUserSpecificNews()` is now called after loading the `userInterests` array with data from the database. Remove the call to this function if one exists outside the `loadUserData()` function.

11. Run the program on the console (in the `bin` folder) to see it in action:

> `node tweeter`

This will fetch user interests from the database, query for all sources, pick out user-specific sources, randomly select one, and tweet the top news article from the selected source:

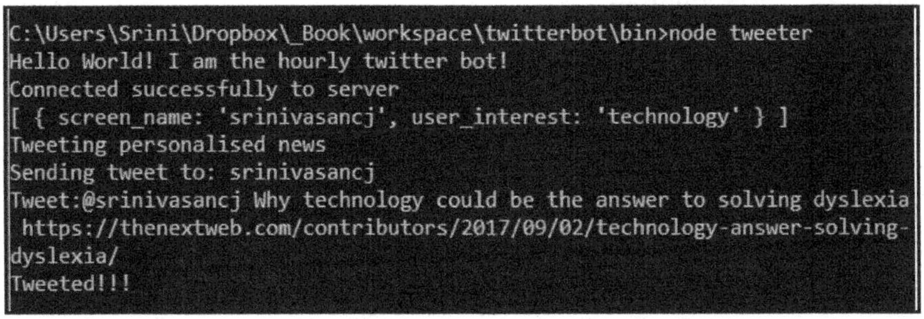

```
C:\Users\Srini\Dropbox\_Book\workspace\twitterbot\bin>node tweeter
Hello World! I am the hourly twitter bot!
Connected successfully to server
[ { screen_name: 'srinivasancj', user_interest: 'technology' } ]
Tweeting personalised news
Sending tweet to: srinivasancj
Tweet:@srinivasancj Why technology could be the answer to solving dyslexia
 https://thenextweb.com/contributors/2017/09/02/technology-answer-solving-
dyslexia/
Tweeted!!!
```

Great! We are now one step closer to a conversational Twitter bot. The only piece of the puzzle that's missing is a way to tell the bot what the user is interested in without having to manually create documents in the database.

Informing the bot of user interests

Wouldn't it be interesting to have users tweet the bot about what they are and are not interested in? The bot could then personalize the news based on what the users say they like. The tweet conversation could go like the one shown here:

```
User > I am interested in politics.
Bot tweets political news every hour.
User > Send me technology news.
Bot tweets technology and political news every hour.
User > Stop sending political news to me.
Bot tweets technology news every hour.
```

To make this Twitter conversation possible, we need a listener that listens to tweets sent to the bot by users informing it of their interests. This information, in natural language, needs to be parsed, understood, and updated in the database. The hourly tweeter would tweet personalized news based on the information it gets from the database. Sound good? Let's get cracking on the tweet listener:

1. Open the `index.js` file. Retain the code for importing the Twitter library and setting up the credentials:

```
var TwitterPackage = require('twitter');
var request = require('request');

var secret = {
  consumer_key: 'YOUR_CONSUMER_KEY',
  consumer_secret: 'YOUR_CONSUMER_SECRET',
  access_token_key: 'YOUR_ACCESS_TOKEN_KEY',
  access_token_secret: 'YOUR_ACCESS_TOKEN_SECRET'
}

var Twitter = new TwitterPackage(secret);
console.log("Hello World! I am a twitter bot!");
```

2. Set up a tweet listener to listen to all tweets sent to the bot. My bot's Twitter handle is @chatbotguru:

```
//listening to incoming tweets
Twitter.stream('user', {}, function(stream) {
    stream.on('data', function(tweet) {
        console.log(tweet);
        var ct = /@chatbotguru/i;
        var userUtt = 'null';
        if (tweet.text.search(ct) != -1){
            userUtt = tweet.text.replace(ct, '');
            console.log('Tweet Msg:' + userUtt);
            console.log('Tweet from:' + '@' +
            tweet.user.screen_name);
        }
    });
});
```

3. Run the code.

```
> node index.js
```

4. Send a tweet from your personal Twitter account to your bot's account. For example, `@chatbotguru I am interested in business news`. This tweet will be received by the listener that we have just set up:

```
C:\Users\Srini\Dropbox\_Book\workspace\twitterbot>node index.js
Hello World! I am a twitter bot!
Tweet Msg: I am interested in business news.
Tweet from:@srinivasancj
```

You should be able to see the tweet received by the bot on your Twitter app, too:

5. Now let's work on the message that we have received from the user. Let's examine the utterance for the topic of interest (politics, business, and so on) and the sentiment conveyed (interested/not interested). This is then used to insert or delete the user interest record in the database:

```
if (tweet.text.search(ct) != -1){
    userUtt = tweet.text.replace(ct, '');
    console.log('Tweet Msg:' + userUtt);
    console.log('Tweet from:' + '@' + tweet.user.screen_name);

    var userInterest = getInterestedGenre(userUtt);
    var userSentiment = getSentiment(userUtt);

    var user = { 'screen_name' : tweet.user.screen_name,
                 'user_interest' : userInterest };

    console.log(user);
```

```
        // Use connect method to connect to the server
        MongoClient.connect(url, function(err, db) {
            console.log("Connected successfully to server");
            var collection = db.collection('users');
            if (userSentiment == 'positive'){
                collection.insertMany([user], function(err, result) {
                    if (err){
                        console.log(err);
                    } else {
                        console.log("Inserted a user interest into the
                                    collection");
                        db.close();
                    }
                });
            } else {
                collection.deleteOne(user, function(err, result) {
                    console.log(err);
                    console.log("Deleted a user interest from
                                the collection");
                    db.close();
                });
            }
        });
    }
```

6. Let's define the `getInterestedTopic()` and `getSentiment()` functions:

```
function getSentiment(text){
    if (text.search('not interested') != -1){
        return 'negative';
    }
    if (text.search('no more') != -1){
        return 'negative';
    }
    if (text.search('don\'t send') != -1){
        return 'negative';
    }
    if (text.search('no ') != -1){
        return 'negative';
    }
    if (text.search('dont like ') != -1){
        return 'negative';
    }
    if (text.search('unsubscribe ') != -1){
        return 'negative';
    }
    if (text.search('don\'t follow ') != -1){
```

```
                return 'negative';
        }
        if (text.search('stop ') != -1){
            return 'negative';
        }
        return 'positive';
    }

    function getInterestedGenre(text){
        if (text.search('tech') != -1 ||
            text.search('technology') != -1 ){
            return 'technology';
        }
        else if (text.search('all kinds') != -1){
            return 'general';
        }
        else if (text.search('politics') != -1 ||
                text.search('political') != -1){
            return 'politics';
        }
        else if (text.search('sports') != -1){
            return 'sport';
        }
        else if (text.search('business') != -1){
            return 'business';
        }
    }
```

These are very simple definitions to start with. You could use NLU toolkits, such as API.AI, to understand user utterances for more complex functionality.

7. For the preceding code to work, we also need to import the MongoDB library and set it up in the index.js file:

```
var MongoClient = require('mongodb').MongoClient;
var url = 'YOUR_MONGO_DB_URI';
```

8. Run the code again, send a tweet, and see how it works. You will be able to see that the bot is now able to insert/delete records from the database. Go back to `mlab.com` and have a look:

That's it! Your hourly tweeter will now be able to pick up the updates in the database and tweet personalized news to all its users. Lastly, push the changes to Heroku Cloud so that you don't have to keep the `index.js` file running on your local machine.

Summary

Hurray! You have built your very own conversational Twitter bot. I would strongly recommend that you take this further and explore other kinds of conversation that you can possibly have with the bot. How about having the bot search and retweet hashtags automatically for you? How would you use metrics, such as retweet counts, follower numbers, and like counts, to qualify a tweet for retweeting? Explore these questions to build better and more useful Twitter bots.

In this chapter, we have covered a lot. We started off with the Twitter API and got a taste of how we can automatically tweet, retweet, and search for tweets using hashtags. We then explored a News source API that provides news articles from about 70 different newspapers. We integrated it with our Twitter bot to create a new tweeting bot. We explored how to personalize it for users by using user interest tags stored in a MongoDB database.

We finally explored how to close the loop by building a mechanism to enable the bot to receive tweets on users' interests and have them stored in the database. I hope I gave you an understanding of how useful Twitter bots can be and motivated you to build more of them. In the next chapter, we will look at how to build a voice bot skill on Amazon Echo.

References

Twitter API documentation: `https://developer.twitter.com/en/docs`

MongoDB documentation: `http://docs.mlab.com/`

8
My TV Guide

In this chapter, we will explore a new genre of assistants that are taking over the world, voice-powered home assistants. These are AI-powered chatbots that assume the functionality of your assistant at home. They sit on a table in your living room and interact with you using voice. They are called *smart speakers* but they are not just speakers. They are assistants, much like the ones we have explored in the earlier chapters, but with an embodiment of their own. One of the more popular ones is called *Alexa*, and is made by *Amazon*. While the embodiment, which is that of a speaker, is called *Echo*, the assistant is called *Alexa*.

There are other smart speakers on the market (for example, *Google Home)*. However, Amazon Echo seems to be leading the race with a market share of around 70% in 2017. The use of smart speaker home assistants is also projected to grow exponentially over time (`https://www.emarketer.com/Article/Alexa-Say-What-Voice-Enabled-Speaker-Usage-Grow-Nearly-130-This-Year/1015812`). In this chapter, let's explore how to extend Alexa's skill set by building our own skills. We will first build a simple skill that can retrieve an inspiring quote to brighten your day. Then we will move on to building a skill where Alexa can help you with your TV schedule for the day.

By the end of this chapter, you will be able to:

- Understand the basics of Amazon Alexa
- Understand and build slot, intents, and interaction models
- Understand built-in slots and intents
- Build a conversation management server on Heroku and integrate it with Alexa
- Integrate data sources, Quote.rest, and the TVMaze API to the conversation manager
- Deploy skills on Amazon Echo

Amazon Alexa

Amazon Alexa has its own development platform that allows developers to teach it new skills. Skills are nothing but conversational capabilities that can be custom-built into Alexa using a combination of Amazon's toolkit with our own. You do not actually need the Amazon Echo smart speaker to get started, but it would be great if you had one. Amazon Echo comes in three sizes: Amazon Echo, Amazon Echo Dot, and Amazon Echo Show. Echo Dot is the most basic version and is priced at £49 at the time of writing. This would suffice for a developer to develop and test custom-developed skills:

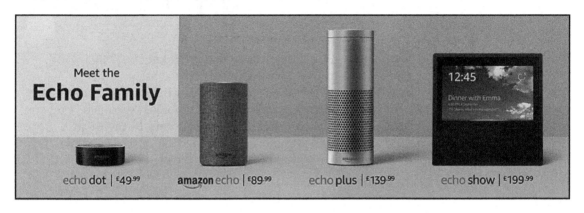

Source:Amazon.co.uk

The Alexa ecosystem also includes a skill store where custom skills can be published. Published skills can be browsed and installed on your Alexa, thereby adding to Alexa's skill set. This can be done either on Alexa's companion website (`alexa.amazon.com`), on the Amazon Alexa app on Google Play/iTunes store, or the Amazon site (`www.amazon.com/alexa-skills/`). Alexa connects to your Amazon account and can have a chat with you about many things: setting timers, weather info, currency rates, making a to-do or a shopping list, playing music, reading a book, ordering from Amazon, and so on. Go on and try the following with Alexa, once you have set it up:

- Alexa, what time is it?</li>
- Alexa, how is the weather?
- Alexa, what is the news update?
- Alexa, tell me a joke.
- Alexa, add eggs to my shopping list.

Warming up with a quotes bot

1. To get started, you need an Amazon developer account. Sign up at the following URL:

   ```
   https://developer.amazon.com/home.html
   ```

2. Once you have signed up, log in.
3. On the dashboard, click **ALEXA**:

4. Choose **Alexa Skills Kit** and click **Get Started**:

5. To create a new skill, click **Add a New Skill**:

Creating an Alexa skill is a two-phase process:

1. Configuring the skill on the developer portal.
2. Creating a conversation management module.

Configuring your skill

In order to explore the toolkit, we will use an example scenario of building a skill that delivers an inspiring quote every day. So the conversation between the user and Alexa may go like the following:

```
User: Alexa! Ask quote master to inspire me.
Alexa: The whole is greater than the sum of its parts.
```

On the developer portal, we will have to go through the following seven step process to configure the skill and its interaction model:

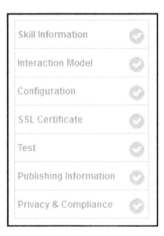

1. In the skill configuration form, leave the skill type as **Custom Interaction Model**:

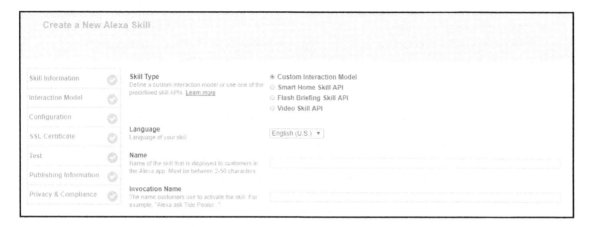

2. Choose the language. This will be the language of your skill. Currently Alexa supports English (US, UK, and India) and German.

3. Give it a name, say, `Quote Master`. This will be the name of the skill as it appears on the Alexa app for other Alexa users to install on their own Echo devices.

4. Give it an invocation name, say, `Quote Master`. The invocation name is how the skill will get invoked by Alexa. Guidelines to choose invocation names are available at the following URL:

```
https://developer.amazon.com/docs/custom-skills/choose-the-invocation-
name-for-a-custom-skill.html#invocation-name-requirements
```

You can install a number of skills on your Alexa, however two skills cannot have the same invocation name. In the case of a conflict, this will be highlighted when installing a new skill whose invocation name is already taken.

5. Leave the other fields to their default values, click **Save**, and then click **Next**:

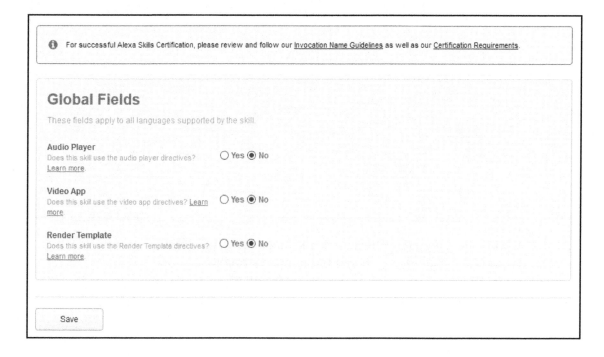

Interaction model

Before we start building the interaction model, let us understand a few basic concepts. The interaction model is the place where we specify the kind of utterances that Alexa needs to be able to decode for the skill. This is specified in terms of intents and examples. Intents represent the number of requests and responses that the user might have when interacting with the skill. Each intent can be expressed in many ways. For instance, the user may want to offer a greeting, and could say any of the following:

- hi
- hi there
- hello there
- what's up
- good day

The aforementioned are examples, while intent can be collectively named as `greet`:

1. Click **Launch Skill Builder**:

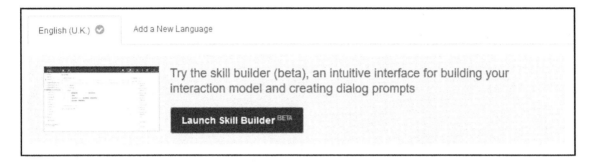

2. This will launch the skills building toolkit and display the dashboard:

Under the **Intents** tab, you can see that the skill already has three intents added by default: CancelIntent, HelpIntent, and StopIntent. These three are built-in intents and are added by default to every skill. This means that your skill can already understand requests to cancel, help, and stop.

The alternative to the dashboard view is to view the same information in code format by clicking the **Code Editor** option:

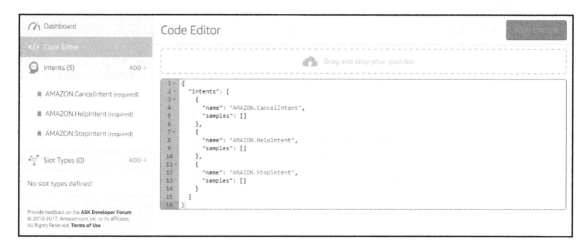

3. To create a new intent, click **ADD +** along the **Intents** tab:

4. There are two kinds of intents that can be created or added to the skill. There are built-in intents that can be added. These are pre-defined intents that can simply be reused. This saves developers a lot of time redefining them for each skill they build. On the other hand, we can custom design intents tailored to the needs of our skill:

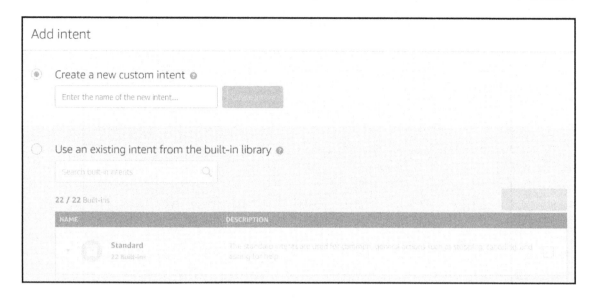

5. Click **Use an existing intent from the built-in library** to browse through the list of predefined intents:

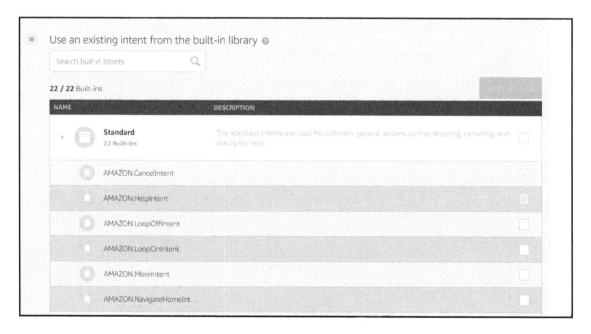

6. Click **Create a new custom intent**. Type the name of the intent, say, `GetQuote` and click **Create Intent**:

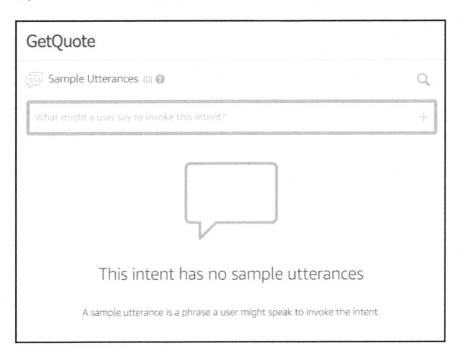

7. Add a few sample utterances. These are the example utterances we discussed earlier. Type each of the utterances and click + or type return to add it to the list of example utterances for a given intent:

8. Let's add one more intent to make this interesting: GetAuthor. This intent will ask Alexa to retrieve the name of the author of the quote it just uttered:

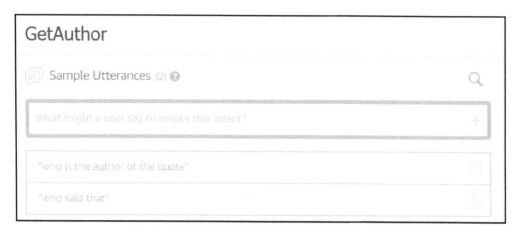

9. Click **Save Model**, then **Build Model**, and allow a few minutes for the interaction model to build:

10. Now that we have specified the requests in terms of sample user utterances and intents, click **Skill Information** to go back to the **Skills Configuration** panel. On the side menu, click **Configuration**:

11. This brings us to the next part of the development, where we need to build a module to manage the conversation. In this step, we are configuring the endpoint where the conversation manager can be found. We have two options: AWS and HTTPS. In the case of AWS, you need to create an AWS Lambda service to host a server endpoint. In case of HTTPS, we can host as a web server in any cloud platform we want. We will take the HTTPS option here.

12. In the following **Default** text field, enter the URL of the web app for your skill's conversation manager. Since we haven't built one, enter an indicative URL for now (for example, `https://my-first-alexa-bot.herokuapp.com/alexa`). Ignore the other parameters for now and click **Next**.

13. On the SSL certificate panel, click **Next** and move forward to **Test**.

14. On the **Test** panel, we can test whether Alexa can recognize the utterances that we want her to recognize and classify their intents accurately. Scroll down to the **Service Simulator** tab:

You will notice the HTTPS endpoint that you set in the **Server Endpoint** is specified.

15. Type an utterance in the **Text** tab and click the `Ask <skillname>` button underneath:

16. You will see that Alexa has parsed the utterance and identified the intent. This is presented in the form of a JSON object on the left (**Service Request**):

```
...
"request": {
    "type": "IntentRequest",
    "requestId": "EdwRequestId.a6845d2d-2901-4e8c-b260-
                  3a3a89bd5068",
    "intent": {
      "name": "GetQuote",
      "slots": {}
    },
    "locale": "en-GB",
    "timestamp": "2017-10-11T07:45:24Z"
  },
...
```

On the right (**Service Response**), there will be an error message, because the endpoint that we have specified does not exist yet. This endpoint needs to process the JSON request and respond with an utterance that Alexa can say back to the user.

Conversation manager - quotes

Conversation manager is a web application that can receive Alexa's intent results and respond with a bot response. Let us create a Node.js web app that can accept the intents that we have specified in our skill and respond appropriately. To build the module, perform the following steps:

1. Create a `package.json` file using `npm init`:

   ```
   > npm init
   ```

2. Install `express`, `request`, `body-parser`, and `hashmap`:

   ```
   > npm install request --save
   > npm install express --save
   > npm install body-parser --save
   > npm install hashmap --save
   ```

3. Create an `index.js` file:

   ```
   /*
   * Alexa
   */
   ```

```
const request = require('request')
const express = require('express')
const bodyParser = require('body-parser')

const app = express()

const Hashmap = require('hashmap');

var userContexts = new Hashmap();

app.set('port', (process.env.PORT || 5000))

// Process application/x-www-form-urlencoded
app.use(bodyParser.urlencoded({extended: false}))

// Process application/json
app.use(bodyParser.json())

// Index route
app.get('/', function (req, res) {
    res.send('Hello world, I am Quote Master.')
})

// Spin up the server
app.listen(app.get('port'), function() {
    console.log('running on port', app.get('port'))
}
```

4. Add a POST route handler to handle the requests from Alexa. The following code has place holders that we will fill in with appropriate code in subsequent steps:

```
app.post('/alexa', function (req, res) {
    console.log('Request from Alexa:');
    console.log(req.body);
    //1. add context code here

    //2. get userIntent from request

    //3. set default return json object
    //4. dialogue management code to decide what to
    //say in response to user intents.
})
```

5. Let's create a local context variable to store all the information that we need. This variable can be used to collect all the data that needs to be shared across a session. To store information locally during the turn, we use the `sessionContext` variable. This gets loaded from a `userContexts` global variable, which is a hashmap holding all session contexts. Alexa presents user intents each time with a session ID that is the same across a session. So, we can use the session ID in order to store and retrieve its context in the `userContexts` global variable:

```
var sessionContext = {
                        'lastUserIntent': 'null',
                        'lastQuote': null
                    };
var sessionId = req.body.session.sessionId;
if (!userContexts.get(sessionId)){
    userContexts.set(sessionId, sessionContext);
} else {
    sessionContext = usercontexts.get(sessionId);
}
```

6. We identify the user intent from the request (`req.body.request.intent.name`). However, when there is a timeout and Alexa ends the session, it returns `SessionEndedRequest`, which needs to be handled appropriately. We handle it similarly to the following `Amazon.StopIntent`:

```
var userIntent = '';
if (req.body.request.type === 'SessionEndedRequest'){
    userIntent = 'AMAZON.StopIntent';
} else {
    userIntent = req.body.request.intent.name;
}
console.log('UserIntent:' + userIntent);
```

7. Let's now prepare a default JSON to return. The following is the format of a return JSON. The `ssml` key contains the **Speech Synthesis Markup Language (SSML)** response with embedded text. The text is what Alexa synthesizes in response to the user's request:

```
var rjson = {
    "version": "1.0",
    "response": {
        "shouldEndSession": false,
        "outputSpeech": {
```

```
      "type": "SSML",
        "ssml": "<speak> Whole is larger than
                    the sum of its parts!</speak>"
      }
    }
  };
```

8. The default SSML response needs to be overwritten with a response appropriate to the user's request. So if the user is asking for a quote, we need to get them a new inspiring quotation, but if they ask for its author, we need to respond with the name of the author. This dialogue management logic is what we will code next. If the user intent is to get a new quote, we make a GET request to fetch a new quote from `quotes.rest`. Notice how we store the quote in context so that if the user asks for the author of the quote, Alexa knows the answer from the context:

```
if (userIntent === 'AMAZON.StopIntent'){
        rjson.response.shouldEndSession = true;
        rjson.response.outputSpeech.ssml = '<speak> Ok.
        Have a good day! </speak>';
        console.log(rjson);
        res.json(rjson);
    }
    else if (userIntent === 'GetQuote'){
        request({
            url: 'http://quotes.rest/qod.json?category=inspire',
            method: 'GET'
        },
        function (error, response, body) {
            //response is from the bot
            if (!error && response.statusCode == 200) {
                var q = JSON.parse(body).contents.quotes[0];
                var quote = {'quote': q.quote,
                            'author': q.author}
                sessionContext.lastQuote = quote;
                usercontexts.set(sessionId, sessionContext);
                rjson.response.outputSpeech.ssml = '<speak>' +
                quote.quote + '</speak>';
                console.log(rjson);
                res.json(rjson);

            } else {
                console.log('Error: ' + error)
                console.log('Statuscode: ' + response.statusCode)
            }
        });
```

```
    }
    else if (userIntent === 'GetAuthor'){

        rjson.response.outputSpeech.ssml =
            '<speak>' + sessionContext.lastQuote.author
            + '</speak>';
        console.log(rjson);
        res.json(rjson);
    }
    else {
        rjson.response.shouldEndSession = true;
        rjson.response.outputSpeech.ssml = '<speak>
        Sorry. I did not get you! </speak>';
        console.log(rjson);
        res.json(rjson);

    }
```

9. Now that we have the web app to manage the conversation, let us push it on the cloud to the server endpoint that was configured in the **Skill Configuration** panel:

```
> git init
> git add .
> git commit -m alexa-quote-bot
> heroku create my-first-alexa-bot
> git push heroku master
```

After carrying out the preceding instructions in your console, you will have the conversation manager running at
`https://my-first-alexa-bot.herokuapp.com/alexa`. This is where Alexa will send a POST request to. The response will be parsed and the SSML utterance will be synthesized to the user.

10. Now go back to the test panel, type a sample utterance (for example, `tell me a quote`), and click **Ask Quote Master**:

11. Continue the conversation. Type who said that and click **Ask Quote Master**:

This request will be identified as the GetAuthor intent and responded to with the name of the author of the quote.

12. Notice that the sessionId for both the preceding requests are the same. Now click **Reset** to reset the conversation. Any new request will have a different sessionId.

Test on Alexa

Congratulations! Your very first Alexa skill is ready. You can test it on your Alexa if you have one at home. All the skills you develop will be added to your Alexa by default. You can see this on your Alexa dashboard (`alexa.amazon.com`), click the **Skills** tab in the menu, and **Your Skills** in the top right:

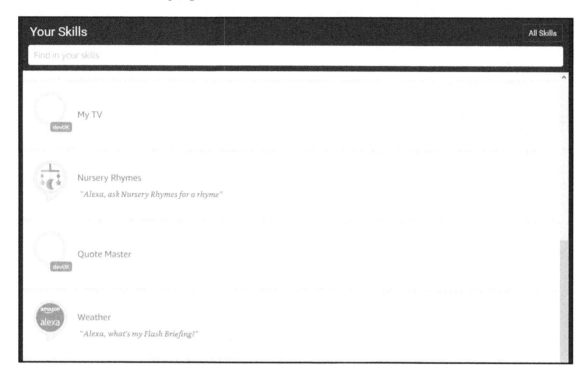

You will notice that Alexa waits after reading the quote for you. This is to allow the user to make a follow-up request. This is enabled by setting `shouldEndSession` to `false` by default. It is set to `true` only when the user says `stop` or times out without saying anything while Alexa is waiting for a response.

My TV guide

Let us move on to a more challenging project: building an Alexa skill to get info on TV shows. In this task, we will build a TV skill that will enable Alexa to answer questions about TV shows. For instance, Alexa will be able to answer the following questions.

- What's next on BBC One?
- What's on ITV now?
- What is the show about?
- Whats on ITV at 2pm?

Building the interaction model

In addition to the concepts we explored in the QuoteMaster skill, in this task we will explore more complex conversational elements: slots. Let us follow the seven step process from earlier to create a new skill called My TV:

1. Fill in the **Skill Information** and move on to the **Interaction Model** page.
2. Click **Launch Skill Builder** and open the dashboard. As before, you will see that there are three intents in the model by default.
3. As you may have noticed, there are elements in the preceding questions that can be enumerated and classified as entity types. For instance, BBC One, BBC Two, and ITV can be classified as networks. In Alexa, this knowledge can be fed into the system as slot types. To create a slot type, here is what you need to do: Under **Intents** on the menu on the left, you will find **Slot Types**. Click **ADD +**:

Img: alexa_slot_types

4. As with intents, there are two types of slots—built-in slots and custom slots:

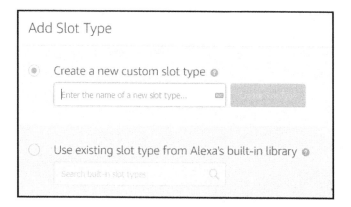

We will create a custom slot called `Network`. Click **Create Slot Type**:

5. On this page, we will have to specify all the networks that we want Alexa to identify during conversations with the user. Let's make a small list: `Channel 4`, `BBC One`, `BBC Two`, and `ITV`. We can add more later.

6. Let's add the first one: `BBC One`. Click **+** at the end of the text field. Add all variations of the the `BBC One` value, `BBC 1`, `BBC One`, and so on, as its synonyms.

7. Add all the other networks in the same way:

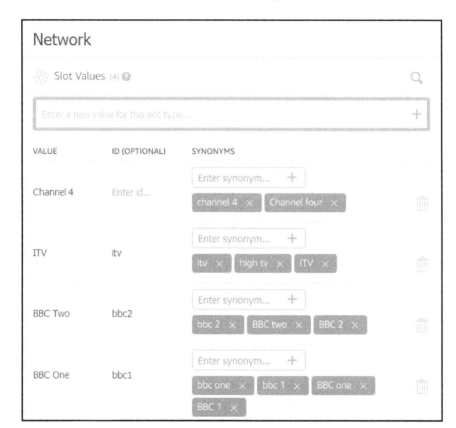

Img: alexa_slot_network_filled

8. Let's now create the intents that use the `Network` slot type. Let's start with `GetNextProgramme`. This intent corresponds to all utterances where the user asks for the next program in a given network. An example utterance would be, `what is the next programme on BBC One?`. Click **Intents +** and add the sample utterances. But instead of mentioning the network in the utterance, we need to use slot types (using `{ }` notation), as shown here:

```
whats on {network} now?
what the next show on {network}
whats next on {network}?
```

When you start entering the slot type in the utterance, the list of slot types pops out from where one can be chosen, as shown here:

Although the slot network is required to carry out the task, keep it unchecked as a required slot (checkbox under **REQ**) for now:

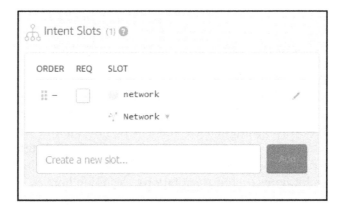

9. Let's add another intent: `GetProgrammeAtTime`. This one is for utterances where the user asks for the show on a particular network at a specific time. An example utterance would be, `what show is on BBC One at 2pm`.

Create a new intent and add the following as utterance samples:

```
what show is on {network} at {time}
whats on {network} at {time}
```

Since time is not a defined slot, we will need to define it later. All slots connected to the intent will be listed on the right, as shown here:

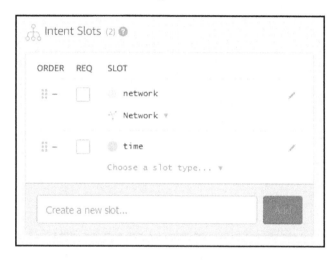

10. Click **Choose a slot type...** and choose **AMAZON.TIME**. This one of the predefined slot types. Click the checkbox to make the slot required and provide a prompt and response, as we did for the network slot:

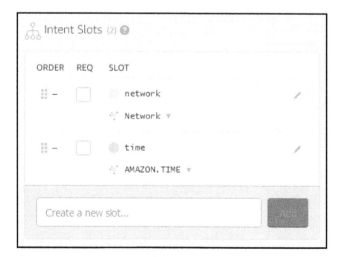

11. Add other utterances and save the model.

12. Add the final intent: `GetDescription`. This intent is for utterances where the user wants to know more about a show. For example, the user could say, `whats the show about` as a follow-up question to the preceding two intents:

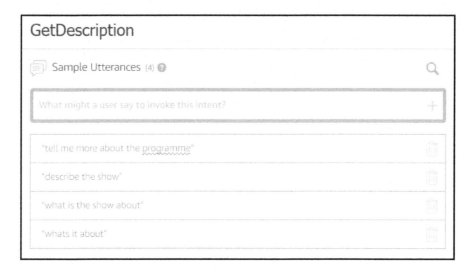

This one does not have any slots attached because we are going to try to keep the information required in the conversational context.

13. Add other utterances for the intent and save the model:

```
tell me more about the show
describe the show
what is the show about
whats it about
```

14. Let's test the model as we did with the QuoteMaster skill. On the test panel, type a few utterances and check out how Alexa analyzes them:

Since you don't have a server set to respond, the response is going to be an error.

Setting up the TV skill server

Now that we have the interaction model, we need a conversation manager that can respond to user intents. Let's now set up the server to respond to the user:

1. On the **Skills Configuration** page, click configuration and choose an **HTTPS** option.
2. Create a Node.js project using `npm` and add the default libraries, as we did for the QuoteMaster server discussed earlier.
3. Create an `index.js` file and import the `request`, `express`, `body-parser`, and `hashmap` libraries.

4. Create a web server using the Express library, as you did before:

```
const request = require('request')
const express = require('express')
const bodyParser = require('body-parser')

const Hashmap = require('hashmap');

var usercontexts = new Hashmap();

const app = express()

app.set('port', (process.env.PORT || 5000))

// Process application/x-www-form-urlencoded
app.use(bodyParser.urlencoded({extended: false}))

// Process application/json
app.use(bodyParser.json())

app.use(express.static('public'))

// Index route
app.get('/', function (req, res) {
    res.send('Hello world, I am the TV Guide.')
})
```

5. We need another library to process dates and times, which we will call a moment. Install it using npm install and add the following code to index.js. This is used to construct today's date for retrieving the TV schedule for the day:

```
const moment = require('moment')

var todaysSchedule = {};
const now = new Date();
var date = now.getDate();
if (date < 10) { date = '0' + date; }
var month = now.getMonth() + 1;
if (month < 10) { month = '0' + month; }
const todaysDate = now.getFullYear() + '-' + month + '-' + date;

loadTodaysSchedule(todaysDate);
```

6. Create a `loadTodaysSchedule()` function to get the TV schedule for the day. This can be stored locally and queried to answer user questions. Note that the schedule will not change every day automatically:

```
function loadTodaysSchedule(todaysDate){
    var url = 'http://api.tvmaze.com/schedule?country=GB&date='
              + todaysDate;
    console.log('URL:' + url);
    request({
        url: url,
        method: 'GET'
    },
    function (error, response, body) {
        //response is from the bot
        if (!error && response.statusCode == 200) {
            // Print out the response body
            todaysSchedule = JSON.parse(body);
            console.log('Todays Schedule: ' +
                        todaysSchedule.length);
            console.log(todaysSchedule);
        } else {
            console.log('Error: ' + error)
            console.log('Statuscode: ' + response.statusCode)
        }
    });
}
```

7. Here is the template for the actual response endpoint:

```
app.post('/alexa', function (req, res) {
    console.log('Request from Alexa:');
    console.log(req.body);
    //1. add context code here

    //2. get userIntent from request

    //3. set default return json object
    //4. dialogue management code to
    //decide what to say in response to user intents.
})

// Spin up the server
app.listen(app.get('port'), function() {
    console.log('running on port', app.get('port'))
})
```

8. Let's save the context and load it up like we did in the QuoteMaster skill. We will be saving the show information that the user asked for so that we can describe it in their subsequent turn:

```
var sessionContext = {
                        'show': null
                };
var sessionId = req.body.session.sessionId;
if (!usercontexts.get(sessionId)){
    usercontexts.set(sessionId, sessionContext);
} else {
    sessionContext = usercontexts.get(sessionId);
}
```

9. Let's get the user intent from the request and prepare the default JSON response:

```
var userIntent = '';
    if (req.body.request.type === 'SessionEndedRequest'){
        userIntent = 'AMAZON.StopIntent';
    } else {
        userIntent = req.body.request.intent.name;
    }
    console.log('UserIntent:' + userIntent);
    var rjson = {
        "version": "1.0",
        "response": {
            "shouldEndSession": false,
            "outputSpeech": {
              "type": "SSML",
                "ssml": "<speak>Hello, I am your TV Guide!</speak>"
            }
        }
    };
```

10. And here is the code for responding to user intents. The JSON user response is reset with information retrieved from the day's schedule:

```
if (userIntent === 'AMAZON.StopIntent'){
    rjson.response.shouldEndSession = true;
    rjson.response.outputSpeech.ssml =
        '<speak> Ok. Have a good day! </speak>';
    console.log(rjson);
    res.json(rjson);
}
else {
    if (userIntent === 'GetNextProgramme'){
        var network =
        req.body.request.intent.slots.network.value;
        var e = getNextProgrammeInNetwork(network);
        sessionContext.show = e;
        usercontexts.set(sessionId, sessionContext);
        rjson.response.shouldEndSession = false;
        rjson.response.outputSpeech.ssml =
            '<speak> The next show on ' + network + ' is ' +
            e.show.name + ' at ' + e.airtime + '! </speak>';
        console.log(rjson);
        res.json(rjson);
    }
    else if (userIntent === 'GetProgrammeAtTime'){
        var network =
        req.body.request.intent.slots.network.value;
        var time = req.body.request.intent.slots.time.value;
        var e = getProgrammeAtTime(network, time);
        sessionContext.show = e;
        usercontexts.set(sessionId, sessionContext);
        rjson.response.shouldEndSession = false;
        rjson.response.outputSpeech.ssml = '<speak> On '
        + network +
            ' at ' + e.airtime +
            ' is ' + e.show.name +
            '! </speak>';
        console.log(rjson);
        res.json(rjson);
    }
    else if (userIntent === 'GetDescription'){
        var e = sessionContext.show;
        var desc = getDescription(e);
        rjson.response.shouldEndSession = true;
        rjson.response.outputSpeech.ssml = '<speak> ' + desc +
            ' </speak>';
        console.log(rjson);
```

```
                    res.json(rjson);
                }
                else if (userIntent === 'Thank'){
                    rjson.response.shouldEndSession = true;

                    rjson.response.outputSpeech.ssml = '<speak>
                    You are most welcome. Goodbye! </speak>';
                    console.log(rjson);
                    res.json(rjson);
                }
                else {
                    rjson.response.shouldEndSession = true;
                    //rjson.response.outputSpeech.ssml = '<speak> Ok.
                    //Have a good day! </speak>';
                    console.log(rjson);
                    res.json(rjson);
                }
            }
        }
```

11. Finally, the part of code that retrieves the necessary info from the schedule:

```
function getNextProgrammeInNetwork(networkName){
    console.log('Getting next programme in : ' + networkName);
    for (var i=0; i < todaysSchedule.length; i++){
        var e = todaysSchedule[i];
        var showtime = moment(e.airdate + ' ' + e.airtime);
        moment().format();

        var a = moment();
        var b = moment(showtime);
        if (a.diff(b, 'minutes') < 0){
            if (e.show.network.name === networkName){
                console.log(e.show.name + ' on ' +
                        e.show.network.name + ' at ' + e.airtime);
                return e;
            }
        }
    }
}

function getProgrammeAtTime(networkName, time){
    console.log('Getting next programme in : ' + networkName + '
            at ' + time);
    for (var i=0; i < todaysSchedule.length; i++){
        var e = todaysSchedule[i];
        if (e.show.network.name === networkName){
            var showtime = moment(e.airdate + ' ' + e.airtime);
```

```
                    var requestedtime = moment(e.airdate + ' ' + time);
                    moment().format();

                    var a = moment(requestedtime);
                    var b = moment(showtime);
                    if (a.diff(b, 'minutes') > -30 && a.diff(b, 'minutes')
                        < 30 ){
                        console.log(e.show.name + ' on ' +
                            e.show.network.name + ' at ' + e.airtime);
                        return e;
                    }
                }
            }
        }

    function getDescription(episode){
        console.log('Getting episode info:' + episode.show.name);
        console.log(episode.show.summary);
        return episode.show.summary;
    }
```

12. Now, let's move this web app on to the Cloud:

```
> git init
> git add .
> git commit -m alexa-tv-bot
> heroku create my-alexa-tv-bot
> git push heroku master
```

After pushing the web app on to the cloud using the preceding instructions, we will have the conversation manager running at `https://my-alexa-tv-bot.herokuapp.com/alexa`. This is where Alexa will send a POST request to. The response will be parsed and the SSML utterance will be synthesized to the user.

Testing the TV skill

Let's now go back to the test panel and test some sample utterances to see how they work:

1. Type `whats next on bbc one` and click **Ask My TV**:

2. **Try** `whats on bbc two at 4pm` **and click Ask My TV:**

3. Finally, let's try to get more information on the show with a follow-up request. Remember not to press the **Reset** button before making a follow-up request as it might reset the conversational context:

The response you get will be a brief description of the show that Alexa previously pulled out. Here is a part of the JSON output:

```
"outputSpeech": {
    "ssml": "<speak> <p>Sarah Moore saves three items from the
    tip in each episode and transforms them into a much more
    valuable piece, before returning the profits back to the
    original owners of the item.</p> </speak>",
    "type": "SSML"
},
```

4. Having tested the skill on the simulator, test it on Echo. Remember, you need to say the invocation name before the request. For instance, `Alexa, ask my TV, whats next on BBC One`.

Built-in intents and slot types

Alexa has a library of built-in intents and slot types that can be used in any skill that we build. Using built-in intents come with their own set of advantages. As a developer, you don't have to provide sample utterances and whenever Alexa gets updated with more sample utterances, your skill gets a boost. Also, it makes it easy for users to remember a simple set of phrases across skills to get things done with Alexa.

Here is a set of standard built-in intents that you can use:

Built-in intents	Description
Amazon.YesIntent	Whenever the user says `yes`, `yeah`, or something similar
Amazon.NoIntent	When the user says `no`, `no thanks`, or something similar
Amazon.CancelIntent	When the user asks to cancel the current task, such as `cancel`, `never mind`, or `forget it`
Amazon.HelpIntent	When the user asks for help (`help`, `can you help me`)
Amazon.StopIntent	When the user says `stop`, `off`, or `shut up`

Alexa also has a number of slot types that you can use:

Built-in slot types	Description
AMAZON.DATE	Any description of a date can be picked up using this slot type. For example, `today` (2017-10-10), `now`, `this weekend` (2017-W40-WE), `next year` (2018), or `this winter`. These phrases will be decoded into the ISO 8601 date format.
AMAZON.TIME	Any reference to time, such as `two o clock`, `tomorrow morning`, or `noon`, will be picked up and stored in the ISO 8601 time format.
AMAZON.DURATION	Duration, such as `ten minutes`, `six hours`, or `seven years`. The decoded info is represented in the ISO 8601 duration format.
AMAZON.NUMBER	Any number, such as `one`, `one hundred`, or `two three four`.
AMAZON.FOUR_DIGIT_NUMBER	Any four digit number.

There are other slot types, such as AMAZON.AggregateRating (for ratings such as best, five star, top ten), AMAZON.Animal (for animals), AMAZON.AT_CITY (for cities across the globe), AMAZON.Color (for colors), and AMAZON.Country (for countries), that can be used. Browse the full list at the following URL:

```
https://developer.amazon.com/docs/custom-skills/slot-type-reference.html
```

Summary

Brilliant! I believe you had fun building your first two Alexa skills in this chapter. We explored the basics of skill building—intents and slots. We explored the process of building the interaction model on the Alexa development platform as well as building the conversation manager web app on the cloud. We have built two skills—one for quotes and another for TV schedules—providing us ample opportunities to explore and understand the various elements of the Alexa skill development process. I would encourage you to take this as a starting point and explore more. There are about 10,000 skills in the Alexa store and it's continuing to grow. With the usage of the home assistance smart speakers projected to grow, there will be a huge market for customizable Alexa skills in the years to come. In the next chapter, we will explore how to build actions for Google Assistant and invoke them on Google Home.

References

Amazon Alexa documentation: https://developer.amazon.com/docs/ask-overviews/build-skills-with-the-alexa-skills-kit.html

9
My Man Friday

Now that we are in the last chapter of the book, let's do something really interesting. How about we build a bot that acts as your very own man Friday. Imagine asking the bot to do tasks such as organizing your to-do list, reminding you of tasks and meetings, and so on. In the last chapter, we developed an Alexa skill to browse through the TV programs for the day. In this chapter, we will explore the process of building skills on Google Assistant. Google Assistant is Google's offering of a personal assistance chatbot like iPhone's Siri and Amazon's Alexa. You can interact with Google Assistant on a variety of channels such as Allo mobile app, Allo for web, and Google Home.

Google Home is a smart speaker similar to Amazon Echo and is powered by Google Assistant. In other words, Google Home is the embodiment in which Assistant lives. This is very similar to the relationship between Alexa and Echo or between Siri and iPhone. Google Home is a direct competitor to Amazon Echo and currently holds a 24% market share. Like Alexa, the skills (or actions, as they call it) of Assistant can be enhanced.

In this chapter, we will build an action for Google Assistant. In an effort to make it man Friday, let's start by integrating it into an online service that can be used to manage your daily tasks easily. We will explore how the action can be enabled to interact with this service to add and retrieve tasks. First, let's explore an online service called Todoist and examine how to add and retrieve tasks using the REST API. Then, we will build an agent with the Dialogflow toolkit and integrate it with Google Assistant as an action. Finally, we will integrate the action with the Todoist service to finish the loop.

By the end of this chapter, you will be able to:

- Build a Dialogflow agent to handle to-do lists
- Integrate to Todoist service using fulfillment webhooks
- Create Google Actions and integrate with Google Assistant
- Test the action on Google Home

Todoist

Todoist is an online service to store and organize lists of items that you plan to do in the near future. Users can add tasks to their account, organize them under projects, and assign deadlines and reminders to their tasks. The account can be accessed on their website as well as apps on Android and iOS devices. The Todoist service can be accessed using their developer API as well. Let us examine two basic services: adding tasks and retrieving the to-do list for the day.

Getting the key

To access Todoist, we need an API key. To get one, follow these steps:

1. Go to `https://todoist.com/`.
2. Sign up for an account.
3. Log in to the account and view the dashboard.
4. Try adding a task by clicking **Add Task**:

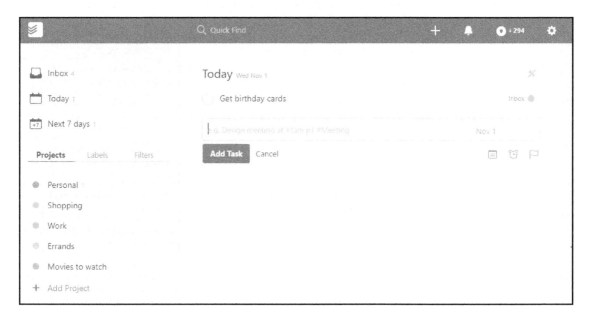

You can see that the tasks can be organized into projects. You can create a new project if you want to. By default, tasks will be added to your inbox and carry the due date of the day they are created.

5. Click the task that you just created and explore the options:

You can change the due date, the project it belongs to, the priority of the task, and set reminders.

6. Now that we have explored the capabilities of the service platform, let's get the API key to your account. Click the settings icon in the top-right corner:

7. Click **Settings**.
8. On the side menu, click **Integrations**.
9. Scroll down to **API token**:

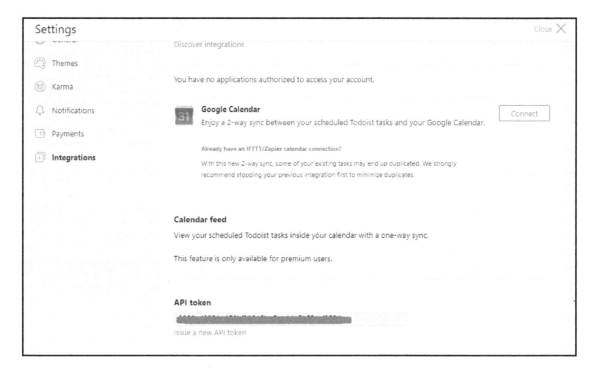

Copy down your token and keep it safe.

Let's now write a Node.js program to add items and retrieve lists.

Adding a task

Using the key, we can add and retrieve the list of tasks to do. Here is the Node.js code to add a task to your to-do list:

```
var task = {'type': 'item_add',
        'temp_id': uuid.v4(),
        'uuid': uuid.v4(),
        'args': {
            'content': taskDescription
        }};
```

```
var url = 'https://todoist.com/api/v7/sync?token=' +
        todoist_token +
        '&sync_token=*&resource_types=["items"]&commands=['
        + JSON.stringify(task) +']';
        console.log('URL:' + url);
request({
    url: url,
    method: 'GET'
},
function (error, response, body) {
    //response is from the bot
    if (!error && response.statusCode == 200) {
        console.log(JSON.parse(body));
    } else {
        console.log('Error: ' + error)
        console.log('Statuscode: ' + response.statusCode)
    }
});
```

Retrieving all tasks for the day

To retrieve all tasks in the to-do list for the day, use the following Node.js code:

```
var url = 'https://todoist.com/api/v7/sync?token='
        + todoist_token +
        '&sync_token=*' +
        '&resource_types=["items"]';
console.log('URL:' + url);
var resp = syncrequest('GET', url);
var allItems = JSON.parse(resp.getBody('utf8')).items;
var allItemsSummary = '';
for (var i = 0; i < allItems.length; i++){
    allItemsSummary += allItems[i].content;
    if (i < allItems.length - 2){
        allItemsSummary += ', ';
    }
    else if (i == allItems.length - 2) {
        allItemsSummary += ' and ';
    }
    else {
        allItemsSummary += '.';
    }
}

response = 'You have ' + allItems.length + ' in your list. '
```

```
                + allItemsSummary;
      console.log(response);
```

The preceding code will later be embedded into the web service that will be called from Dialogflow to get the response utterance generated dynamically from the webhook. To explore the full range of possible actions within Todoist, refer to the documentation here: `https://developer.todoist.com`.

Building an action

To build a *Google Assistant Action*, we need to start from *Dialogflow*. Broadly, the steps are as follows:

1. Build a Dialogflow agent.
2. Create a web app that accesses the *Todoist* service.
3. Integrate the agent with *Google Actions*.
4. Test it in the simulator.
5. Test it on Google Home.

Building a Dialogflow agent

To build a Dialogflow agent, follow these steps:

1. Go to `dialogflow.com` and sign in using your Google account.
2. Click the drop-down menu on the left and click **Create new agent**:

3. Add agent info and click **SAVE**:

4. This will create a new Google project assigned to the agent. You can view the settings info by clicking the Settings icon next to the agent's name on the drop-down list.

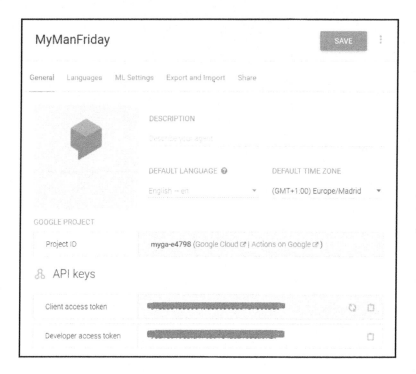

5. Let's add four intents to the agent to begin with:

- `greet`
- `add_task`
- `inform_task_description`
- `list_all_tasks`

We assume here that the user will begin the conversation with a greeting (the `greet` intent) followed by a request to either add a task (`add_task`) or list all tasks for the day (`list_all_tasks`). In the following request to add a task, the agent will ask the user to describe the task for which the user will respond with a task description (`inform_task_description`).

6. Add a few example utterances for the greet intent:

   - hi
   - hello there

7. Let's work on the add_task intent. This is the intent that a user would use to add a task to this list. Now add a few utterances here:

   - i want to add a task
   - add new task
   - add a task to my list

8. We need to follow this up with a request for a description of the task that needs to be added. So let's ask for the task description in response and also set the context to `asked-for-task`:

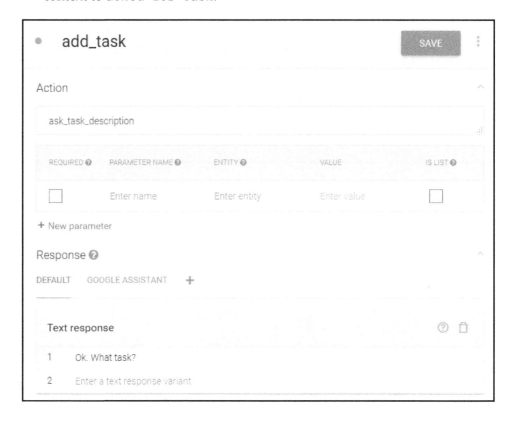

9. The user will naturally respond with a task description. We need to capture that description and send it to a web app that can record it in your Todoist list. Let's do this with the `inform_task_description` intent in the `asked-for-task` context:

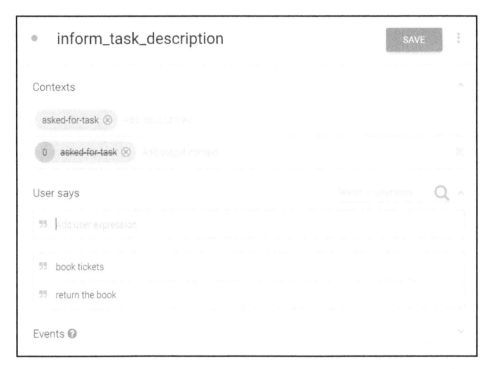

10. All utterances in `inform_task_descriptions` can be considered task descriptions and therefore sent to Todoist as they are. To capture the whole utterance in a parameter (say `task`), select the whole utterance and select `@sys.any` in the drop-down menu that appears:

11. This will create a parameter called `any` associated with the intent. Let's rename it `task`. Click `any` and change it to `task`:

12. Do the same for a few other example utterances. The following are task descriptions:

- `buy gifts for christmas`
- `send a birthday card to Jones`
- `have tablet after lunch`

13. Add `Sorry. I could not add new task.` as a response to the intent. This response will be delivered only when the agent fails to add a new task using the web app. We will enable the webhook for this intent in a short while. Save the intent by clicking the **SAVE** button.

14. Create a new `list_all_tasks` intent to list all the tasks in the to-do list of the user. Add the following utterances:

    - `what tasks do i have still`
    - `list all my tasks`
    - `get me the list of all tasks`

    Give the response action a name: `inform_all_tasks` and set a default response to `Sorry. I cannot get the list of tasks just now.` We will enable a webhook for this intent later as well.

15. Let's now set up the web service to call for the `list_all_tasks` and `add_task` intents. Click **Fulfillment** on the menu to the left.

16. Enable a webhook and type the URL of the web app to call. Since we don't have one yet, just create a placeholder for it (`https://my-home-bot.herokuapp.com/home`):

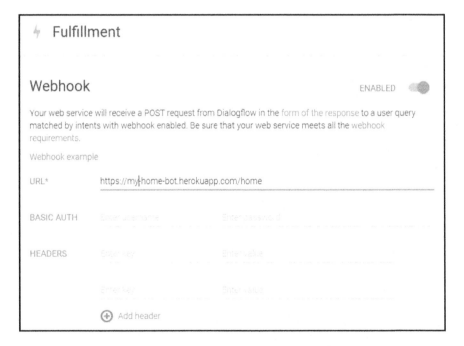

Scroll down to the end of the page and click **SAVE**.

17. Go back to the `list_all_tasks` and `add_task` intents. For each of these intents, scroll down and click **Fulfillment**. This ensures that the intent and parameters are sent to the web app that generates appropriate response utterances.

Creating a web app

Now that we have a Dialogflow agent to understand user utterances, we need to build a web app that it can interact with. The agent will send user intents and parameters to the web app so that appropriate responses can be generated. For instance, when the user wants to add a new task, the task description needs to be sent to the web app, which will in turn will add a new task in your to-do list using the Todoist API. To create the web app, follow these steps:

1. Create a new Node.js project using `npm` and create a home bot project:

   ```
   > npm init
   ```

2. Install the necessary libraries:

   ```
   > npm install request --save
   > npm install sync-request --save
   > npm install express --save
   > npm install body-parser --save
   > npm install moment --save
   > npm install node-uuid --save
   ```

   `request` and `sync-request` are libraries that will be used to interact with the Todoist service. `express` and `body-parser` will be used to spin up a web server. `moment` will be used for time/date-related computations. Finally, `node-uuid` will be used to generate UUIDs for tasks.

3. Create a file called `index.js`. Add the import statements, as shown here:

   ```
   'use strict'

   /*
   * Google Home Bot
   */

   const request = require('request')
   const syncrequest = require('sync-request')
   const express = require('express')
   const bodyParser = require('body-parser')
   ```

```
const moment = require('moment');
const uuid = require('node-uuid');
```

4. To spin up a server, we need to add the following code:

```
const app = express()

app.set('port', (process.env.PORT || 5000))

// Process application/x-www-form-urlencoded
app.use(bodyParser.urlencoded({extended: false}))

// Process application/json
app.use(bodyParser.json())

app.use(express.static('public'))

// Index route
app.get('/', function (req, res) {
    res.send('Hello world, I am your man Friday.')
})

// Handle the intents
app.post('/home', function (req, res) {
    // Handling the intent code
}

// Spin up the server
app.listen(app.get('port'), function() {
    console.log('running on port', app.get('port'))
})
```

5. Add the following code in the /home POST handle to handle the intents:

```
console.log('Request from DialogFlow:');
console.log(req.body);
var intent = req.body.result.metadata.intentName;
var botSpeech = 'hello world';
if (intent === 'inform_task_description'){
    var taskDescription = req.body.result.parameters.task;
    addTask(taskDescription);
    botSpeech = 'Adding new task.';
}
else if (intent === 'list_all_tasks'){
    botSpeech = getAllTasks();
}
```

```
var out = {speech: botSpeech,
        displayText: botSpeech,
        data: null};
var outString = JSON.stringify(out);
console.log('Out:' + outString);
res.send(outString);
```

6. Finally, we need to create the two functions that are called from the /home handle. To add a new task, first we add the following code:

```
function addTask(taskDescription){
    var todoist_token = 'YOUR-TODOIST-TOKEN';
    var task = {'type': 'item_add',
            'temp_id': uuid.v4(),
            'uuid': uuid.v4(),
            'args': {
                'content': taskDescription
            }};

    var url = 'https://todoist.com/api/v7/sync?token='
            + todoist_token +
              '&sync_token=*&resource_types=["items"]&commands=['
            + JSON.stringify(task) +']';
    console.log('URL:' + url);
    request({
        url: url,
        method: 'GET'
    },
    function (error, response, body) {
        //response is from the bot
        if (!error && response.statusCode == 200) {
            console.log(JSON.parse(body));
        } else {
            console.log('Error: ' + error)
            console.log('Statuscode: ' + response.statusCode)
        }
    });
}
```

And next, to get a summary of all tasks, we add the following code:

```
function getAllTasks(){
    var todoist_token = 'YOUR-TODOIST-TOKEN';
    var url = 'https://todoist.com/api/v7/sync?token='
            + todoist_token +
                '&sync_token=*' +
                '&resource_types=["items"]';
```

```
        console.log('URL:' + url);
        var resp = syncrequest('GET', url);
        var allItems = JSON.parse(resp.getBody('utf8')).items;
        var allItemsSummary = '';
        for (var i = 0; i < allItems.length; i++){
            allItemsSummary += allItems[i].content;
            if (i < allItems.length - 2){
                allItemsSummary += ', ';
            }
            else if (i == allItems.length - 2) {
                allItemsSummary += ' and ';
            }
            else {
                allItemsSummary += '.';
            }
        }
        var alltasks = 'You have ' + allItems.length + '
                       in your list. '
                        + allItemsSummary;
        return alltasks;
    }
```

7. Let's push it into the cloud now:

```
> git init
> git add .
> git commit -m initial-commit
> heroku create my-home-bot
> git push heroku master
```

Once pushed, the web app is ready to talk to our Dialogflow agent.

Testing the agent on Dialogflow

Now we are ready to test our man Friday on Dialogflow. On Dialogflow, you can test your agent using the simulator. If you have created a Dialogflow agent (previously called API.AI) in one of the previous chapters, you may already know how to carry out this process. If not, follow these steps:

1. Go to dialogflow.com.

2. On the right, you will see a frame with a **Try it now** text field at the top. Type `hi` and hit return. Here is where we will type our inputs to the agent. The agent will return a textual response as well as the intent of the user and the system action:

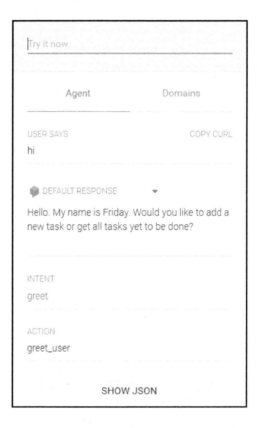

3. Now add a task. Try the `add a new task` utterance. The agent should now ask for a task description. You will also notice that the context is updated to `asked-for-task`:

4. Provide a task description. The agent will now add a new task to your to-do list and get back with an acknowledgement:

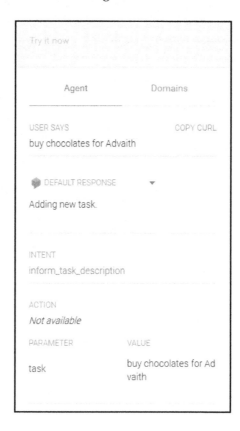

If it fails to contact the Todoist service for some reason, it will return the default response message.

5. Add a couple more tasks in the same manner.

6. We can now check out the tasks added to our to-do list by logging on to
   todoist.com or using the Todoist app:

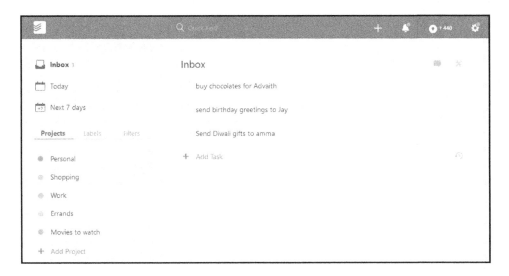

7. Now try to retrieve all the tasks. Try the get all tasks utterance:

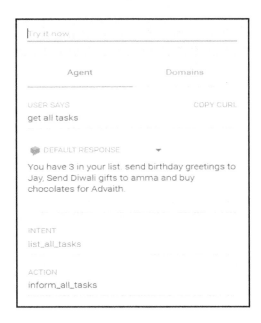

Hurray! You have successfully integrated the Dialogflow agent with Todoist.

Integrating with Google Assistant

Now that the agent is ready, our next step is to integrate it with Google Assistant. Perform the following these steps to carry out this integration:

In order to test your actions on the web without a hardware device, you may need to turn on the **Web & App Activity**, **Device Information**, and **Voice & Audio Activity** permissions on the **Activity Controls** page (`https://myaccount.google.com/activitycontrols`) for your Google Account.

1. On the Dialogflow menu on the left, click **Integrations**:

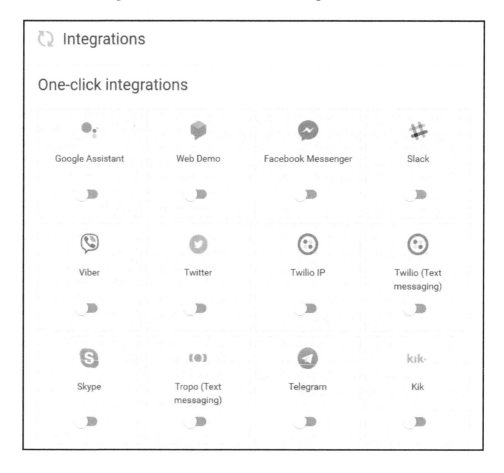

2. Click **Google Assistant**:

3. On the **Google Assistant** dialog box, move the slider in the top-right corner to the enable position.
4. Choose a `Welcome` intent. Choose the `greet` intent that we have defined.

5. Click **TEST** and then **VIEW** to open the **Actions Simulator**:

This will open another tab and take you to `console.actions.google.com` where the agent can be tested in simulation as an action on Google Assistant:

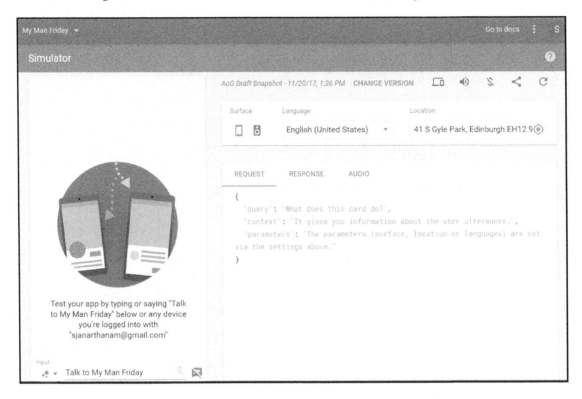

6. Change **Surface type** to **Phone** and **Input type** to **Keyboard**.

7. Type `Talk to my test app` and hit return. This will open the test version of the action and you should be able to have the same conversation with the agent as we had on Dialogflow. All tasks will be added to your to-do list, which can be checked by visiting `todoist.com` or asking to `get all tasks` once the test tasks have been added:

 Note that `talk to my test app` is the default invocation phrase. We will define invocation phrases for the action in a moment.

8. After testing the agent, go back to Dialogflow, click **Update Draft**, and click **Visit Console** in the dialog box that opens:

9. On the **Overview** page for the action, you will notice that the actions are linked to Dialogflow. The next step is to provide some essential app information.
10. Click **Edit**:

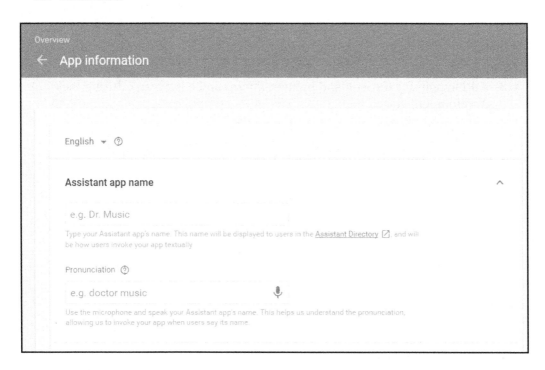

11. Type a name, pronunciation, and description.

12. Scroll down to find default invocations for the action. You can add more if necessary:

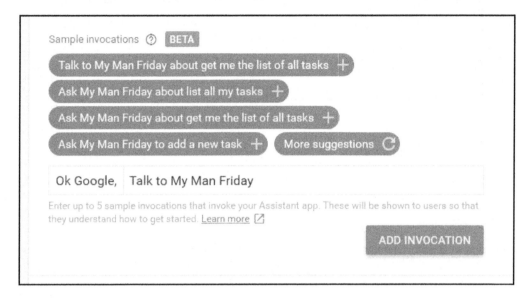

13. Add images for the icon and banner. These can be left blank during the development stage.

14. Scroll down to the bottom and click **SAVE**.

Now the action is available to test for the Google Account associated with the developer. In order to make it available to other users you have to submit the action for approval at the following URL:

```
https://developers.google.com/actions/distribute/
```

Test on Google Home

Now that the action is all set up, you can test it on your Google Home device. You need to be set up on the same Google Account that was used to build the agent and the action, as it is still under development and not published yet. So turn on your Google Home and say, `Hey Google, talk to my man Friday`:

Source: store.google.home

You should now be able to have the same conversation that you had on the simulator, on Google Home using voice. Although the accuracy of the speech recognizer is pretty high when it comes to common words and phrases in the English language, it may still not be able to recognize unusual names and non-Western concepts. The conversation will start with a disclaimer message stating that the action is still a test version. Try adding a task and reviewing all the tasks you still have left to do. Go on the Todoist app to strike off tasks completed and review them again on the device. Have fun. Congratulations on building your very own action for the Google Assistant!

Summary

Brilliant! Great work building a Google Assistant action to manage your to-d0 list. I believe you will extend the functionality of the agent to organize tasks by projects and also be able to create and retrieve tasks for specified times. Such extensions can make the agent much more powerful. Imagine being able to manage your daily tasks using a voice-powered assistant at home or at work. A Global Market Insights (June 2017) report stated that voice powered assistants on smart speakers are poised at an estimated CAGR of 50% from 2017 to 2024. These assistants will not only interact with services over the cloud but also with IoT and smart home devices, such as smart bulbs, smart thermostats, and smart plugs, making them voice-controlled. Following Amazon, Google, and Apple, more players are joining in to capture their share of the market. The number of Google Actions and Alexa Skills are expected to grow in the coming years to satisfy growing market demand. I hope this chapter got you started on your journey to building more interesting and innovative capabilities for voice-powered assistants.

Conclusion

I hope you enjoyed working through all the projects building exciting and interesting chatbots and voicebots. Great work! But remember, we have barely scratched the surface of what is yet to be unleashed. There is more to building chatbots and conversational UI than just plugging tools, services, and data together. It takes practice and a deeper understanding of underlying concepts to get the design right and build bots that give users a great experience. The user should be able to get the job done by having a conversation with the bot without having to think too much and with a smile on their face. Great conversational experience, the experience that the user gets when interacting with or at the thought of doing so, is what we should always aim for. And only with practice and mindful design can we achieve that.

Remember that this technology is evolving at a rapid pace and so are the tools, services, and our collective understanding of underlying concepts. To keep yourself up-to-date, I would recommend you become part of groups on social media (such as Facebook pages and LinkedIn groups) dedicated to chatbots and AI, participate in local meetups, subscribe to journals and magazines, and participate in chatbot hackathons and conferences (see Appendix). Many brands across the world are introducing chatbots as a new channel of customer contact. Keep an eye out for the news and interact with them, if you can, to experience and understand their design principles.

I believe that this book has given you a fundamental understanding of concepts, tools, and techniques that you can build upon in the future. I hope you had fun building all the bots whilst also being inspired with new ideas to build more in the days to come. And as a closing note, I wish you exciting days ahead designing and building great conversational experiences.

References

Google Actions documentation: `https://developers.google.com/actions/extending-the-assistant`

More Resources

Articles

Here are some articles that you might find interesting and useful:

- *Chatbot Design Canvas* by Srini Janarthanam [https://chatbotslife.com/chatbot-design-canvas-c3940685ca2c]
- *Designing Chatbots* by Yogesh Moorjani [https://uxdesign.cc/how-to-design-a-robust-chatbot-interaction-8bb6dfae34fb]
- *25 Chatbot Platforms: A Comparative Table* by Olga Davydova [https://chatbotsjournal.com/25-chatbot-platforms-a-comparative-table-aeefc932eaff]
- *The Ultimate Guide to Designing a Chatbot* by Sébastien Fourault [https://chatbotsmagazine.com/the-ultimate-guide-to-designing-a-chatbot-tech-stack-333eceb431da]
- *19 Best UX Practices for Building Chatbots* by Eunji Seo [https://chatbotsmagazine.com/19-best-practices-for-building-chatbots-3c46274501b2]
- *The Tools Every Bot Creator Must Know* by Ron Levinson [https://chatbotsmagazine.com/the-tools-every-bot-creator-must-know-c0e9dd685094]

List of conferences

Here's a list of popular conferences where you can learn more about the state of the industry and network with chatbot designers, developers, and investors:

- Chatbot Summit (chatbotsummit.com)
- ChatbotConf (https://orat.io/chatbotconf)
- Re-work AI Assistant Summit (www.re-work.co/events/)
- Intelligent Assistants Conferences (http://opusresearch.net/wordpress/events/)

List of magazines

Here is a list of magazines and newsletters that publish insightful articles and news about the happenings in the world of chatbots:

- Chatbots Magazine (`chatbotsmagazine.com`)
- Chatbots Journal (`chatbotsjournal.com`)
- Chatbot's Life (`chatbotslife.com/`)
- Chatbot News Daily (`chatbotnewsdaily.com/`)
- Chatbots Weekly (`www.chatbotsweekly.com/`)

Groups on social media

Here's a list of social media groups to sign up to in order to network with and keep abreast of the latest in the industry:

- UX for Bots (`https://www.facebook.com/groups/uxforbots/`)
- ChatBots (`https://www.facebook.com/groups/aichatbots/`)
- Chatbots Developers (Global) (`https://www.facebook.com/groups/chatbotsdevelopers/`)
- Messenger Platform Developer Community (`https://www.facebook.com/groups/messengerplatform/`)
- Chatbot Professionals (`https://www.linkedin.com/groups/7052578`)

Index

Made in the USA
Middletown, DE
20 July 2019